D1423635

THE BOLSHEVIK REVOLUTION:

*Its Impact on American Radicals, Liberals,
and Labor*

BY PHILIP S. FONER

History of the Labor Movement in the United States VOLUME I: *From Colonial Times to the Founding of the American Federation of Labor* VOLUME II: *From the Founding of the American Federation of Labor to the Emergence of American Imperialism* VOLUME III: *The Policies and Practices of the American Federation of Labor, 1900–1909* VOLUME IV: *The Industrial Workers of the World, 1905–1917*

Helen Keller: Her Socialist Years
The Case of Joe Hill
The Letters of Joe Hill
A History of Cuba and Its Relations with the United States (2 vols.)
The Life and Writings of Frederick Douglass (4 vols.)
The Complete Writings of Thomas Paine (2 vols.)
Business and Slavery: The New York Merchants and the Irrepressible Conflict
The Fur and Leather Workers Union
Jack London: American Rebel
Mark Twain: Social Critic
The Jews in American History: 1654–1865
The Basic Writings of Thomas Jefferson
The Selected Writings of George Washington
The Selected Writings of Abraham Lincoln
The Selected Writings of Franklin D. Roosevelt

★

THE
BOLSHEVIK
REVOLUTION

*Its Impact on American
Radicals, Liberals, and Labor*

A Documentary Study

by PHILIP S. FONER
Professor of History, Lincoln University

INTERNATIONAL PUBLISHERS · NEW YORK

PREFACE

A half century has passed since John Reed, the most famous reporter of the scenes in Petrograd in 1917, wrote in his great work, *Ten Days That Shook the World:* "No matter what one thinks of Bolshevism, it is undeniable that the Russian revolution is one of the great events of human history, and the rise of the Bolsheviki a phenomenon of world-wide importance." Reed pleaded for understanding of this phenomenon, but in most circles in the United States his plea went unheeded. From the outset, the Socialist revolution in Russia was greeted in these circles with hatred, fear and open hostility often based on ignorance, misinformation and misunderstanding.

Yet there were many Americans who did not share the moral abhorrence of the Bolshevik revolution, and in the present volume, I have attempted to present through representative editorials, reports of meetings, speeches, articles and resolutions (either in full or in excerpt form) the impact of the Russian revolution on this section of the American population. Here the reader will find various views. Among the radicals included here many were convinced from the beginning that the Bolshevik revolution would prove a blessing to the Russian people and to the world. Liberal opinion, though critical of various aspects of the upheaval, either believed it to be primarily an experiment in social justice which should be encouraged, and credited the Bolsheviks with sincere aspirations for a better world, or held that the revolution was here to stay and that all efforts to crush Bolshevism by force were doomed to fail, and that peace, trade and economic assistance were the only logical policies to pursue. Among trade unionists were those who hailed the revolution as a victory for the working class of the world and Soviet Russia as the first workers' republic, and others who, while not ready to accept this position, were prepared to join in demanding that an end be put to the intervention in favor of the counter-revolution and that trade relations be resumed with Russia: There were also many in business, government and labor who favored relations with the Soviet government, not because they approved of the revolution but because they believed it would be in the national interest.

The period treated in this book extends from the outbreak of

5

the Socialist revolution in November 1917 to the opening months of 1921. There have been books devoted to the impact of the Russian revolution on American opinion during this period.* But there has been as yet no documentary collection revealing the support for the revolution and the opposition to intervention against the Soviet Socialist Republic. It was with a view to filling this gap that the present volume was conceived.

Because of the wide variety of spellings of Russian names I have made them uniform throughout. The heads for each item are for the most part as they appeared in the original publication.

Sources for the documentary section are cited at the end of each document. In a number of cases in the introduction explanatory notes are placed at the bottom of the page, but mostly they will be found in the section of reference notes. Biographical sketches, arranged alphabetically, will be found at the back of the book.

In preparing this volume I have had the assistance of the staffs of the Library of Congress, the New York Public Library and Duke University Library, and I wish to express my thanks. Perhaps of the greatest importance to this book were the files of the New York *Call*. The *Call* was the only daily English-language Socialist paper published in this period, and its reports of meetings held by supporters of the Russian revolution were rarely duplicated in the non-Socialist press. I wish to thank the staff of the Tamiment Institute Library of New York University for making the files of the paper available.

January 1967

PHILIP S. FONER

* *See especially* Meno Lowenstein, *American Opinion of Soviet Russia,* Washington, D.C., 1941; Paul H. Anderson, *The Attitude of the American Leftist Leaders Toward the Russian Revolution,* Notre Dame, Ind., 1942; Winton U. Solberg, "Impact of Soviet Russia on American Life," unpublished Ph.D. thesis, Harvard University, 1952; Christopher Lasch, *The American Liberal and the Russian Revolution,* New York, 1962; E. Malcolm Carroll, *Soviet Communism and Western Opinion, 1919–1921,* edited by Frederic B. M. Hollyday, Chapel Hill, 1965; Peter Gabriel Filene, "American Attitudes Toward Soviet Russia, 1917–1933," unpublished Ph.D. thesis, Harvard University, 1965. Two specific studies of the Russian Revolution and American labor are: Bernard Gronert, "The Impact of the Russian Revolution Upon the AF of L, 1918–1928," and D. F. Wieland, "American Labor and Russia, 1917–1925." Both are unpublished Master's theses (1948) at the University of Wisconsin.

CONTENTS

7

10 *Contents*

ILLUSTRATIONS

"I know what this Bolshevism means, Bill—it means us!"

—Clive Weed

The Liberator, July 1919

INTRODUCTION

For decades before the Revolution of 1917, tsarist Russia had become a symbol of reaction, tyranny, injustice and persecution in the United States. That such a country would be the scene of the most sweeping revolution in the history of the world was something few Americans would have dared to predict. Certainly it was too much to expect that a land with a semi-feudal structure and with an underdeveloped bourgeoisie and a relatively small working class would be the one in which the first socialist state would be established. Contrary to the opinions of Marx and Engels,[1] and of Lenin himself,[2] it was the more or less common view among American Socialists that Russia was not ready for socialism and that before the working class could take over the government, the country would first have to go through the state of fully developed capitalism.

Nevertheless, there were Americans who had confidence that despite the tsarist tyranny, the Russian workers and peasants would ultimately overthrow the autocracy and usher in a socialist society. "Socialism in Russia, though in its fledgling years, gives evidence of robust development," commented the *International Socialist Review* as early as June 1901. When the unrest that gripped Russia exploded in rebellious students' demonstrations, strikes and widespread acts of peasant violence and finally culminated in the Revolution of 1905, some American radical journals were convinced that the revolution would triumph—if not immediately, then eventually. "The Russian people are demanding industrial liberty, and the fires of revolution will never be quenched until the people are supreme," the *Miners' Magazine* (November 9, 1905), official organ of the militant Western Federation of Miners, predicted. The *Industrial Worker*, official journal of the newly organized Industrial Workers of the World (IWW), ventured the prediction (March 1906) that "The sun of the socialist republic will first cross the horizon of the Slavic empire." The *International Socialist Review* (January 1906) was convinced that if the revolution were successful in Russia, it might usher in an era of "European revolutions that will end with the dictatorship of a Socialist society."

Even after the Revolution of 1905 was crushed, the radicals were not completely discouraged. Their great hope for Russia

13

had to be postponed, but only for the present. The revolution had clearly indicated the great potential power of the Russian workers, and in due time that power would achieve a victory.* When World War I broke out, some radicals were certain that in Russia the reaction against the war would provide the impetus for a successful revolution. "At the risk of shocking some of our readers," declared *Solidarity*, the IWW journal (September 12, 1914), "we are offering to bet on Russia as the hope of Europe." (Even some liberals shared this viewpoint and believed that Russia was ripe for revolt.[3]) The Tsar had led Russia into the war, but the workers would lead the nation out of the conflict and into a new social system. By 1916, as the strain of the war opened ever-increasing cracks in the Russian economy and tsarist failures aroused widespread discontent both in the army and on the home front, many American radicals awaited the coming of the revolution.

The long-awaited explosion came with a suddenness that surprised even some of the radicals. In February 1917, spontaneous strikes swept Petrograd and Moscow as workers complained of lack of bread and the mounting inflation.† On February 27, the Tsar ordered the workers back to the factories and shops, but the garrison of Petrograd joined the strikers. The Tsar abdicated and on March 1, 1917, a Provisional government under Prince George E. Lvov, a liberal nobleman, assumed power. Alexander Kerensky, soon to become Minister of War and Premier of the Provisional government, occupied the post of Minister of Justice under Prince Lvov. The Provisional government had been created by the Duma, established as part of a new semi-constitutional system after the Revolution of 1905. At the same time, however, the Petrograd Soviet of Workers' Deputies was created,‡ and began to function as a sort of dual government, issuing its own proclamations.

* On April 13, 1918, the *Industrial Worker* noted that after the Revolution of 1905, it had expected another one in ten years. "And it came. Not in 1915, nor in 1916, as we expected, but in 1917—it came."
† On February 23, 90,000 workers went on strike in Petrograd and by the following day, the number had swelled to 200,000. These dates are based on the old-style Russian calendar which is 13 days behind the Western one.
‡ The name was soon changed to Petrograd Soviet of Workers' and Soldiers' Deputies. The word "soviet" means "council." A Soviet of Workers' Deputies was first formed in St. Petersburg on October 26, 1905, in which each deputy represented 500 workers.

The February revolution in Petrograd (March 9–14, 1917, by the Western calendar) aroused widespread rejoicing in the United States. Tsarism, bureaucracy, the oppression, all seemed to have been torn away. "The most corrupt government, the most detestable despotism which has survived among the nations of the modern world, is by way of perishing," *The New Republic* (March 24, 1917) cheered. At its national convention in April 1917, the Socialist party of the United States sent "fraternal greetings to the Socialists and workers of the Russian republic, and hearty felicitations upon their glorious victory in behalf of democracy and social progress."[4] The American Federation of Labor, the largest national labor body in the United States, hailed the revolution and saluted "freedom in Russia," while the tiny Knights of Labor heralded the revolution as "the most wonderful step out of the darkness of absolutism towards the light of freedom and democracy ever known in human history."[5]

The forces in the United States favoring participation in World War I were especially pleased by the news from Russia. The February revolution had solved a dilemma for them. The "Unholy Alliance" with the Tsar in a "crusade for democracy" would have given credence to the charges of the anti-war forces, who maintained that the conflict was an imperialist war and that the United States should stay out. Now the blood of revolution seemed to purge Russia of past sins.[6]

Samuel Gompers, president of the AF of L, sent a cable to the "representatives of the working people of Russia," cautioning the Russian workers to solve their problems "practically and rationally" and not attempt further revolutionary activity. Freedom could not be "established by revolution only—it is the product of evolution," Gompers wrote.[7] But *The New Republic* (March 24, 1917) noted that it would require more revolutionary activity "to eradicate the old regime in Russia," and a meeting of radicals in New York City on April 29, 1917, declared that the February revolution "had solved the political problem only, and has yet to solve the most important social and economic ends of said Revolution." To achieve these ends a second revolution, a real revolution, would be required.[8] It was naive to imagine that Russia, having in the middle of a brutal war emerged from centuries of autocracy, with its people yearning for peace, with a land-hungry peasantry, with a militant, class-conscious working class, would be satisfied with a liberal republic, especially if it yielded to Allied pressure and promised to go on with the hated war.[9]

While most Americans concentrated their attention on the Provisional government, the radicals watched the Petrograd Soviet of Workers' and Soldiers' Deputies. When, on March 27, the Soviet advised the workers of all countries to take matters into their own hands and put an end to the war, the pro-war forces were horrified, but American radicals were thrilled.[10]

Little excitement was caused in the United States by the news from Petrograd that on April 3 Vladimir Ilyich Ulyanov—Lenin —had arrived at the Finland Station, ending years of exile.[11] But excitement was created by news from Petrograd later that month. On April 25, 1917, a *New York Times* headline read: "Anti-American Outburst. Extremists Attempt to Demonstrate at Petrograd Embassy." The article, datelined Petrograd, April 23 (via London April 24) stated:

"An effort by a small group of ultra-radicals to make an unfriendly demonstration before the American Embassy today was frustrated by militiamen as the radicals marched down the Nevsky Prospect on their way to the Embassy.

"The demonstration was led by Nikolai Lenin,* the radical Socialist leader, who recently arrived here through Germany from Switzerland with a safe-conduct from the German authorities.

"The demonstration is said to have been due to the alleged killing in America of an anarchist named Mooney, who was under sentence in San Francisco.

"A guard was sent by the authorities to protect the embassy."

It was this protest meeting in Petrograd which first drew the attention of most Americans to the frame-up of two militant trade unionists, Thomas J. Mooney and Warren K. Billings, following the explosion of a bomb, July 22, 1916, during a Preparedness parade in San Francisco, killing nine persons and wounding about 40 more.[12] As *The New Republic* (May 5, 1917) observed: "Is it not a remarkable commentary upon the attitude of the American press toward labor that one of the most significant and dramatic events should have come to the attention of American newspaper readers through a mass meeting in the Nevsky Prospect?"

Despite widespread evidence of the longing for peace in Russia

* Nikolai was the first name given to Lenin by others. He never used it himself, although he did use the initial "N."

and the demoralization of the army, the United States put pressure upon the Provisional government to keep Russia in the war. To arouse enthusiasm among the Russians to continue the fight, survey the situation and make policy recommendations, the Wilson Administration sent a mission to Russia headed by Elihu Root, former Secretary of War and Secretary of State and a leading spokesman for big business. Wilson wished to have the mission include a labor representative, but feared that "Gompers and the leaders immediately associated with him are known to be pronounced opponents of Socialism and would hardly be influential in the present ruling circles in Petrograd. And yet we shall have to be careful, if we are to send a real representative of American Labor, not to send a Socialist."[13] The dilemma was solved by choosing a Gompers-type bureaucrat, 79 year-old James Duncan, president of the Granite Cutters' International Union and AF of L vice-president. Also chosen was Charles Edward Russell, the pro-war, right-wing Socialist.[14] The other members of the mission were representatives of business, finance, the army and philanthropy.

The Root mission spent the latter part of June and the beginning of July in Petrograd, "wined and dined by all sorts of respectable elements."[15] Russell had been expelled from the Socialist party for his stand on the war and for accepting a place on the Root mission.[16] This did not stop him from holding up his red card of the Socialist party when he addressed the Soviets and told the Russians: "I come . . . from the plain people of America, from the workers, the radicals, the American socialists, the champions of democracy." Russell urged the Russian workers to give up their opposition to the war, arguing that only "through victory against Germany" could socialism be built.[17] Duncan, viewing the Russians as a group of children who with childlike enthusiasm were seeking to build a better world, lectured the Petrograd workers on the union label.[18] But Elihu Root got down to the real purpose of the mission. He told the Provisional government that unless Russia continued to fight in the war, no money would be forthcoming from the United States. "No fight, no loan," he declared in Petrograd.[19]

Bowing to this pressure (coupled with more from London and Paris) the Provisional government launched the summer offensive into Galicia which ended in appalling disaster.[20] The decision to continue the war caused a series of violent demonstrations in Petrograd. Soldiers refused to be sent back to the front. On July

16–18 occurred the demonstration of the Kronstadt sailors, the Petrograd workers and soldiers against the Provisional government. Urging the end of dual power, the crowds in the streets shouted Lenin's slogan, "All power to the Soviets!"

Instead of drawing the correct conclusion from the military disaster and the convulsion of the "July days" in Petrograd, the Provisional government, now headed by Prime Minister Alexander Kerensky, a lawyer and Socialist-Revolutionary, but a man who really had no revolutionary conviction,[21] denounced the Bolsheviks for demoralizing the troops and causing the failure of the offensive. The Bolshevik party was driven underground; Lenin, falsely branded a traitor and paid agent of the German General Staff,[22] was forced into hiding in Finland, and many Bolshevik leaders were imprisoned.[23]

But repressive measures could not satisfy the Russian people's demand for peace, land and bread. Moreover, Kerensky did not go far enough in suppressing the Left to satisfy influential Russian bankers, industrialists and generals nor the Allied embassies in Petrograd. They decided that more was needed to keep the people from pushing the revolution to the Left, and backed General L. G. Kornilov to do the job. No sooner had Kerensky become Prime Minister than he appointed Kornilov Commander-in-Chief of Russia's armed forces, hoping to use him against the Bolsheviks and the Petrograd Soviet. But in August the general began to work for the overthrow of Kerensky's government as well as for the suppression of the Soviet and the parties of the Left, and for the establishment of a military dictatorship. The military coup of August 25 to 30 (September 6 to 10 by the Western calendar) was defeated without firing a shot, because Kornilov's soldiers refused to fight for him, and the workers, led by the Petrograd Soviet, resisted *en masse*. The Provisional government was saved, but only for a few weeks. Its end was inevitable. As D. F. Fleming points out:

"The Kerensky government was doomed not only because it was a moderate group, but above all because it wanted to carry on the war. . . . The nation was already deeply disgusted with the war before the revolution. After it the revolution was the main interest of the people, not the war. The Red slogan, 'Peace, Bread and Land!' was far more effective than appeals to continue the endless agony and humiliation of the war."[24]

During the spring and summer of 1917 the Petrograd Soviet had been dominated by the Socialist-Revolutionaries and the

Mensheviks.* But in September the Bolsheviks, the only group which reflected the mood and wishes of the country, commanded a majority. In Moscow and in other industrial cities, the Soviets too showed a Bolshevik majority.

Lenin succeeded in convincing his comrades to move toward seizure of power, and on October 23, sensing that the Kerensky government was falling to pieces, the Bolshevik Central Committee decided to organize an armed revolt. On November 5, the Fortress of Peter and Paul in Petrograd was captured without bloodshed. On November 7 (October 25 by the old-style Russian calendar) the Bolsheviks captured the Winter Palace and overthrew the Provisional government in Petrograd. Lenin wrote his famous proclamation, "To the Citizens of Russia," which read:

"The Provisional Government has been deposed. State power has passed into the hands of the organ of the Petrograd Soviet of Workers' and Soldiers' Deputies, the Revolutionary Military Committee, which heads the Petrograd proletariat and the garrison.

"The cause for which the people have fought, namely, the immediate offer of a democratic peace, the abolition of landed proprietorship, workers' control over production, and the establishment of Soviet power—this cause has been secured.

"Long live the revolution of workers, soldiers and peasants!"[25]

On November 8, the Council of People's Commissars, consisting of Bolsheviks, was established. Lenin, Chairman of the Council, read the decrees on nationalizing the land and on peace, calling upon the warring peoples and governments to enter into immediate negotiations for a peace without indemnities and annexations.

On November 15 the triumph of the Bolsheviks occurred in Moscow. After the failure of his counter-attacks, Kerensky was forced to flee in disguise to England. The Provisional government had ceased to exist. Soviet power had come into being.

At first many American radicals adopted a "wait and see" attitude toward the Bolshevik revolution. Some Russian Socialists

* At the Second Congress of the Russian Social-Democratic Labor Party in 1903, two conflicting trends emerged, the opportunist and the revolutionary, with the latter, led by Lenin, in the majority. Since then one wing has been known as Mensheviks (from the Russian word *menshinstvo*, minority) and the other as Bolsheviks (*bolshinstvo*, majority). The Bolsheviks remained a faction of the R.S.-D.L.P. until 1912, when they organized a separate party under the same name. At the Seventh Congress in 1918, the name of the party was changed to Russian Communist Party (Bolsheviks).

in the United States tried to explain it, but news from Russia was so confusing that there was simply no great clarity about what had taken place. Then on November 22, 1917, the headline in the New York *Call* read: "John Reed Cables The Call News of Bolshevik Revolt He Witnessed," and the subheading: "First Proletarian Republic Greets American Workers." The dispatch, dated Petrograd, November 13, but delayed by the censor in the United States, carried the stunning words:

"This is the revolution, the class struggle, with the proletariat, the soldiers and peasants lined up against the bourgeoisie. Last February was only the preliminary revolution. . . . The extraordinary and immense power of the Bolsheviki lies in the fact that the Kerensky government absolutely ignored the desires of the masses as expressed in the Bolsheviki program of peace, land and workers' control of industry."

A tremor of hope ran through the American radical movement. What did it matter that some leading Marxian theorists had insisted over and over again that Russia was not ready for a Socialist revolution, and that even now Karl Kautsky maintained that "the proletariat in Russia is still too weak too underdeveloped to rule the nation, to accomplish a revolution in the Socialist sense of the term."[26] The workers and peasants of Russia, under the leadership of the Bolsheviks, had proved that it was possible for the masses to seize power, and the seizure of power in Russia, it was felt, would be the signal for a European-wide, perhaps even a world-wide, revolution.

The formation of the first Socialist government thrilled and inspired the American radicals. Subjected to unprecedented harassment because of their anti-war stand especially after the United States entered the war in April 1917, many of the radicals were becoming discouraged as to their ability to continue activity. Now in backward Russia, symbol of oppression, there had occurred the most successful Socialist revolution the world had yet seen. Now, at long last, the champions of socialism could point to an example of success.

With but a few exceptions, almost all Socialist party members, officials and journals praised the Russians for what they had achieved, and expressed enthusiasm for the Bolsheviks. Three months after the October revolution, the National Executive Committee of the Socialist party hailed the fact that "the revolution of the Russian Socialists threatens the thrones of Europe and makes the whole capitalist structure tremble." Commenting on the ability of the Bolsheviks to accomplish their revolution "with hunger stalking in their midst, without credit, without international recognition, and with a ruling caste intriguing to regain control," the NEC welcomed the Soviets' "message of proletarian revolution," and gloried "in their achievement and inevitable triumph."

These sentiments were voiced by almost every Socialist leader. Eugene V. Debs consistently praised the Bolsheviks from the beginning of the revolution, and expressed himself very clearly in 1919 when he announced that "from the crown of my head to the soles of my feet I am a Bolshevik, and proud of it." Morris Hillquit, in June 1918, saw Russia "standing in the vanguard of democracy, in the vanguard of social progress, in the hands, all through from top to bottom, of the people themselves, of the working class, the peasants." Victor Berger, too, praised what the Bolsheviks had done in Russia. On the first anniversary of the revolution, the Milwaukee Socialist wrote that "the Russian people love the Soviets. They are the Soviets. Here is a government of the people and for the people in actual fact. Here is a political and industrial democracy." The Soviets' survival, "in the face of all attacks," proved that "it has satisfied its own people. It has fitted their immediate needs, it has maintained their interests, and they are with it."[27]*

Even Socialists who had supported the war, or who had been unenthusiastic about the party's anti-war stand, showed their support for the Russian revolution. Max Hayes wrote in his *Cleveland Citizen* (May 7, 1919) that the Soviets were the "most extreme democratic government that has yet been inaugurated." Several months later, Dan Hogan of Milwaukee announced that all Socialists gave "unqualified support to Soviet Russia."[28]

Although the wealthy Jews in the United States joined with others of their class in opposing the new Soviet government, none were more enthusiastic in welcoming the end of the rule of landlords and capitalists in Russia and its replacement by the rule of the workers and peasants than was the Jewish community. B. Charney Vladeck spoke for the mass of the Jewish people when he declared: "Life is strange: my body is in America. My heart and head and soul and life are in that great wonderful land, which was so cursed and which is now so blessed, the land of my youth

* Debs was close to the left-wing of the Socialist party; Hillquit, a moderate Socialist, occupied a center position between the right and left wings, and Berger was a leader of the right-wing of the party.

and revived dreams—Russia." The Jewish Socialist Federation and Jewish unions were represented at every celebration greeting the Soviet republic. In his study of the Yiddish press of this period, Joseph Rappaport concludes with the observation that "the Leninists of Russia came to be looked upon in 1918 as the hope of the world for Socialism. . . . Sympathy for the Bolsheviks mounted in the succeeding months as Leninist efforts to stabilize conditions appeared to be the only alternative to chaos and a Rightist reaction."[29] This is reflected in the stand of the *Jewish Daily Forward*, the Socialist Yiddish-language daily edited by Abraham Cahan. Up to May 1918, Cahan had been cold to the Bolsheviks, but on May 17, 1918, he announced his support of the revolution and wished "our victorious comrades in Russia further success and happiness." On May 25, the *Forward* editorialized:

"Every friend of the Russian Revolution, every Socialist who cherishes Socialism regardless of his criticism of the Bolsheviks, must support the present Bolshevik regime with all his energies, because the struggle now being waged against the Bolshevik government is a struggle against Socialism and against the government of the Russian people."

Negro Socialists joined their Jewish comrades in supporting the Bolshevik revolution. *The Messenger*, a Negro Socialist journal edited by A. Philip Randolph and Chandler Owen,* ended a long editorial (May–June 1918) on "The Soviet" with the ringing declaration: "Long Live the Soviet." *The Crusader*, another Negro Socialist journal, praised the Russian revolution and declared (October 1919): "If to fight for one's rights is to be Bolshevist, then we are Bolshevists, and let them make the most of it." The Negro Socialist press devoted much space to Lenin's famous doctrine of "national self-determination" under which every nationality within Russia could be autonomous or, if it wished, enjoy independent political and cultural existence, and contrasted this with lynching and mob violence against Negroes in the United States. Writing in *The Messenger* (September 1919), W. A. Domingo, a Negro Socialist, asked: "Will Bolshevism accomplish the full freedom of Africa, colonies in which Negroes are the majority, and promote human tolerance and happiness in the United States by the eradication of such disgraceful occurrences as the Washington and Chicago race riots?" He replied:

"The answer is deducible from the analogy of Soviet Russia,

---

* *The Messenger* was billed as "The only Magazine of Scientific Radicalism in the World Published by Negroes."

a country in which dozens of racial and lingual types have settled their differences and found a common meeting ground, a country which no longer oppresses colonies, a country from which the lynch rope is now banished and in which racial tolerance and peace now exist."

All this does not mean that there were no differences among Socialists concerning the Russian revolution. Some Socialists criticized the party press for not showing more enthusiasm for the Bolsheviks, insisting that several capitalist papers "endorse the Bolshevik with more virility than the New York *Call* or any representative Socialist periodical in America," as one county organizer in New Jersey complained.[30] But the basic difference among Socialists revolved about the question of applying the lessons of the Bolshevik revolution to the United States. Right-wing and centrist Socialists, led by Berger and Hillquit, respectively, opposed the idea of applying Bolshevik theory and methods to the United States while left-wing Socialists, led by Charles Ruthenberg, Louis G. Fraina, John Reed, Louis B. Boudin, Ludwig Lore and Nicholas Hourwich insisted that the Bolshevik program had world-wide significance and should be applied to the United States as quickly as possible. Some left-wingers saw revolution in the United States as the order of the day and put forward as the immediate aim for the Socialist party the slogan of Soviet power. They received the support of the overwhelming majority of the foreign-language Socialists, especially those in the Russian and other Eastern European Federations.[31] Other left-wingers, however, felt that the slogan of Soviet power in the United States would find no echo among the American workers and the American people and would be used as a club by reaction to destroy the party. The lessons of the Bolshevik revolution should be applied to revitalize the party without calling for immediate revolution. Both groups of left-wingers felt that the right-wing and center Socialists were merely giving lip-service support to the Bolsheviks since they had no other choice. For to condemn the October revolution would isolate them from the rank and file of the Socialist party. Still words were not enough. "The 'representatives' of the party cannot completely avoid the Bolshevik issue," wrote Fraina in *The Class Struggle* (February 1919), "so they adopt the policy of words, of camouflage. The Bolsheviks are acclaimed—miserably, in words; not daringly in deeds. . . . Action is necessary. Emphasizing the implications of accepting the Bolsheviki is necessary—the necessity for the revolutionary reconstruction of socialism."

However, it should not be forgotten that to acclaim the Bolsheviks—even in words—required courage. For this was the era of the great Red Scare and of the infamous Palmer Raids. Attorney General A. Mitchell Palmer and J. Edgar Hoover, director of the newly-created "Radical Division" in the Department of Justice, saw red "behind every bush and every demand of an increase in wages."[32] In one night, January 2, 1920, more than 4,000 suspected radicals in 33 cities were seized, arrested and thrown into jail. Some hundreds of aliens were deported to Russia and the only charge against many of them was that their names sounded Russian. The Federal government and state authorities persecuted and repressed pacifists, Socialists and radical trade unionists under esiponage and state criminal syndicalist laws. Mass indictments under the Espionage Act were returned against Socialist party and IWW members and leaders. These indictments were obviously designed directly to hamper the party organization and activity and the IWW organizing drives among the exploited lumber and agricultural workers and miners. Socialists who were elected to the New York State Legislature were not permitted to take their seats. Victor Berger was indicted in the middle of his campaign for senator in Wisconsin in March 1918, was sentenced to 20 years' imprisonment in January 1920, and was prevented by action of the Congress of the United States from taking the seat in the House of Representatives to which he was twice reelected.[33]

To acclaim the Bolsheviks and the Russian revolution in this atmosphere was to run the risk of being accused of "treason" and imprisonment. Yet the vast majority of American Socialists did hail the revolution—not a few, like Eugene V. Debs, from their prison cells.*

Socialists were not alone in supporting the Russian revolution. Arnold Peterson, national secretary of the small Socialist Labor party, in the *Weekly People* (November 24, 1917) questioned whether "up-to-date Socialism" could be established in Russia "woefully behind in capitalist development," the majority of whose population was "composed of peasants, a large number of

---

* Arrested after a meeting where he had spoken on the Russian revolution and charged with violating the Espionage Act, John Reed declared: "If people are to be imprisoned for protesting against intervention in Russia or for defending the workers' republic in Russia, I shall be proud and happy to go to jail." (New York *Call*, Sept. 16, 1918.)

whom are illiterate, and wholly ignorant as regards the object of the labor movement, and the nature of the social revolution," and whose industrial proletariat was "not organized into industrial unions, the condition *sine qua non* of the Socialist Republic." But most party members rejected this attitude, and letters to the official SLP organ, called upon the party leadership to support the Bolsheviks. "To declare their cause as hopeless is to adopt the role of a prophet," wrote a member in the *Weekly People* (December 22, 1918), "and I for one am content to leave the matter in the hands of the apparently competent Bolsheviki and await developments." The fact that the Bolsheviks had earned "the bitter enmity of the whole capitalist world" was sufficient to prove the socialist character of the new regime in Russia. Hence he wished the Bolsheviks success. The *Weekly People* agreed with its correspondent and announced its support of the revolution. Even Arnold Peterson changed his mind and announced in the party journal that the Bolshevik revolution was a truly socialist phenomenon.[34]*

The IWW saw in the victory of the Bolsheviks the triumph of the very class and principles for which the Wobblies were working. Thus an IWW publication (*Defense News Bulletin,* December 8, 1917) concluded that "in broad essentials, the now famous Bolsheviki stand for about the same thing in Russia as our IWW stands for in America," specifically workers' control of industry through industrial unions. On January 26, 1918, the *Industrial Worker* announced: "The trend of events in Russia sustains the IWW contention that the power of the workers lies in industry and in their unions on the economic field. None but actual producers can function there and the laws that are passed in the union hall have behind them the strength of the organized toilers." Noting that the Bolsheviks were a minority, the *Industrial Worker* held that they represented, nevertheless, the majority, the peasants, workers, and soldiers, who, because they were the wealth producers, were "the only groups which can and do control the situation. . . . It is they who are the revolution, not

* Peterson's change was influenced by reports that Lenin regarded Daniel De Leon, the late ideological leader of the SLP, as the father of the Soviets. The *Weekly People* proudly featured these reports under headlines like "The American Who Lenin Says Originated the Soviets" (May 11, 1918, Feb. 9, 1919). Actually, Lenin never made this statement. He did express interest in De Leon's theories, but at no time regarded him as the originator of the Soviets.

Lenin and Trotsky as the capitalist press would try to have American workers think." From this truly democratic society a new freedom would arise, based on the sturdy backs of the Russian workers who because they controlled the all important element in society, the means of production, would be able to carry out this new freedom.[35]

Since the IWW saw World War I as an imperialist conflict among capitalist nations for profit, and of no concern to the working class, the Bolshevik demand for peace and an end to Russian participation in the war, appeared completely justified. So, too, was the Bolshevik refusal to abide by treaties made by the tsarist government. A freed slave could not be expected to pay debts incurred by his master. If capitalists and their governments wanted to exact promises made during the Tsar's rule, let them redeem these promises from the men who made them. The new Russian government owed no debt to the nations of the world.[36]

The Bolshevik emphasis on political action and the necessity of capturing the institutions of the state went counter to the IWW insistence that only economic action is important because the state is only a reflection of "the economic." But while the Soviets and the formation of a Bolshevik government were "admittedly political [and] not the establishment of a society of labor based on the principles of industrial administration," this was regarded as necessary "for the time being."* In any case, the IWW did not condemn the Soviets.

"We understand them, we understand why they acted so, and moreover, we approve of their actions. It was impossible to act otherwise. We think that while it is necessary for the workers to participate in political questions, and while at the heads of foreign nations there are capitalists and autocrats, the working class of Russia must have a government of its own, based on strictly working class lines.

"As soon as the capitalist governments of other European countries fall into decay through the growth of working class

---

* It was too much to expect, many Wobblies noted, for the Bolsheviks, facing military invasion and blockade, to institute the "correct" economic organization. But on January 24, 1920, *The New Solidarity*, official journal of the IWW published in Chicago, ended an editorial entitled, "All Hail to the Bolsheviki," with the observation: "With all military resistance practically ended and the blockade raised, Soviet Russia now enters the second period of the revolution—the period of construction. And the working plan of the new social order which it shall build will be—the industrial unionism of the IWW."

power, there will be no more need for political governments of any kind. The international relations of workers will be based on industrial lines, and regulated by the economic needs of the people."[37]

By 1920, however, the strong anti-Soviet faction which then dominated the IWW General Executive Board was no longer willing to accept "the state character of the Soviets." The Board banned further distribution of Harrison George's pamphlet, *The Red Dawn: The Bolsheviki and the I.W.W.*, extolling the Bolshevik revolution and explaining its background.[38] But many Wobblies still continued to show their enthusiasm for the Bolshevik revolution by singing the new chorus for the famous IWW song, "Don't Bite the Hand That's Feeding You":

> *All hail to the Bolsheviki*
> *We will fight for our Class and be free.*
> *A Kaiser, King or Tsar, no matter which you are*
> *You're nothing of interest to me.*
>
> *If you don't like the red flag of Russia,*
> *If you don't like the spirit so true,*
> *Then just be like the cur in the story*
> *And lick the hand that's robbing you.*[39]

Even the anarchists joined in hailing the Russian revolution. Though it could not accept the Bolshevik conception of the power of the Soviets and though Lenin had made it quite clear that the movement he headed was not in favor of anarchism,[40] *Mother Earth*, edited by Emma Goldman, was filled with praises of the Bolsheviks. "Though they were Marxists and therefore governmentalists," Emma Goldman wrote years later in her autobiography, "I sided with them because they had repudiated war and had the wisdom to stress the fact that political freedom without corresponding economic equality was an empty boast."[41]

In short, for the first time in the history of American radicalism, all radical groups had a similar stand on a single issue: support of the Bolshevik revolution. To be sure, each group interpreted the revolution to fit into its own theory of revolutionary struggle and the nature of the future society. To be sure, the amount and intensity of support for the revolution varied from group to group. To be sure, this coincidence of view proved temporary and some of the early supporters of the Bolsheviks were to become their bitterest enemies. But in the months immediately following the October revolution practically all radicals were in sympathy with the Bolsheviks and regarded the revolution as shedding "the first ray of hope upon an otherwise hopeless world."[42]

A strong feeling permeated radical groups that it was not enough to extol the Russian revolution. It was also necessary to protect it. "We may help the cause of the Russian revolution along considerably by replying to slanderous attacks of the reptile press on the Bolsheviki," a member of the Socialist Labor party urged in the *Weekly People* as early as December 22, 1917. Although the press attacks on the Bolsheviks began immediately after the October revolution, emphasizing that their leaders were paid agents of the Kaiser and/or anarchists, there was still some restraint. As long as there was hope that the Bolsheviks would continue Russia's participation in the war, many newspapers were willing to hold back their attacks and the "war liberals" even spoke out in favor of the revolution.[43] During the peace negotiations with the Germans which began on December 9, 1917, at Brest-Litovsk, there was still hope that the Russians would not abandon the war. But with the signing of the treaty of Brest-Litovsk on March 3, 1918, and the ratification of the harsh terms (under which Russia was to lose its Baltic, Polish and Ukranian regions) on March 15, 1918, it was obvious that the Bolsheviks would not resume hostilities against Germany. The era of relative restraint was over. Robert K. Murray describes what occurred next:

"Horror stories of every kind filled the columns of American newspapers. It was claimed that in Petrograd the Bolsheviki had an electrically operated guillotine that lopped off five hundred heads an hour. Bolshevik rule was said to be a 'compound of slaughter, confiscation, anarchy and universal disorder . . . the paradise of IWW's and the superlative heaven of anarchists and direct-action Socialists.' The nation's cartoonists had a field day; one portrayed the Bolshevik government as a smoking gun, a bomb, and a hangman's noose, while others painted scenes of wealthy and cultured women cleaning the streets, and officers of high rank, businessmen, and professors selling newspapers to keep from starving. The Bolsheviki meanwhile were described as riding around in automobiles, dining in fashionable restaurants, and otherwise amusing themselves."[44]

The Allied blockade of Soviet-controlled territory severed most of the means of communication, including the telegraph, telephone and mail. This provided an opportunity for the invention of all sorts of horror stories. On October 31, 1918, the New York papers were filled with reports that the Bolsheviks had designated November 10 as the day of mass terror, a "St. Bartholomew's eve" on which the bourgeoisie would all be slaughtered. When November 10 passed without violence, only one paper, the New York *World,* reported this fact.[45]

Obvious forgeries, like the so-called Sisson Documents which purported to prove that the Bolsheviks were hired agents of Germany, were palmed off on the American people. Hundreds of stories were published about supposed decrees on free love. The Bolsheviks at Saratov on the Volga were reported to have issued a decree requiring all women over the age of 18 to register with a "Bureau of Free Love." Then these women were said to have been parceled out among various husbands, an unlimited supply of women to each husband. The only restriction, one paper reported, was that "men citizens have the right to use one woman not oftener than three times a week for three hours."[46]

It did not matter that these stories were exposed as lies; they continued to appear in one form or another. No wonder *The New Republic* asked wearily in November 1919: "Is the case against the Bolsheviki so weak that it has to be sustained by lies?" On August 4, 1920, *The New Republic* published its famous special supplement, "Test of the News" by Walter Lippmann and Charles Merz, which demonstrated the unreliability of reporting on Russia in *The New York Times* from 1917 to 1920. They concluded that "on every essential question the net effect of the news was almost invariably misleading."

To speak seriously of Bolshevism, noted a writer in *The New Republic* (November 2, 1918), "no matter whether one is going to condemn them or not, is considered if not a crime at least an indecency." It is to the credit of the American radicals and their press that they did speak "seriously" of the Russian revolution and exposed as best they could the incessant flow of lies about it. A few of the nation's liberal journals, such as *The Nation, The New Republic, The Public,* and *Dial,* while often critical of the Bolsheviks, did dare to insist upon publishing truthful facts concerning Russia and evidence of constructive work done by the Soviet government.[47]

At first President Wilson came in for warm praise in many radical circles because of his advocacy of the principles of no annexations, no indemnities in his December 8, 1917, address to Congress, which caused many to equate his diplomacy with the foreign policy of the Bolsheviks. Then came the Fourteen Points in which Wilson set forth his peace program, which seemed to offer sympathy and consideration to the Bolsheviks. Many Socialists who had opposed the war changed to supporters of the Administration. This trend was accelerated by the German offensives against Russia eventually culminating in the Treaty of Brest-Litovsk. Convinced that there was a need to protect the Russian revolution from the German invaders, many radicals began to take a new view of the war, or at least, the desirability of German defeat. They rallied around Wilson when he affirmed on May 18, 1918, America's determination to "stand by Russia."[48]

The Amalgamated Clothing Workers of America, formerly opposed to the war, announced in March 1918 that they stood by President Wilson "in his efforts for a democratic and durable peace, as shown by his message to Russia and by his steadfast opposition to militarism." The union had come to believe that the role of "heroic Russia" in "this frightful world tragedy" gave the "struggle against German militarism new meaning," and that German militarism now stood as "the brigand of the world." Max Eastman, editor of the Socialist literary magazine, *The Masses,* echoed this idea at his sedition trial in April. Announcing that Wilson had "placed himself directly beside the Russians" with respect to their platform of no annexations, no indemnities, and that the Germans had ignored these principles and were gaining ground in Russia, Eastman revealed that he now supported the Allied powers.[49] Morris Hillquit, who had run for mayor of New York City in the fall of 1917 on an anti-war platform, reversed himself and called upon Socialists to support the war so that "Prussianism and Austrian junkerdom . . . the foe of liberty and peace" might be overthrown and the Russian revolution saved.[50] A strong movement arose for repeal of the anti-war St. Louis Socialist platform adopted in April 1917.

But it soon became clear that the Wilson Administration, for all the President's high-sounding declarations of friendship for the Russian revolution, was bent, like the other Allied Powers, upon destroying the Soviet government. There were two "cornerstones" of the Administration's policy toward the new Soviet regime, notes William Appleman Williams: "(1) As long as the Bolsheviks remained in power the United States would refuse to establish normal intercourse and would under no circumstances recognize Lenin's government. (2) Washington would do all in its power to aid any serious and conservative leader or group whose aim was the destruction of the Soviet State."[51]

While it took some time for them to do so, most American radicals saw through Wilson's words by the summer of 1918. On August 10–12, a Conference of Socialist state secretaries and party officials met in Chicago and rejected proposals to repeal the anti-war St. Louis platform. Instead, the conference issued a "Proclamation on Russia" in which the party welcomed the Soviets as "an advanced form of democracy," and praised the Russians for having "cast aside the false idols of secret diplomacy and imperialism." "Economically and socially as well as politically," the conference declared, "the Russian Socialist Federated Soviet Republic is a government of the workers, by the workers and for the workers," which the "forces of capitalism and reaction throughout the world" were "determined to crush."

Since both sides in the war were intent on destroying the Russian revolution, the party declined to choose between them. "German imperialism," the proclamation continued, "has attempted to crush Russia from the West," after wresting the Russian border provinces and the Ukraine from Russia under a "brigand's peace." On the other hand, "imperialists in the countries at war with Germany have adopted an attitude toward Russia similar to that of the Prussian junkers," and were "demanding an invasion of Russia" and the "crushing of the Soviet Republic by Allied armies." Condemning both sides, the party called on Americans to join with it in urging the Administration to recognize the Soviet republic. "The Socialist party of America," the proclamation concluded, "declares itself in accord with revolutionary Russia and urges our government and our people to co-operate with it," to the end that the "democratic forces of the world may be victorious and autocracy and imperialism banished forever."[52]

Actually, the "imperialists" were doing more than "demanding an invasion of Russia." Although the Japanese landed two companies of marines in Vladivostok on April 5, 1918 (and the British landed a party of 50 sailors on the afternoon of the same day), the formal start of Allied intervention in Siberia began in August 1918 with the appearance of their men of war in Vladivostok. At anchor in the harbor were three Japanese warships, a British cruiser, a Chinese cruiser, and the *Brooklyn* from the U.S. Asiatic fleet. Stationed in the city were some 25,000 Allied troops, half of them Japanese.

Two contingents of American troops were landed at Vladivostok in August 1918. A month later, approximately 2,000 more men under the command of General William S. Graves arrived. At the same time, a company of infantry, a company of engineers, and some hospital units were landed in North Russia at Archangel. By late 1918, the United States had approximately 7,000 soldiers on duty in Russia.

According to the statements made at the beginning of the intervention by the powers participating in it, various purposes were proclaimed. The British announced their aim was to bring economic relief to the Russians and to assist them in the struggle against the Germans. The purpose of the Americans was "to render protection and help" to the 45,000 Czechoslovaks "against the armed Austrian and German prisoners" who were preventing their return to the western front via Siberia,* to help the Russian people "regain control of their own affairs, their own territory, and their own destiny," and eventually "to extend economic aid." Echoing the sentiments expressed by the Allies, the Japanese government announced that its purpose was to assist the Allies in accomplishing their stated mission, and in addition, to protect the lives and property of Japanese nationals residing in Eastern Siberia.[53]†

But all this was just for the record. In reality, the purpose of the intervention was to destroy Soviet power. Allied manpower, money and supplies were furnished to the counter-revolutionary forces. (By the end of the summer of 1918 there were at least 18 counter-revolutionary governments, most of them set up and supported by the Allied powers, throughout Russia.)[54] The statement that American intervention was designed primarily to rescue the Czech Legion from the German prisoners of war omitted the fact that the Czechs were counter-revolutionary factions who had

* The Czech units had been organized in the Tsar's army at the beginning of the war to aid in liberating their country from Austro-Hungarian bondage which supposedly was one of the aims of the Russian government in the war. Those units were swelled by Czech and Slovak war prisoners, and the entire body of Czechoslovaks were supposed to be moved out of Russia to assist the Allied war effort.

† Japan's official declaration emphasized that "upon the realization of the objects above indicated, they will immediately withdraw all troops from Russian territory, and will leave wholly unimpaired the sovereignty of Russia in all its phases whether political or military." (K. K. Kawakami, *Japan and World Peace,* New York, 1919, pp. 80–81.) This declaration was followed by four years of Japanese military intervention in Siberia.

aligned themselves with the parties opposing the Bolsheviks, and were not fighting Germans but Russians. The truth is that American intervention, as William Appleman Williams points out, "was undertaken to provide direct and indirect aid to the anti-Bolshevik forces in Russia. It was thus anti-Bolshevik in origins and purposes. The men who made the decision viewed the Bolsheviks as dangerous social revolutionaries who threatened American interests and the existing social order throughout the world.[55]

The United States insisted throughout the intervention that its troops were not to be used for interference in Russia domestic affairs. But American troops in Siberia did what they could to assist the White Armies. Large supplies of war material were sent to Admiral Alexander Kolchak's counter-revolutionary forces, while private banks in the United States helped to finance his war against the Soviets. In November 1918, the U.S. Treasury allowed the payment of $1,239,000 from funds accredited to the Kerensky government for printing paper currency to be used by Kolchak. Boris Bakhmetev, officially recognized by Washington as the Russian representative until June 1922 even though the government he represented had been overthrown, supported the White forces with funds derived from the sale of supplies purchased with American credits.[56]

American radicals conducted a tireless campaign to end the intervention against Soviet Russia. The "Hands Off Russia" campaign encompassed all radical groups: Socialists, Socialist Labor, IWW, and the newly-founded Communist and Communist Labor parties. While each group conducted its own campaign, the struggle to defend revolutionary Russia was a unifying force in the American radical movement. For while the Socialist party was split apart in 1919 in a dispute between the right and left wings and while the issue of how to apply the lessons of the Bolshevik revolution to the United States intensified the split, the question of defending the Russian revolution against the interventionists was not an issue that divided the different elements in the party at that time.

In the first week of September 1919, two groups of left-wing members of the Socialist party met in Chicago and formed the Communist party and Communist Labor party, respectively. The Communist party of America made its first campaign "the struggle to arouse the workers against the blockade of Soviet Russia." All branches were urged to hold mass meetings from November 7 to 9, 1919, adopt resolutions against the blockade, and distribute a "Break the Blockade of Russia" declaration issued by the Central Executive Committee of the party. The declaration stated boldly:

"The war against Russia, the blockade of Russia, is an expression of the international class struggle between the workers and the capitalists. Force is used against the Russian workers, but force is also used by these governments—British, French, Italian, Japanese, American—against their own workers. The war against Soviet Russia is a war against the workers of the world.

"Let the workers determine: We must break the blockade of Soviet Russia. . . .

"Workers, men and women! Come to the aid of your fellow-workers! Break the blockade of Soviet Russia!"[57]

The Communist Labor party entered the campaign against the blockade and intervention, distributing its "Hands Off Soviet Russia" appeal which urged American workers to emulate their brothers in Britain, France, and Italy who were "refusing to load ships with ammunition and provisions destined for the foes of Soviet Russia.[58]

Meanwhile, the Socialist party, though its ranks were decimated by the split of 1919,* continued the campaign against the intervention. Socialists, Hillquit wrote in the *Socialist World* (August 1920), had "always supported the Soviet government of Russia" because it was "the government of the working class of Russia," a government striving to "abolish every remnant of capitalism and for that reason" one which was "being persecuted by every imperialistic and reactionary power on the face of the globe." The reasons that impelled the U.S. government to "make war upon Russia," Hillquit pointed out, were "exactly the same reasons" that impelled American Socialists to "support Soviet Russia in all its struggles."

Liberal journals and progressive Senators like Hiram Johnson of California, Robert M. La Follette of Wisconsin and William E. Borah of Idaho joined the campaign against the intervention, demanding to know what American boys were doing in Siberia and Archangel; why, if the war was over, they were not being brought home. "In this day when intolerant newspapers imperatively demand immediate and complete endorsement of prevailing opinion, it is a dangerous and delicate thing to speak of

* The Socialist party lost three-fourths of its membership in two years after the split and was down to 24,587 members in 1921. (New York *Call*, Feb. 22, 1921.)

Russia, or to inquire concerning our activities there," declared Senator Johnson.[59] Nevertheless, these men did speak of Russia and exposed the Administration's Russian policy.

Radicals and liberals differed sharply on many aspects of the Russian revolution, but, in general, they agreed that the intervention was totally unjustified and against the best interests of the American people. As Senator La Follette declared on the floor of the Senate: "We have as much as we can do in the United States to restore self-government and make living conditions tolerable without further aggression in Russia.[60] Norman Thomas, writing in *The World Tomorrow* (February 19, 1919), carried this point a step further:

"If the Russians are left alone the whole world may learn valuable lessons from the great experiment, both from their failures as well as from their successes. An order of society which has come so near to the verge of collapse and ruin as our own must not crush out new hope and plans through which life and liberty may come to mankind."

The Administration's interventionist policy, however, received enthusiastic support from the top leadership of the American Federation of Labor. Gompers sadly admitted that "all our efforts to prevent the second Russian revolution failed." But this did not stop him and his associates from trying to destroy the revolution after it was successful. Although Gompers conceded that the Soviets were "undoubtedly" the *de facto* government of Russia, he warned the Administration against any friendly overtures. At the Paris Peace Conference of 1919, Gompers was the U.S. representative on the Commission of Labor Legislation. Through an intermediary, he presented the American peace commissioners with a long list of grievances against the Soviets and urged that the Russian government not be recognized. He protested that certain individuals attached to the American peace delegation seemed to support "the policy of favoring both directly and indirectly the Bolshevists."[61]

On his return to the United States, Gompers was honored at a dinner given by the National Civic Federation, an organization dominated by the leaders of big business, which stood at the head of the anti-Soviet drive.* Amidst thunderous applause, Gompers told the businessmen at the dinner that he opposed Bolshevism in

---

* The National Civic Federation saw in the anti-Bolshevik crusade "an opportunity to benefit the position of organized capital." (Robert K. Murray, *Red Scare: A Study in National Hysteria*, Minneapolis, 1955, p. 85.)

theory and in fact. In theory he considered it a mental impossibility, and he warned that if it were put into operation, it would mean the "decadence and perversion of the civilization of our time."[62]

Despite Gompers' bitter opposition to the Bolshevik revolution, delegates to the AF of L conventions insisted on voicing their members' support for the Soviet republic. At the 1919 convention at Atlantic City, resolutions were introduced calling for recognition of Soviet Russia, for the lifting of the blockade, and an end to intervention by outside governments. One resolution, introduced by the central labor union of Portland, Oregon, urged withdrawal of American troops from Russia, and another, proposed on behalf of the central labor unions of Cleveland and Akron, Ohio, asked that all American troops be withdrawn as speedily as possible, and that the Russian people "be left to regulate their own affairs." The Pennsylvania Federation of Labor called for the lifting of the blockade on Russian ports so that food and clothing might reach the Russian people. On behalf of the Seattle Central Labor Council, James A. Duncan, its secretary, introduced a resolution demanding both withdrawal of troops and recognition of the workers' government. The resolution proposed that the question of recognition be referred by ballot to members of the AF of L, so that policy might be determined by the rank and file.

These resolutions were rejected by the committee on resolutions to which they were referred. However, bowing to the sentiment of the delegates, the committee reported out a resolution which recommended withdrawal of American troops "at the earliest possible moment," but, reflecting the viewpoint of the AF of L leadership, refused to endorse the Soviet government until the people of Russia had established "a truly democratic form of government." John P. Frey, secretary of the committee on resolutions, advanced an astounding explanation for the committee's refusal to endorse the Soviet government: since the Russians claimed that their government represented only the workers such as government was unrepresentative of the nation as a whole. The committee could not approve of sending food to the Russian people because "it would simply strengthen the Bolshevik government that controls the transportation of food." A delegate from the International Ladies' Garment Workers' Union then asked if the AF of L, having refused to support sending food to the Russians, would "approve of sending ammunition to the Kolchak government to kill the Russian workers."[63] The remark infuriated Gompers, but the delegate's comment revealed the disgust many workers felt at the position adopted by the AF of L leadership toward the Russian revolution.

At the Montreal convention of 1920, resolutions on Russia were again placed before the delegates. Delegate Luigi Antonini of the ILGWU introduced a resolution praising the people of Russia for having established a government which was "based on the universal duty to work and the right of all toilers to have and enjoy the full produce of their labor, thereby doing away with industrial slavery and economic injustice, the elimination of which we hold to be the ultimate aim and finality of the organized labor movement," and calling for lifting of the blockade against Russia, the resumption of trade relations with her, and recognition of the Soviet government by the United States. Duncan of the Seattle Central Labor Council introduced a resolution which expressed admiration for "the noble defensive fight waged against tremendous odds by the workers of Russia for the right to work out their own salvation, without outside interference," called upon the government to urge the immediate withdrawal of all foreign troops from Russia, to lift the blockade and furnish credits to the Russian government.

Once again the Administration-dominated committee on resolutions rejected these resolutions. Instead it recommended a resolution which not only did not call for withdrawal of foreign troops, but went beyond the 1919 resolution in criticizing the Soviet government, adding to the previous charge of its non-representative character an indictment of its attempt "to create revolutions in the well-established, civilized nations of the world" and to interfere in the functioning of trade unions. Duncan announced himself "astounded" by the report, and urged the delegates not to be taken in by imperialist propaganda against the workers' republic. "I know that possibly it is unpopular in an American Federation of Labor convention, at least, to say one word in behalf of my Russian brothers, but regardless of the cost I am going to undertake at least one sympathetic voice in this convention." Duncan expressed the hope that the convention would go on record in a very definite way as being opposed to any further blockade, for the resumption of trade with Russia, and demand the right of the Russian people to have the opportunity "to work out their own salvation without outside interference."

But the AF of L leadership refused to budge. Frey, speaking for the committee on resolutions, disclosed the fact that on the eve of the convention, Gompers had wired Secretary of State Bainbridge Colby asking if the government sanctioned trade relations between the United States and Russia. Colby had replied that "there is no licensed or regular trading between the United States and Russia at present," added hypocritically that while the government "had no desire to interfere with the international affairs of the Russian people or to suggest the kind of government they should have," it could not approve of "the existing regime in Russia," nor recommend trade relations with it. The AF of L leadership emphasized that Colby's stand was sufficient to justify the convention in refusing to recommend relations with Russia. The convention then proceeded to adopt the resolution proposed by the committee on resolutions.[64] One-third of the votes cast, however, were in favor of trade relations with Russia, and *Justice* reported in its issue of July 2, 1920, that "The Negroes [at the Convention] in general voted to extend the helping hand to the Russians." The Philadelphia *Public Ledger,* conservative Republican organ, hailed the AF of L leadership for having defeated the rising tide in the American labor movement for recognition of and support for the Russian Soviet government. "It is a matter for congratulations," it declared enthusiastically on June 17, 1920.

While the national AF of L refused to take a stand in support of Soviet Russia and, instead, allied itself with the interventionist drive to destroy the Socialist republic, many international unions, local unions, city centrals and state federations of labor rallied to the support of the embattled Russian workers and peasants. The International Ladies' Garment Workers' Union and the Amalgamated Clothing Workers of America, a large percentage of whose membership were Jewish immigrants from tsarist Russia and identified themselves with the Socialists in the United States, took the lead. At the ILGWU's 14th convention which met in May 1918, the delegates pledged themselves to the following program:

"The members of the International Ladies' Garment Workers' Union will follow the struggle of their brothers in Russia with intense interest and sympathy, not only because many are linked to them by ties of kinship and sentiment, but also because the fate of the first great working class republic in the world cannot but be a matter of prime concern to the organized and progressive workers of all countries."[65]

The ILGWU condemned the blockade and called for the reestablishment of trade relations with Russia. The union attacked Wilson's policy toward Russia as "pathetic and lacking in vision," and condemned the AF of L's stubborn opposition to the Soviet government. It called the resolution adopted by the 1920 AF of L convention "condescending" toward the workers' republic.

President Benjamin Schlesinger of the ILGWU spent several weeks in Russia prior to attending the International Federation of Trade Union's Conference at Copenhagen. On his return to the United States in November 1920, he predicted that the Soviet government would "not fall before the blows of international capitalism," and declared that the "great suffering in Russia is not due to failure of the workers' Republic, but is due to the blockade that has kept Russia from importing necessaries." Schlesinger praised the admirable attempts to regenerate the poorer classes, the absence of exploitation of labor, and the magnificent role of the trade unions in determining the nation's destinies.[66]

The Amalgamated Clothing Workers were even more firm in support of the Russian revolution. "The interest in Russian affairs among our members is intense," Joseph Schlossberg, general secretary of the union declared in June 1918. "Many of them have been citizens of Russia in the past, and they are familiar with conditions there and know what the revolution means to the great mass of the Russian people." At its convention that same month, the Amalgamated hailed "with joy free Russia" and sent her its "most fraternal greetings." "It is our fervent hope," the union resolved, "that our own country and all other civilized nations will come to the assistance of free Russia by recognizing the Russian people's Soviet government, and giving the Russian people all aid in working out their own destinies."[67]

The Amalgamated endorsed the Russian Soviet Recognition League, formed in June 1918, to influence the government to establish relations with the Soviet republic. It opposed intervention on the ground that the Bolshevik government was supported by a majority of the Russian people and was successfully establishing order. The union denounced American participation in the blockade against Russia, and at its 1920 convention called upon the government to enter into friendly relations with Russia to offset the untold hardships created by the blockade.

The Amalgamated felt that it was the duty of all American workers to stand by Russia because, regardless of certain faults, the Soviet republic embodied the principle of a workers' government. The union viewed Russia's struggle against her capitalist enemies as an industrial strike on a vast scale, and insisted that world labor should adopt the same attitude toward Soviet Russia as it would toward any sister organization in the industrial world. The enemies of Russia were also the enemies of labor. The Amalgamated regarded the Russian experiment as a test of whether labor was able to take over the reins of government or whether it must resign itself to a secondary position. It admired Russia's progress in the face of a hostile world, believing that the workers' republic held out a promise of a better day for workers everywhere.[68]

Sidney Hillman, president of the Amalgamated, returned from a visit to Soviet Russia in 1921 full of enthusiasm for the workers' republic. He found "order preserved even in economic ruin," efficient factories producing clothing fit to wear in the United States, and an incomparable appreciation by labor of its duties in society. "Labor understands its mission in Russia, and its mission in life is to build." Referring to his contact with various officials if the Soviet government, Hillman declared: "I have never met a group of people so realistic, so practical, so courageous as the group of people who have charge of the destinies of the Russian nation today." And he concluded: "I want to tell you that the power of that Russian group is greater than any group anywhere, because it has a power that comes from the willing cooperation of the peoples of Russia."[69]*

No labor body was a more consistent defender of the Russian revolution than the Seattle Central Labor Council. Its official journal, the Seattle *Union Record,* published and distributed 20,000 copies of Lenin's speech, delivered in April 1918 to the Congress of Soviets, on the next tasks of organizing power. It was "avidly read by radicals up and down the Pacific Coast as well as in Seattle's shipyards."[70] Since little or no authentic news about Russia was printed in the Seattle commercial press, the *Union Record* opened a Bureau of Russian Information which published from time to time reports of constructive work under the Bolsheviks.

---

* Although it lies outside the scope of the present discussion, it is worth mentioning the intensive campaign the Amalgamated waged during 1921 and 1922 to raise funds for relieving the famine in Russia and its activity in founding the Russian-American Industrial Corporation, organized in 1922 to develop the clothing industry in Russia.

The educational work conducted by the *Union Record* helps explain the fact that while most unions opposed intervention against Russia through speeches and resolutions, the workers of Seattle went further. In September 1919, the longshoremen of the city noticed a mysterious shipment by rail, a trainload of 50 freight cars, destined for Vladivostok, and labeled "sewing machines." When a longshore crew, suspicious of the cargo, allowed a crate to crash on the dock, out came stacks of rifles, bound for the Kolchak counter-revolutionary government. The longshoremen's union announced that its members would not touch the cargo, and that any dock that attempted to move it would be put under permanent ban. The union notified other ports of their action. The Central Labor Council backed up the longshoremen.[71]

The Allied intervention and blockade caused widespread suffering in Russia, but so far as overthrowing the Bolshevik government, they proved fruitless. To be sure, the interventionist press repeatedly reported the intervention to be a success and the fall of the Bolshevik government was a regular weekly feature. "It fell with a regularity that in time became tedious," writes Christopher Lasch. "Altogether, if *The New York Times* was to be believed, it fell or was about to fall 91 times in a period of two years from November 1917 to November 1919."[72] But by the beginning of 1920 the failure of the intervention was obvious. In January, the blockade against Russia was lifted by the Allied powers—the United States, however, waited until July 7, 1920, before announcing the nominal lifting of the blockade—and later that year Allied warships and troops, including American troops, were withdrawn.[73]

Justice, official organ of the ILGWU, declared that the failure of the intervention was caused by the fact that, while Russia had to conduct a war "amidst untold sufferings," the Russian people had been "prepared to make these sacrifices for the triumph of the workers' republic," and this spirit had caused the inevitable triumph of Soviet power. Others attributed the failure of the intervention to divisions among the Allied powers. But there was general agreement that the "Hands Off Russia" campaign conducted by American radicals, liberals and trade unionists (and similar campaigns in other countries) had contributed to ending the intervention. On the second anniversary of the October revolution, L.C.A.K. Martens, the Soviet government's official representative in the United States, hailed American labor for its support of his country and opposition to the intervention: "I want to thank the American workingmen and women in behalf of Soviet Russia for the sympathy and helpfulness which they have shown during the past year in their protests against the attacks on Soviet Russia. I feel confident that the more the American workers learn the truth about the republic of the Russian workers, the stronger will be our bonds of sympathy and solidarity."[74]

Martens, a Russian engineer living in the United States since 1916, had been appointed on January 2, 1919, as the first "Representative of the People's Commissariat for Foreign Affairs in the United States of America." On March 18, 1919, he dispatched his first note to the State Department in which he informed it of his appointment as official representative of the Russian Soviet Federated Socialist Republic. The memorandum stressed: "Being fully aware that the prosperity of the whole world, including that of Soviet Russia, depends on the continuous exchange of goods between different countries, the Soviet government wishes to take up trade relations with other countries and the USA especially." The memorandum contained a long list of goods the Soviet government was ready to buy and sell including railway equipment, farm implements, mining and electrical machinery.

"The Soviet government," the memorandum stated, "is willing to acquire immediately in the USA large amounts of manufactured goods on a payments agreement satisfactory to both sides and to enter into an agreement for the export from Russia of raw materials, required by other countries, of which there is an enormous surplus in Russia. In the event of trade relations with the USA being resumed, the Soviet government is ready to deposit immediately in European and American banks gold to the value of $200,000,000 as payment for the initial purchase."[75]

Martens was ignored by the State Department. Acting Secretary of State Frank L. Polk informed him on April 17, 1919, that the United States had on July 5, 1917, recognized the representative of the Provisional government as Russian ambassador, and would continue to consider him the sole representative. The letter stated that "the Government of the United States has not received nor recognized Mr. Martens in any representative capacity in the United States on behalf of the Government of Russia, or of any other Government." Despite this rebuff, Martens tried to establish normal relations with the United States. He set up the Bureau of the Russian Soviet Federated Socialist Republic in

New York on March 19, 1919, and after December 20, 1919, in Washington, achieved contacts with American business firms and made some $30,000,000 worth of tentative contracts. He reported that within the short period from April to December 1919, 941 firms in 32 states "expressed a readiness to enter into trade relations with Soviet Russia."[76]

But the anti-Soviet forces in the United States would not permit the establishment of normal relations with the socialist government. In January 1919, *Bankers' Magazine* carried a report of a speech delivered by Prince George Lvov, first premier of the Provisional government, under the auspices of the American-Russian Chamber of Commerce. Prince Lvov appealed to the assembled bankers and businessmen for help to crush the Bolsheviks so that American capital could come to Russia. He warned: "If the disease which we call Bolshevism is not stopped in Russia, it will threaten the healthy economic development of other civilized countries, and none of them can claim immunity. Bolshevism is a universal danger and must be crushed by the joint forces of the Allies." *Nation's Business* agreed that the basic condition for resumption of trade with Russia was the overthrow of the Bolsheviks. American capitalists were quite ready to invest in Russia and trade with her. But the Bolshevik government was "upsetting the business tradition of ages" and turning things topsy-turvy. Russia's chances to get foreign trade and capital "depended completely upon the fall of the Bolsheviki."[77] Little wonder then that Martens' overtures for the establishment of normal relations were brusquely rejected.

Martens was subjected to continual harassment both in New York and Washington. On June 12, 1919, representatives of the Lusk Committee (a New York Joint Legislative Committee Investigating Seditions Activities, headed by state senator Clayton R. Lusk) raided the Soviet Government Bureau in New York City. On November 14, Martens was subpoenaed by Lusk, and although he replied at first that he was only answerable to the State Department, he consented to appear. The hearings went on before the Lusk Committee through November and into December. Martens answered questions freely about his diplomatic mission and his political beliefs, but declined to reveal the channels through which he was in communication with his government. Judged in contempt by Lusk, Martens went to Washington which put him out of the state senator's jurisdiction.[78]

In December 1919, the Department of Justice issued a warrant for Martens' arrest. But before the warrant could be served, Martens appeared before a sub-committee of the Senate and obtained the protection of its hearings, which continued from January 19 to March 29, 1920. After the hearings, the sub-committee concluded that Martens had no status as a diplomat or other type of governmental representative, had not received recognition from the U.S. government, and was guilty of having conducted propaganda against the United States.

The persecution of Martens continued. He was subjected to still more hearings, this time before an immigration inspector. On December 25, 1920, the Department of Labor ordered Martens' deportation from the United States. The action was taken even though Secretary of Labor William B. Wilson ruled that "Mr. Martens was not proved to have done anything unlawful as an individual."[79] Martens reported to his government that the deportation order was "undoubtedly politically dictated by the policy of the present Government toward the Soviet Government," and was "based on no actions ascribed to me but only on the circumstances that I am representing the Soviet Government."[80] Ultimately the deportation warrant was canceled, and Martens was allowed to leave the country quietly on January 29, 1921. As he departed, *The Toiler,* official organ of the Communist Party of America, noted (February 5, 1921) that he left "amidst the cheers and well wishes of thousands assembled upon the docks and piers of New York's harbor." It predicted that the day would come when normal relations would be established between the United States and the Soviet Union:

"The demand for recognition of and trade with Russia has not been stifled by this act of deportation. A matter of this importance is not settled in that manner. The causes which created the demand for a favorable settlement of this question are growing larger and larger. A country of the size and economic quality of Russia cannot be left out of this country's trade calculations and all be well. Conditions demand the opening of trade relations, this, aside from humanitarian reasons, will have the say-so and settle the question in favor of trade."

Even while Martens was being persecuted, the demand for relations with Russia was mounting.[81] Radicals and liberals joined in denouncing the treatment of Martens, and urged a policy of friendship with the Soviet Union. On January 2, 1921, 10,000 workingmen and women and liberal-minded citizens met in New York's Madison Square Garden to protest the plan to deport

Martens and to urge recognition of and trade with the Soviet republic. Sponsored by a large body of trade unions, the meeting condemned the deportation order and the continuing blockade of Russia, and requested that Martens "take to the Russian workers the greetings of their American brothers, and the assurance that we are utterly opposed to the treatment by the administration of the accredited representative to this country of the Russian Soviet Republic, as well as to the policies of the administration regarding relations between the United States and Russia."[82]

A year earlier, in January 1920, the American Commercial Association to Promote Russian Trade was organized by 45 American business firms. Pointing out that England, France, Italy and even Germany were "making strenuous efforts to corral Russian trade," the Association asked the State Department "to permit the shipment of American goods into Russian ports."[83] The request was rejected, but the movement for trade with Russia continued to gain strength. Following the wartime boom, business received a sharp setback in 1921. The number of unemployed mounted, reaching three and a half million by the fall of 1921. Business and labor urged that trade with Russia would serve a two-fold purpose: alleviate famine conditions in Russia and cut down on unemployment in the United States. "We have come to realize now," declared Joseph Schlossberg of the Amalgamated Clothing Workers, "because the hundred and thirty million human beings in Russia are badly in need of the things which we can produce for them, that they will be excellent customers and give us employment if Washington will permit us to work for them."[84]

On November 21, 1920, a conference of authorized delegates of New York's labor unions founded the American Labor Alliance for Trade Relations with Russia. (Originally the organization was called the American Humanitarian Labor Alliance.) The delegates, representing 800,000 organized workers, chose Timothy Healy of the International Association of Firemen and Oilers as chairman of the Alliance, and Alexander Trachtenberg of the ILGWU as secretary. A resolution adopted by the conference stated:

"Resolved, That we demand that the State Department take immediate steps to remove all obstacles to trade with Russia, to establish communication by post, cable, and wireless, to restore the right to travel between the United States and Soviet Russia, and to permit the transfer of funds from Russia to be used in the purchase of American goods, to allow authorized representatives of the Soviet government to act in its behalf regarding all commercial transactions and otherwise establish complete and unrestricted relations with Russia."

The objectives of the Alliance were endorsed by 12 international and national unions, more than a score of state federations of labor, and the central labor unions of 72 cities in 29 states, all of them affiliated with the American Federation of Labor, and representing a membership of 2,500,000 workers. (When one realizes that the total membership of the AF of L was about 4,000,-000, it is clear that the aims of the Alliance received the endorsement of a substantial section of the Federation.) Leaders in the support of the Alliance's program included the Central Trades and Labor Council of New York City (600,000 members); the Chicago Federation of Labor (400,000 members); Seattle Central Labor Council (600,000 members); the ILGWU (115,000 members), and the Amalgamated Clothing Workers (175,000 members).[85] All of the organizations, except the Amalgamated, were affiliated to the AF of L.

A resolution for reopening trade relations with Russia was introduced into the Senate on February 27, 1920, by Senator Joseph I. France of Maryland. The resolution was referred to the Senate Committee on Foreign Relations, dominated by reactionary anti-Soviet Republicans, Henry Cabot Lodge and Philander Knox, and remained buried there for a whole year. The Committee finally got around to holding hearings on Senator France's resolution, and on January 26, 1921, representatives of the American Labor Alliance for Trade Relations with Russia appeared to plead the cause of American labor for the resumption of trade with Russia. Timothy Healy told the Committee that he had sounded out labor opinion on relations with Russia on his recent trip throughout the East and Midwest, "held meetings in 25 or 27 cities between Maine and Nebraska and Kansas," and found that everywhere workers were "anxious that trade should be resumed with Russia. . . . I believe that the average workingman today in this country is in favor of the recognition of the Soviet republican government of Russia." However, the Alliance was not pressing for recognition of Soviet Russia at this time. But it was convinced that the resumption of trade with Russia was an urgent necessity in order to relieve "the steady growing unemployment in this country, which has already, according to our Department of Labor report just published, reached 3,473,466."

But the plight of American workers did not concern the members of the Senate Committee. Nor were they impressed by the number of trade unionists who supported the Alliance's program; all they wanted to know was how many of these workers were American citizens, as if it were impossible for any one but an alien to favor normal relations with Soviet Russia.[86] Although rebuffed by the Senate Committee on Foreign Relations, the Alliance received increased impetus to continue its work in favor of reopening trade with Russia by the negotiation of a trade agreement between the British and Soviet governments in 1921. So great was the movement now favoring trade with Russia that the AF of L leadership became alarmed. Even though his own organization, the Cigar Makers' Union, joined the campaign for trade relations with Russia, Gompers determined to crush the movement. In this he had the full cooperation of the U.S. government.

On March 15, 1921, Gompers wrote to Secretary of State Charles Evans Hughes requesting information on the status of trade between the United States and Russia, and asking whether it was possible to establish an effective trade relationship between the two countries, thereby reducing unemployment in the United States. Hughes, as was to be expected, replied that Russia did not possess "important quantities of commodities which might be exported," that it represented "a gigantic economic vacuum," and that no evidence existed that "the unfortunate situation above described is likely to be alleviated so long as the present political and economic system continues." Hughes then voiced the yearning of leading American capitalists: "It is the sincere hope of this government that there may be readjustments in Russia which will make it possible for that country to resume its proper place in the economic life of the world." Translated into simple English, this meant that the U.S. government hoped that the day would soon arrive when the Soviet system would be overthrown and Russia once again would be free for capitalist exploitation.

Gompers promptly published Hughes' letter in the *American Federationist* and distributed it to all national and international unions, state federations and city central labor unions and to the entire labor press. "The information contained therein," he emphasized, "ought to be given the most careful attention and it should be brought to the attention of the people everywhere." He called particular attention to Hughes' remark that there was little likelihood of any change in Russia's economic picture as long as the Soviet system continued.[87]

In *A Letter to American Workers,* first published in *The Class Struggle* of December 1918, Lenin called Gompers the American Scheidemann, comparing him with the German Social-Democratic leader who served the interests of the Kaiser and the imperialists.[88] In the eyes of many American workers Gompers' efforts to crush the movement for trade relations with Russia justified this condemnation. In its March, 1922 issue, the *Locomotive Engineers Journal,* organ of the conservative Brotherhood of Locomotive Engineers, bitterly condemned Gompers for permitting his hatred of the Soviet Union to blind him to the needs of American labor:

"We are not concerned with Mr. Gompers' private opinion about the Russian government. That is his own affair. . . . We are only amused by his inconsistency when in one breath he preaches disarmament and good will among the nations, and in the next he calls for the isolation and extinction of the largest country in Europe. Like the gold-braided generals of France, he wants peace, but first he wants his bucket of Bolshevik blood. But we are rightly concerned when Mr. Gompers, claiming to speak for American labor, officially urges our government to adopt a policy toward Russia that will take bread and butter out of the mouths of American workers and sow the seeds of chaos in Europe."

Europe, the *Journal* pointed out, needed cessation of military activity to achieve economic reconstruction and this was essential for American economic recovery. "Peace with Russia" was thus the first step toward economic reconstruction.

"Like the multiplication table, this is not a matter of sentiment, but a cold fact, upon which well-informed labor leaders, political economists, and statesmen of Europe are agreed. Opposing them are the blood-thirsty tsarist generals, the hordes of ex-Russian landlords, no-account counts, ignoble nobles, and other jobless remnants of autocracy, together with a Russian propaganda bureau in New York sponsored by eminent Wall Street bankers and labor haters. Truly Mr. Gompers has chosen strange bedfellows.

"Were Mr. Gompers an ordinary citizen, his lack of knowledge about Russia would excuse him from severe censure. He has never been to Russia. . . . His information about Russia is second-hand, and often obtained from very unreliable second-hand dealers. But in Mr. Gompers' case this ignorance is no excuse. The leader who attempts to lead without knowledge is morally responsible for the consequences of his blunders.

"Mr. Gompers may not know much about conditions in Russia, but he ought to know and care about the situation in the United States. Between four and five million workers are walking our streets searching for jobs. Miners are starving in West Virginia and dodging bayonets in Colorado. The Supreme Court tears up labor's safeguards built up by years of struggle. Millions of unorganized workers are ruthlessly exploited by the Steel Trust and its allies. Groups of organized workers are rent asunder by jurisdictional disputes. The open shop campaign and the drive to slash wages is in full tilt. While American labor is being crucified, Mr. Gompers takes time to stick pins into the hide of the Russian bear."

But these words of wisdom were lost on the AF of L leaders. At the 1921 convention, the Executive Council took the lead in opposing any move the delegates might make in favor of trade with Russia by submitting a report entitled "America and the Soviets," which condemned the campaign for trade relations as a camouflage for *de facto* recognition of the Soviet government, and conducted "with a redoubled intensity both in the subsidized revolutionary press and in certain pro-Bolshevist newspapers and weeklies." Ignoring the fact that over 2,000,000 AF of L members had demanded trade relations with Russia, the report emphasized that it was all part of a Bolshevik plot "within the labor unions with a view of overthrowing the bona fide labor movement of America as a condition precedent for the overthrow of the republic of the United States." The report was vigorously opposed by many delegates, led by the ILGWU delegation. But the Gompers' machine had the necessary votes, and the report was adopted by the convention.[89]

"AF of L: Gibraltar of Reaction" read the title of an editorial in the June 1, 1922 issue of *Advance,* official organ of the Amalgamated Clothing Workers. The journal attacked the Federation's leadership for having "reaffirmed its open and bitter antagonism to Russia," and dismissed the reasons advanced for opposing recognition of and trade with Russia as "fraudulent":

"The true reason is that the Civic Federation and the powers that be are against recognition of Soviet Russia. That is the law for Gompers. . . . Let it be clearly understood that with the AF of L leaders the determining factor in the Russia question is not the conduct of the Soviet government but the wishes of American capital."

The Soviet Union had survived the bitter opposition of the American government, American capital and the leaders of the American Federation of Labor. Few indeed, were those anywhere, who during the first critical years after the October revolution, foresaw the survival of the Soviet government. At one point during the civil war and the war against Western and Japanese invasions, its territory was down to about a tenth of what was formerly the Russian empire. Its end was regarded as certain. But the Bolshevik leadership, headed by Lenin, and a self-sacrificing spirit of the people in support of the new government, produced victory for the world's first Socialist government. In 1921, the Soviet republic was an established fact. To be sure, six and a half years of war, revolution, civil war, and foreign intervention had left large parts of Russia in ruins. But armed intervention was a lost cause. Great Britain had granted *de facto* recognition of the Soviet government. Soviet trading delegations were established in many countries. Although full diplomatic recognition was withheld in most cases, Soviet Russia was no longer isolated.

The United States, the first nation to recognize the Provisional government established after the February revolution, was the last great power to accord recognition to its Soviet successor. On October 30, 1923, in a speech in New York's Harlem on "The Negro Workers," Eugene V. Debs once again hailed the Russian revolution and predicted the ultimate recognition of the Soviet republic by the government of the United States.

"The reason we do not recognize their Republic is because for the first time in history they have set up a government of the working class; and if that experiment succeeds, good-bye to capitalism throughout the world! That is why our capitalist Government does not recognize Soviet Russia. We were not too proud to recognize the Tsar nor to have intercourse with Russia whilst Siberia was in existence and human beings were treated like wild beasts; when women were put under the lash and sent to Siberia and brutalized and dehumanized. We could calmly contemplate all this and our President could send congratulations on his birthday to the imperial Tsar of Russia. We could then have perfect intercourse with that Government, but we are now so sensitive under our present high standard of moral ethics that we cannot recognize Soviet Russia. But the time will come when the United States will recognize the Soviet Republic of the Russian people."[90]

Ten years later, Debs' prediction came true. For 16 years, Soviet Russia was officially a nonentity in the eyes of the government of the United States. Finally, on November 16, 1933, full diplomatic relations were established between the United States and the Soviet Union.[91] On that day, President Franklin D. Roosevelt wrote to Maxim Litvinov, Soviet Foreign Minister: "I trust that the relations now established between our peoples may forever remain normal and friendly, and that our nations henceforth may co-operate for their mutual benefit and for the preservation of the peace of the world."[92]

American radicals, liberals and trade unionists who had championed the cause of friendly relations between the United States and Soviet Russia in the years immediately following the October revolution, could take pride in their contributions.[93] Although it spoke only for its own organization, in its issue of December, 1933, *Advance* also expressed the views of these early advocates of normal relations between the two countries:

"After 16 years 'we' finally recognize the Soviet Union. 'We'— the USA not the ACWA. Our union did not require that much time to recognize a fact of world-wide significance—the establishment of a labor regime over one-sixth of the globe and a population of 160 million. . . .

"It is legitimate pride for the Amalgamated to say that during these sixteen years of diplomatic break between the USA and USSR, the clothing workers have done a good deal toward breaking down current prejudices against the Russian people and the fear of industrial and business relations with the Soviet government. . . .

"That the government of the United States has taken our position, now 16 years old, may not be a matter of undue humiliation for the spokesman of that government, but we just aren't modest enough to refuse to emphasize our pride and joy on this occasion."

An Interruption

The Liberator, March 1918

—BOARDMAN ROBINSON

THE FIRST YEAR

November 1917 to November 1918

1. FIRST PROLETARIAN REPUBLIC
GREETS AMERICAN WORKERS

*John Reed left New York for Russia in August 1917, repre-
senting* The Masses, the New York Call, *and* Seven Arts. *He
was accompanied by his wife, Louise Bryant. Reed arrived in
Petrograd in September, and began attending meetings of committees of the Petrograd Soviet and of shop committee delegates
at Smolny Institute, once a fashionable academy for daughters of
the tsarist nobility. He interviewed Kerensky, heard Lenin speak
at the Smolny Institute, and was present at the All-Russian Congress of Soviets on November 7 when the workers, peasants and
soldiers in the Congress hailed the seizure of power by the Bolsheviks. He witnessed the capture of the Winter Palace by
soldiers, sailors and the Red Guard, and on November 8 heard
Lenin announce at Smolny, "We shall now proceed to construct
the Socialist order." On the morning of November 13, when news
reached Smolny of Kerensky's defeat, Lenin gave Reed a short
statement for American Socialists. On November 15, Reed received permission to cable this message, together with an account
of Kerensky's downfall, to the New York* Call, *the Socialist daily
newspaper. The dispatch was held up by the censor in the United*

*States, and was released on November 21. On the following day,
the* Call *published it under a seven-column banner.* (For his full
account of the revolution, first published in 1919, *see* John Reed,
Ten Days That Shook the World, New York, 1967.)

by JOHN REED

Petrograd, November 13.—The Petrograd garrison, the Kronstadt sailors and the Red Guard,[1] comprising as a whole the Bolsheviki army, last night defeated Kerenski's army of 7,000 Cossacks, junkers (students in military schools) and artillery, who were attacking the capital.

The attempted "junker" insurrection on Sunday, directed by the committee of salvation, comprising Mensheviki (moderate Socialists) and Cadets (Constitutional Democrats)[2], was put down by the Kronstadt sailors, who took an armored car and telephone station by assault, and also the "junior" school.

Hundreds of delegates arrived at Smolny Institute, the headquarters of the revolutionary government and of the councils, to report the solidarity of the army at the front with the Bolsheviki.

This is the revolution, the class struggle, with the proletariat, the workmen, the soldiers and the peasants lined up against the bourgeoisie. Last February was only the preliminary revolution. At the present moment the proletariat are triumphant.

The rank and file of the Workmen's, Soldiers' and Peasants' Councils are in control, with Lenin and Trotsky leading. Their program is to give the land to the peasants, to socialize natural resources and industry and for an armistice and democratic peace conference. The extraordinary and immense power of the Bolsheviki lies in the fact that the Kerenski government absolutely ignored the desires of the masses as expressed in the Bolsheviki program of peace, land and workers' control of industry. . . .

No one is with the Bolsheviki except the proletariat, but that is solidly for them. All the bourgeoisie and appendages are relentlessly hostile. . . .

The news from the front and from all over the country shows that although some fighting is still going on in various cities the masses are pretty solid for the Bolsheviki, except in the Don region where General Kaledin[3] and the Cossacks have proclaimed a military dictatorship.

The Workmen's, Soldiers' and Peasants' councils through *The Call* send to the American International Socialists a greeting from the first proletarian republic of the world.

——*New York* Call, *November 22, 1917.*

2. CLEVELAND SOCIALISTS GREET
BOLSHEVIK REVOLUTION

At an emergency convention, the Cleveland local of the So-cialist party adopted the following resolution, drawn up by Charles E. Ruthenberg. The resolution was distributed through-out Cleveland in leaflet form. The resolution reflected the excite-ment caused by the news that the first act of the Russian Councils of Workers and Soldiers, after seizure of power, was to call for an end to the war.

The effort of the Bolsheviks to establish peace through the action of the workers of all countries, a peace not based upon the interests of the ruling classes of the nations involved nor attained through the trading of diplomats, but based upon the interests of the workers and established through the aggressive action of the workers, a peace without annexations and without indemni-ties, offers the only hope of saving our civilization from destruc-tion. In this effort we pledge to the workers of Russia our earnest support. We hail the policy of their present government as the true expression of proletarian action, and pledge ourselves to do all in our power to assist in wiping out capitalist imperialism and in establishing the civilization of the future, the commonwealth of the workers united irrespective of nationality.

——*Cleveland* Socialist News, *November 25, 1917.*

3. "THANK GOD FOR THE RUSSIAN REVOLUTION"

One of the first statements issued in the United States hailing the Bolshevik revolution appeared in the sermon delivered by Dr. John Haynes Holmes, the Socialist pastor of the Church of the Messiah in New York City.

"Thank God for the Russian revolution." Dr. John Haynes Holmes, pastor of the Church of the Messiah, raised this prayer of thanksgiving yesterday morning during his sermon on "Thanksgiving or Penitence: Which?"

Holmes said his spirit "is swinging between penitence and thanksgiving," that his "mind and heart are confused," but later declared that his hope in a better world, seconded by such events as the Russian revolution, was triumphing in his spirit.

His voice registered exultation when he declared. "This is the Day of Revolution. They are going to do away with kaisers and tsars everywhere," and he made it clear that he included with the political kaisers and tsars the industrial kaisers and tsars of democracies. . . .

Speaking of the Russian revolution, he said:

"The spirit of Tolstoy today is ruling Russia. This is a thing for which we cannot offer too much thanksgiving. The peasants of Russia have overthrown the tsar, and with him the spirit of autocracy, war, Siberia and oppression."

———*New York* Call, *November 26, 1917.*

4. BOLSHEVIKS' PEACE PLAN URGED ON SENATE

Among the first American organizations to support the Bolshevik revolution was the Friends of the Russian Revolution. It was organized less than a month after the revolution primarily to support the Soviet demand for an immediate peace without annexations or indemnities.

A mass meeting to urge support of the peace move of the Bolsheviki, and recognition of the strategic value of Lord Lansdowne's suggestion that the Allies restate their terms of peace with a view to winning the confidence of the German people,[4] is the first move in what its sponsors describe as a "political offensive for the settlement of the war."

The announcement of the meeting is signed by a committee calling itself the "Friends of the Russian Revolution," consisting of Roger Baldwin, Mary Ware Dennett, Crystal Eastman, Vida Milholland, Lou Rogers, Rebecca Shelly, Alexander Trachtenberg, James P. Warbasse, Margaret Sanger, Dr. A. Goldwater, Pauline K. Angell, Merrill Rogers, and others.

In a statement issued today it is said that the purpose of the meeting is to urge upon Congress "that the friendly relations between America and the Russian democracy be continuously maintained, and that food supplies, money, and such assistance as can be given by America to the builders of the New Russia be offered without reserve. There is every evidence that the leaders in Russia today are prompted in everything they are doing by the will of the Russian people, and it is believed that such democratic action should be vigorously encouraged by nations fighting for the ideals of democracy."

Congress will also be urged "to support the demand of the Russian democracy for a peace parley and to immediately co-operate with new Russia in arranging a time and place where representatives of the people of all belligerent nations can undertake a sane solution of this world problem." And Colonel House is to be instructed by Congress "to press this point of view upon the envoys of the allied powers now assembled in Paris and to demand from them a clear statement of war aims."

It is said further that the publication of the secret treaties by the Russian foreign office disclosing "the bargain made by the allies to fight for Italy's territorial ambitions"[5] has emphasized the need for such a restatement of terms.

"The American people have a right to know how far the motives of the allies are consistent with our own avowed ideals in the war. Moreover, as Lord Lansdowne has pointed out, an unequivocal statement by the allies that they do not intend to crush the German people will put courage into the forces now in revolt in Germany, and will thus do more than a military drive to overthrow the power of the military autocracy."

Miss Rebecca Shelly, well known for her connection with various peace organizations, is in charge of the meeting.

"There is a growing discontent among the people of all nations," she said, "because one opportunity after another for the opening of peace negotiations is cast aside by those in power without serious consideration, or any earnest effort to utilize the opportunity. The platitude that the time is not yet ripe for peace negotiations no longer satisfies. When will the time be ripe? We can see no reason for continuing the war one single hour until it has been positively demonstrated that Germany will not yield to an agreement which will insure a just and lasting peace, and this can only be discovered when envoys of all belligerents have gathered to discuss the issues."

——*New York* Evening Call, *December 3, 1917.*

5. HOURWICH TELLS OF BOLSHEVIK REVOLT

"Peace, peace, we want peace," cried 3,000 people at New Star Casino, 107th street and Park avenue, last night when Dr. Isaac Hourwich, speaking on the Russian revolution, said:

"We were told it was a bloodless revolution started by the liberals. It was started by the workers marching through Petrograd crying for bread, as the women of this city marched to the city hall last year, but the Russian workers also cried for peace."

The meeting was held under the direction of the Friends of Russian Freedom to support the Bolsheviki peace terms.[6] Mary Ware Dennett, formerly National Secretary of the Women's Bureau of the National Democratic Committee, acted as chairman.

Dr. Isaac Hourwich was the first speaker. He explained the internal situation in Russia, the meaning of the names of the different parties, and described the growth of the Bolsheviki since the revolution.

"The Constituent Assembly[7] of the Milyukov party met and formulated plans for conquest, they wanted territory, they wanted Constantinople, but the Russian people did not want Constantinople or any other nation's territory and so they were forced to resign.[8]

"Then came Kerenski, and the peace without annexations or indemnities.[9] Kerenski thought that in order to secure peace he must start an offensive, so he ordered the soldiers to go west, but they went east. In their ignorance they did not want to fight.

"The people were promised an early peace, but eight months passed and no peace came. So the Bolsheviki leapt into power and within three weeks plans for an armistice and a general peace were already formulated."

He predicted that the Bolsheviki would remain in power till the Constituent Assembly meets in a few weeks, and that the new government of Russia would be a Socialist government.

Miss Vida Milholland, who was introduced as one of the women fighters for democracy in this country, sang the song *Russian Freedom,* a song inspired by the revolution, the audience rising while she sang. Wild encores recalled her when she finished, and when she sang for the second time, the audience, catching the spirit she put into the song, sang with her. . . .

"To me," said Art Young of the *Masses,*[10] "it seems that the lesson of the Russian revolution is that you can't kill an idea by either prosecution or persecution. The tsar thought by banishing scholars and thinkers and censoring the press that he could put an end to the spirit of liberty. . . ."

"What are we thinking of?" asked Rebecca Shelly. "What do we want? We want peace!" Here the audience again rose to its feet and awoke the echoes with cries for peace. When the applause died down she continued.

"When do we want it and how? We want it now, and by the Bolsheviki plan, for the Bolsheviki plan means that the people rule supreme."

A resolution endorsing the Bolsheviki peace terms, and calling on the government to support the demand for an immediate armistice on all battle fronts, was passed unanimously and a delegation will present it to congress.

————*New York* Call, *December 5, 1917.*

6. THE RED DAWN

The first pamphlet published in the United States explaining and supporting the Bolshevik revolution was Harrison George's The Red Dawn: The Bolsheviki and the IWW. *It was written early in December 1917 and published in Chicago that same month by the IWW Publishing Bureau. George was in prison awaiting trial along with other IWW members when he decided to write about the background of the Bolshevik revolution. He obtained much of his information from a fellow Wobbly and fellow prisoner, Leo Laukki, who had participated in the Russian revolutionary movement before leaving for the United States. Like most Wobblies at this time, George saw in the Bolshevik revolution a victory for the ideas of the IWW and its concept of the Industrial State in which the industrial unions would operate the government. He concluded his pamphlet with an appeal to American workers to join the IWW if they wanted to show their support for the Bolsheviks. Later George became a Communist and wrote regularly for the Communist press. (See Art Shields, "The Story of a Communist Columnist," Daily Worker, August 10, 1937.) The following is the introductory section of George's pamphlet.*

by HARRISON GEORGE

Today, locked behind several sets of steel bars in one of those dungeons Capitalism has prepared for workers who challenge its rule, the writer watches the play of social forces in the greatest of crises ever yet facing this stage of civilization. Someone has said that the people of any given period do not grasp the significance of events transpiring under their eyes; that events are only historically understood as they move into the past and afford perspective. It may be that my interested isolation, my severance from active participation in the great drama affords such perspective. But, be that as it may, the writer feels constrained to point out what, in his opinion, is the lesson to the workers contained in recent and current history—what means that inspiring light that penetrates even the prison windows and floods my cell with the glory of the Red Dawn?

For, out of the bloody mist that rises off the quagmires of mangled men that have fought each other like wild beasts and have ended by mixing their blood and bones in Death's Democracy, there marches, upright and unafraid, rebellious Labor, and the hope of the ages, the Industrial State, approaches realization as at this hour the fighting proletariat of Russia, the herald of a new world, presses its victory to completion and binds and consolidates its 175,000,000 people into a cohesive unit of Industrial Democracy.

And if it can be, as if it is possible, that by outer intrigue and inner treachery, the brave workers of Russia now under the Bolsheviki, valiantly fighting these dark forces are betrayed, beaten and go down heroically in seas of blood as did Ennus, Spartacus and the Communards, yet the world of Labor will have profited and—success or failure—their brave attempt, their magnificent spirit and bold deeds will live forever and their story shall be told "in lands remote and accents yet unknown."

. . . . To clarify the Russian situation in the minds of the workers of other lands is a duty. To explain to those who read the lies of the capitalist press and who believe that the Bolsheviki rule is a mushroom growth to be lightly swept aside by shooting Lenin and Trotsky who are pictured as the long-haired stage anarchist and "East Side vendor of collar buttons" is a service to the working class.

——The Red Dawn: The Bolsheviki and the IWW, *pp. 1–4.*

7. LENIN, MASTER STATESMAN

So little was known about Lenin in the United States that his name was most often incorrectly spelled. (His name at birth on April 22, 1870, was Vladimir Ilyich Ulyanov.) The article below attempted to dispel the notion that Lenin seized leadership of the Russian revolution by sheer accident, and traced his long career in the revolutionary movement. Although it appeared originally in Truth, *a British publication, it was widely reprinted in the United States. (The article contains inaccuracies which are corrected in the notes.)*

At last the world witnesses the ascendancy of a real statesman —Nicolai Ilyich Ulyanov, known to the world as Nicolai Lenin, premier of the world's first industrial democracy—mighty Russia!

A meteor across the political sky as Lenin appears to the uninformed, this doughty champion of real democracy has long been known in the Socialist movement as orator, organizer, author and Maximalist economist.

As early as 1897, Lenin, then a resident of St. Petersburg, was at the very front of the Socialist movement, being honored by the exploiters with the appellation "dangerous nihilist." The appearance of a radical article in a Russian journal, treating boldly of the economic development of Russia, served as an excuse for the Tsar's agents to arrest its author, and he was sent on a long and bitter journey to Siberia. . . .[11] Despite the hardships of prison camp, Lenin wrote his scholarly work on *The Development of Capitalism in Russia.*[12]

After four years of suffering, the astute Lenin managed to outwit his keepers and escaped from Siberia, making his way to western Europe, where he remained in exile, part of the time in France and some of the time in Switzerland.[13] In the latter republic Lenin gained fame as one of the editors of the *Iskra* [Spark] central organ of the Russian Social-Democratic Labor party. In 1912, a split took place in the party, Lenin resigning from the editorial staff of the paper. . . .[14] Lenin was strongly opposed to any compromise tactics, or dallying with governmental officials. He was openly and above board in opposition to the government and against any and all who were willing to support the government. He was not a "patriot," judging him from ruling class standards. He despised the Russian autocracy, heading a radical group known as "Porashenzi" who were anti-patriots, hoping for the defeat of the "little Father's" army in the great conflict. Only after such a defeat, he declared, could the democratization of Russia be effected. It was in this sense only that Lenin could be called pro-German. He was pro-anything that would lead to the overthrow of the Russian autocracy. Now that the insane Tsar and his soothsayers are relegated to the farm, Lenin is a patriot to the limit, as well as an international-ist, ready to fight for the world as the workers' country and defend their homes from capitalist aggressions.

In 1905, when the first revolutionary outbreak occurred, bring-ing with it some measure of freedom and amnesty to political exiles, Lenin promptly returned to St. Petersburg, and was made editor of the Socialist daily, the *New Life*. Later came the reac-tion, and Lenin was obliged to flee the country.

Lenin is well known to European Socialists as a member of the International Socialist Bureau, and as a permanent delegate to the International Socialist congresses.

Among his published works is an excellent Russian translation of Webb's *The History of Trade Unionism*.[15]

From the foregoing brief sketch, it may be seen that the premier of free Russia is no upstart demagogue or politican, but a tried and true soldier in the fight for world-wide industrial Democracy.

——Truth, *December 12, 1917.*

8. CALL ON U.S. TO RECOGNIZE BOLSHEVIKS

The Friends of the Russian Revolution changed its name to the Friends of New Russia and sponsored a mass meeting in Carnegie Hall to ask for recognition of the Soviet government. Despite the efforts of the Police marshal to intimidate the gather-ing, the audience refused to be swerved from expressing its opin-ion that the United States should recognize the Bolshevik gov-ernment.

Marshal Thomas D. McCarthy was present . . . at a mass meet-ing of the Friends of New Russia, held in Carnegie Hall, at which it was resolved to ask the government of the United States to recognize the Bolshevik government of Russia, and to back up their attempt at an armistice and general peace.

The speakers of the evening were Rebecca Shelly, Dr. A. Goldwater, chairman; Joseph D. Cannon, organizer for the International Mine, Mill, and Smelter Workers' union; Ludwig Lore, associate editor of the *Volkszeitung*,[16] and Patrick Quinlan.

The marshal did not interfere with the meeting in any way, but his own particular form caused a thrill as he marched down the aisle during the proceedings and took a seat in the front row. It is not known if he became converted as a result of the arguments he heard advanced, but when Vida Milholland sang the new Russian national hymn and the audience arose, the marshal retained his seat. After a while he must have become bored, because he left before the meeting was over.

"We are going to ask the government to recognize the Bolshevik government as the authentic spokesman of the Russian people," Rebecca Shelly declared to applause in explaining the purpose of the meeting, "and ask that the government back up the Bolsheviki in their demand for an immediate armistice and general peace."

Ludwig Lore referred to Kerensky as "the Russian Scheidemann."[17] Narrating the events which led to Kerensky's fall, he said that the Russian people had been driven to the conclusion that the only way to get peace "is to force peace." The mention of Lenin and Trotsky was wildly cheered by the audience.

"Revolutionary Socialists in Germany are very active," he said, and he declared that that radical group, in common with the Socialists of the world, will force peace eventually.

Joseph D. Cannon declared that the world will never go back to ante-bellum conditions. "No nation can withdraw from the war," he continued, "but we can devise ways and means by which it may be brought to an end." He declared that "the hope of an early peace" lies in the familiar Russian formula of no annexations, etc.

"I won't quote the Declaration of Independence," he said, "they're throwing men into jail in Philadelphia for that."[18]

He read the audience a portion of the President's last war message, in which it was said that if the purposes of the allies in the war had been made clear, the sympathy and aid of the Russian people would not have been lost.[19]

"President Wilson conceded that if we had taken the position in the earlier part of the war in favor of Russia's terms, Russia might not have been lost to us. Why don't we take that stand now and win Russia back?"

He declared that Congress should be made publicly to resolve that the United States wanted no territory either for herself or for her allies. Such a stand would unite the German Socialists on our side, Cannon said, and the result would be that "the German people would stand with the Bolsheviki of Russia and the radicals of the world." He made a plea for Ireland at the peace conference, declaring that she must be included with the other small nations which are entitled to choose their own government.

Resolutions were passed favoring the recognition of the Bolsheviki and the support of their peace aims by the government. A resolution was also passed which will be sent to Russia and given to the people there through Maxim Gorky's paper,[20] in which it was said that "we pledge our cooperation with your efforts to defeat all imperialist aims and to secure a people's peace which will abolish the cause of international war."

Patrick Quinlan introduced a resolution from the Irish Progressive League favoring the granting of a place to Ireland at the peace conference. All the resolutions were passed unanimously.

——*New York Evening* Call, *December 22, 1917.*

9. SEATTLE LABOR COUNCIL SENDS GREETINGS TO WORKERS OF RUSSIA

The Russian transport Shilka, *steamed into Elliot Bay, Seattle, around Christmas of 1917, carrying a cargo of licorice root, peas and beans. Rumors were widespread that it carried gold in its hold and munitions to aid in starting a Bolshevik revolution in the United States. "All of us are Bolsheviki," the committee of the crew told a group representing the Seattle Central Labor Council. Through the aid of a Russian interpreter, the Central Labor Council learned of conditions in what the Seattle Union Record called "the world's newest and most advanced democracy" (February 2, 1918). When the* Shilka *left harbor on January 8, 1918, it carried a letter from the Central Labor Council to the workers of Russia.*

During their stay in the United States, the crew of the Shilka *visited the halls of the IWW in Seattle and Tacoma. When the ship left it also carried a message from the IWW local of Tacoma.*

To the Workers of All Russia, Who Are Sincerely Endeavoring to Establish Democracy, In Care of the Crew of the Russian Steamship *Shilka*.

Brothers and Sisters: The Central Labor Council of Seattle, representing upwards of 40,000 organized workers of this city, an integral part of the American Federation of Labor, whose membership is composed of 2,000,000 men and women, welcomes the opportunity presented by the visit of the Russian steamship *Shilka* to this port to send you our fraternal greetings and express to you our sincere hope for the success of your efforts to make of Russia a free republic conditioned upon both political and industrial democracy.

Having no direct means of communication with you, and compelled to rely upon other sources for our information, including perverted news through a capitalist controlled press, and consequently misled as to Russian internal conditions, we make no effort nor have we any desire to address ourselves exclusively to any one faction, but we extend to all factions of workers alike our hearty good will, firm in the belief that in the end (which we trust is not far off) the rule of the workers will be absolute, and the affairs of your great country, the first of any in modern history, placed to remain in the hands of the only necessary and responsible class in society—the working class.

Again expressing to you our profound sympathy with you in your efforts to establish true democracy and pledging you our hearty support in hastening that end, we are, yours fraternally,

—*Central Labor Council of Seattle, A. E. Miller, G.M. Welty, Leon Glasser, Committee; James A. Duncan, Secretary, January 3, 1918. Seattle* Union Record, *February 2, 1918.*

10. TACOMA IWW GREETS REVOLUTIONISTS

To the Revolutionary Movement of All Russia, and Especially the Crew of the Transport *Shilka*, Now in the American Port of Tacoma, Washington:

Fellow Workers: We, the members of the Tacoma Branch of the IWW, wish to extend to you our heartiest greetings and best wishes, and wish to compliment all the revolutionists who took part in the successful crushing of the autocrats of your part of the world. But we wish above all to commend you for your wonderful example in building the New Society and raising the Proletariat to its rightful place as rulers of its own destiny, in which we recognize you as co-workers with the Industrial Workers of the World in our attempt to establish the world wide Industrial Commonwealth and the great idea of the Brotherhood of Man, to the end that the human race may be able to continue to progress higher and greater unhampered by parasites of any kind.

You no doubt realize that we, the revolutionists of America, being still in the minority, are unable as yet to follow your example in freeing ourselves from the terrible slave system in which we are enthralled, but confidently look forward to the time when we can reach across the Pacific Ocean and grasp the hands of our Progressive Fellow Workers in Russia and say WE ARE WITH YOU!

The prosecution of the members of the Industrial Workers of the World becomes more severe each day,[21] and our organization grows accordingly. We have nothing but great hopes for the future Freedom of ALL MANKIND. LONG LIVE THE RUSSIAN REVOLUTION!

Yours for the Freedom of the Workers.

———*A. R. Tucker, W. H. Harrington, K. McClennon, Committee, January 5, 1918.* Industrial Worker, *Seattle, January 12, 1918.*

11. NY SOCIALISTS GREET REVOLUTION

The convention of the Socialist party of Greater New York extends its heartiest greetings to the Russian revolution and its de facto Socialist government, who so valiantly uphold the principles of international Socialism and are therefore the living refutation of the capitalistic hope that revolutionary working class solidarity is dead.

We are highly gratified over the fact that the first Socialist government ever established has brought about the beginning of peace negotiations and was instrumental in forcing the imperialistic world powers and their capitalistic governments to pay homage, in words if not in deeds, to the Socialist peace formula of: No annexations, no punitive indemnities and the self-determination of nationalities.

The convention takes great pride in the courageous and consistently international attitude that the revolutionary government of Russia has taken in the peace negotiations with the central powers[22] and expresses its special satisfaction over the decided refusal to sanction annexation in any form.

——*New York* Evening Call, *January 7, 1918.*

12. BOSTON SOCIALISTS GREET REVOLUTION

The members and friends of the Socialist party and of the Workmen's Council of Greater Boston, assembled in mass meeting this 13th day of January, hail the Russian revolution as the greatest achievement for humanity in this century. We send greetings of working class fellowship and solidarity to the revolutionary government of Russia and indorse the struggle of Russian revolutionists against the imperialists of all countries.

We greet the Russian revolution as the dawn of a new era for the workers of the world. The heroic struggle of our Russian comrades against the lying press of the imperialists of other nations, their success in thwarting the counter-revolution of the reactionaries and their service in publishing the secret treaties of the capitalist governments with the old tsarism are additional proofs of their proletarian statesmanship in this hour of world travail.

We commemorate the martyrs and the heroic dead of our class who fell victims of the hated regime of the Romanovs. We remember with reverence the grim lines of revolutionists that walked their weary way in exile to frozen Siberia; the Comrades who rotted away in the vile dungeons of the autocracy, and the brave fighters who went to the scaffold with songs on their lips.

We also send heartfelt greetings to the revolutionaries in all countries who have gone to prison, some to their death, in the glorious struggle against the imperialists and international exploiters. We send special greetings to Karl Liebknecht and the increasing numbers associated with him in the struggle against Prussian domination of Europe. Their fight is an inspiration to the workers of all nations who oppose the rise of autocracy at home.

We further welcome with joy the increasing signs of the decay

of capitalism in all advanced countries and the increasing power
of the working class. The peace of the world will not be dictated
by the professional diplomats and imperialists, but by the
workers through the international that grows stronger every
day. The old order of capitalism is passing, and the commonwealth of useful labor will yet be established on its ruins.

——*New York* Evening Call, *January 15, 1918.*

13. BANKER PRAISES BOLSHEVIK LEADERS

*Upon his return from Russia, Colonel William Boyce Thomp-
son, a member of the American Red Cross mission, was interviewed by Charles W. Wood. The report Thompson gave of
conditions in Russia differed sharply from that found in most
commercial newspapers.*

"Russia is not anarchistic. Russia is not lawless. The despised
Bolsheviki are not and never have been pro-German, and the
attitude of the American press in failing to understand them has
tended to aid the kaiser's cause. The fact is that Russia has been
under the leadership for several months of the most radical
socialist group, but this fact is neither unnatural nor a thing to
provoke despair. It simply means that Russia is pointing the way
toward a new order of society throughout the world, a larger
freedom, a more complete equality and what I believe to be a
purer democracy than the world has ever known before. The
Russian people have made tremendous sacrifices for this ideal,
but they have been happy in their suffering and would not
exchange their new found freedom for the conditions that obtain
anywhere else on earth."

It was not a socialist who spoke. It was a Wall Street millionaire, a banker, a captain of industry, a "mining king," Col.
William Boyce Thompson, who had just returned from a six
months' trip to Russia as one of the heads of the American Red
Cross mission. Unlike most Americans of wealth, he had made
it a point while there to get acquainted with the Russian people,
not merely with that 10 per cent who have made up the so-called
respectable element. When he spoke of Russia, he spoke of the
90 per cent. They were the happy ones, that 90 per cent of
no-accounts who are most decisively counting now.

"And the real pro-German element in Russia," said Col. Thompson, "is not found among the mass of workers and peasants who were supposed to be conspiring for a separate peace. It is found among the very respectable capitalists and landlords, who have been loudest in their cries that Lenin and Trotsky were German spies. The price of real estate jumped in Petrograd when Riga was captured by the Germans. . . .

"I must say for the Bolsheviki that they have maintained a most surprising degree of order in Russia. The impression must prevail here that they sprang like a mob upon Petrograd, terrorizing the order-loving people, looted the homes and indulged in a general melee of riot and bloodshed. As a matter of fact, the change of government was announced officially in every section of Petrograd. The city was divided into regional headquarters, and every person in Petrograd knew the headquarters of the region in which he lived. Instructions were issued in case assistance were needed to send word to these headquarters. An appeal always, within a few minutes brought a motor car filled with soldiers to the spot. Looting was absolutely prohibited and during the first month of the November revolution, I can say from my personal observation, there was better order than at any other time during my four months' stay.

"This is the situation which in the American press has so generally been called 'anarchy.' There has been the greatest opportunity for the reigning of anarchy in Russia that has ever existed since men began to wear boots, and yet, considering the temptations to lawlessness and to indulgence in license rather than liberty, the order and good behavior which prevailed are astounding. At no time since the Tsar was overthrown has there been anything for a single moment comparable to the excesses of the French revolution.

"Yet the Russian revolution must be looked upon as an equally great transition. Consider the wrongs that had been endured from time immemorial, the complete negation of liberty and human rights. A workingman in Russia was considered no better than a dog. In many respects he was treated worse. Then suddenly these 180,000,000 downtrodden human beings found themselves in possession of absolute liberty, and there were 10,000,000 of them under arms. In the face of this situation the intelligent classes were talking of placing a grand duke on the throne, or in some way preserving a measure of the old regime. But, notwithstanding this additional incentive to violent revenge, Russia was practically free of massacres of the upper classes. This is all the more wonderful when we remember that the country had just passed through three years of brutalizing rule. . . .

"I sincerely believe that Russia is pointing the way to general peace, just as she is pointing the way to great and sweeping world changes. It is not in Russia alone that the old order is passing. There is a lot of the old order in America and that is going, too. We may just as well open our eyes to it—all of us. The time has come everywhere when affairs must be handled for the benefit of the many—never again for the comparatively few, and what I call legislation by proxy must cease.

"I'm glad it is so. When I sat and watched those democratic conclaves in Russia, I felt that I would welcome a similar scene in the United States. Some cultured professor or some great captain of industry now in Congress might be answered by some locomotive fireman in hobnail boots; and often Hobnails would have a shade the better of the oratory. I'd like to see a lot of workingmen in the United States Senate; not merely attorneys for workingmen, but men whose rough hands or rough and ready ways show that they are actually doing the world's work. Then I'd like to see real employers side by side with them instead of their paid attorneys. I believe we'd all come to a better understanding then."

Colonel Thompson blamed natural conservatism, not German propaganda, for our misunderstanding of Russia. But he insisted that this misunderstanding had been giving aid and comfort to the Kaiser.

"President Wilson," he said jubilantly, "has shown that he appreciates the full situation. His message to Congress is one upon which the common people of all nations can come to a common understanding.[23] It should be received by the workers of Germany with the same enthusiasm that it was received in Petrograd; and it is not beyond my expectations that it may prove a death blow to German imperialism."

————*San Francisco* Examiner, *January 19, 1918.*

14. PROCLAMATION ON RUSSIA

On February 4, 1918, the National Executive Committee of the Socialist party adopted two resolutions supporting the Bol-

*shevik revolution and the program of the Soviet government,
both of which are reproduced below.*

The revolution of the Russian Socialists threatens the thrones
of Europe and makes the whole capitalist structure tremble. With
hunger stalking in their midst, without financial credit, without
international recognition and with a ruling caste intriguing to
regain control, the Russian Socialists have yet accomplished their
revolution, and they inspired the working class of the world with
the ideal of humanity's supremacy over class rule.

They come with a message of proletarian revolution. We glory
in their achievement and inevitable triumph.

The Socialist Party of the United States offers its encouragement and pledges its support to the fundamental revolutionary
aims and purposes of the enlightened workers of every country.

——*Archives of the Socialist Party of the United States,
Manuscript Department, Duke University Library.*

15. RUSSIAN PEACE PLAN ENDORSED

The war frenzy, which has gripped many nations, including
our own, is waning. The Socialist party, therefore, through its
national executive committee, deems it to be its duty to state its
views as to the best methods of obtaining a speedy, general and
democratic peace.

We indorse unreservedly the peace program of the Russian
Socialist government, based upon the demand for the evacuation
of all territory occupied by hostile forces and its restoration from
an international fund, the right to all nations and inhabitants of
disputed territories to determine their own destinies; the unrestricted freedom of travel and transportation over land and sea;
full equality of trade conditions among all nations; universal
disarmament; open diplomacy, and an effective international
organization to preserve peace, to protect the rights of the weaker
peoples (including the natives in the colonies) and to insure the
stability of international relations.

We are unalterably opposed to all annexationist and imperialistic designs, all plans of enforced geographical or political readjustments, and all punitive measures included in the war aims of
the contending ruling circles and their governments.

We emphatically deny that it is necessary for the people of the United States to spill their blood and waste their treasure in order to rearrange the map of Europe. If rearrangement is necessary, it can be more speedily and more effectively accomplished by the peace conference.

The present situation demands more than the mere statement of war aims or peace terms. An agreement to enter into peace negotiations is now imperative. To agree upon the details of peace is impossible until the representatives of the belligerent nations meet one another in conference.

The statement of detailed conditions is futile. Such details are quite as likely to multiply the causes of disagreement, magnify the difficulties and delay peace as they are to bring peace.

We earnestly urge you to recognize officially the present Russian government, and to accept immediately its invitation to take part in the peace conference of the Russians and the central powers. We also urge you to make every effort to secure the participation of the allies in the conference.

A decision by our country and the allies to join in the conference will electrify the peoples of the world. It will take the ground from under the crowned robbers of the central powers. It will deprive the autocrats of all arguments now used to deceive the people and maintain themselves in power.

This is the road to peace.
——*New York* Call, *February 5, 1918.*

16. SMALL NATIONS' CITIZENS GREET RUSSIANS

The League of Small and Subject Nationalities was organized in 1917 to secure a democratic peace treaty in which the rights of small nations and the colonial possessions would be recognized. At its second annual dinner the subject of the Russian revolution dominated the proceedings.

The League of Small and Subject Nationalities was addressed by a distinguished number of speakers at its second annual dinner, held in the Grand hotel, 31st street and Broadway. Among those heard were Dr. Frederic C. Howe, president of the League; Joseph D. Cannon, Socialist candidate for Congress; Dr. Patrick McCartan, Ireland; Rev. E. S. Noll, Albania; Lajpat

Rai, Asia; Lincoln Steffens, Russia; Ivan Konigsberg, Slesvig, and Dr. W. E. B. Du Bois, Africa.

The principal address of the evening was made by Steffens, who, while scheduled to speak on Russia, spoke on behalf of the workers of the world.

A notable message was unanimously adopted at the gathering, heartening Russia in the present crisis the proletarian republic faces. The telegram which was sent to the Russian government follows:

"The League of Small and Subject Nationalities meeting in New York tonight voted a message of sympathy for new Russia in this crisis of the revolution; sorrow that the German people permitted the German invasion, and a prayer that the Russian people shall not forget that they are struggling, not for themselves alone, but for all the subject people in this subject world."

The evil in the world, Steffens said, is not moral, but it is physical; it is economic.

He assured his audience that though there is much sorrow in Petrograd and Moscow, the revolutionists do not believe that their theories have failed. "They believe you have failed," he said.

"In Russia they do not call it the Russian revolution," he said, "but the revolution, because it is not only for themselves they want freedom, but for all peoples. Last May day I was in Petrograd and the workers marched through the streets in celebration, not of the day of their own deliverance, for they do not celebrate that day, but have adopted the day the other workers have chosen. In the streets I heard them say, 'The workers of France, England, Germany, America, Japan and the whole world are out today.'"

Dr. Howe said that "we are here to contemplate the progress we are making." He said that for the first time subject and small nations were being recognized as having the same rights as great nations, and that the peoples of the world, also for the first time are formulating terms to end the war.

Patrick McCartan, speaking for Ireland, said that "we of the small nations are more or less skeptical of fine talk." He denounced the British rule of his country, and denied the truth of press reports stating that American sailors have been wantonly attacked in Ireland. "We ask England to withdraw from Ireland," he declared.

——*New York* Evening Call, *February 28, 1918.*

17. RADICALS HERE OFFER LIVES TO RUSSIA

Although Lenin believed that it was essential for the future of the revolution that Russia sign a peace with Germany at Brest-Litovsk, Trotsky, who headed the Soviet delegation, rejected this position, and declared that the Soviet government would not make peace with capitalist governments. He favored a policy of passive resistance—"neither peace nor war," neither sign the peace treaty nor fight—a position which Lenin denounced as "lunacy or worse." As a result of Trotsky's actions, the peace negotiations at Brest-Litovsk collapsed, and on February 18, 1918, ten days after the breaking off of peace negotiations, the German high command launched a great offensive along the entire Eastern front. As news reached the United States of the German advance through the Ukraine, through Poland toward Moscow, and in the North toward Petrograd, support for embattled revolutionary Russia was expressed by various groups. The messages to the Bolsheviks are printed below as they appeared in the press.

Radicals throughout the nation, stirred by the invasion of revolutionary Russia by the Germans, pledge their moral support, money and life to the great cause—the preservation of the Russian democracy.

Cablegrams have been sent to the Council of People's Commissars and the revolutionary committee, promising not only sympathy but immediate aid.

Algernon Lee, educational director of the Rand school[24] and Alexander Trachtenberg, Russian Socialist, both felt that the situation was by no means hopeless.

"I cannot doubt that the part which the kaiser's government is playing is a desperate one, and that it must fail. For the present the effective leadership has passed into the hands of the British labor movement," said Lee.

Alexander Trachtenberg felt that it was the duty of every Socialist to spread the doctrine of optimism throughout the country in regard to the Russian revolution.

"I shall lend all my powers to interpret the true version of the revolution to the workers of this country," he said.

Asked if he felt that the governments of the allies and the United States were not quick enough to grasp the situation, Trachtenberg said:

"These governments are doing the greatest possible injury to true democracy by not aiding Russia in her bitter struggle."

Some of the telegrams sent to the Bolshevik government follow:

"Council of People's Commissars, Smolny Institute, Petrograd —Bolshevik information bureau organized here two months ago to interpret actions of commissaries and to arouse solidarity of American workers with Russian proletariat. Widespread sympathy of American workers with Russian proletariat. Widespread sympathy of American workers with you. Have taken steps to organize a Red Guard[25] here. Louis Fraina, Bolshevik Information Bureau."

"Council of People's Commissars, Petrograd—The first united Russian convention in America held in New York February 1 to 4 sends greetings to revolutionary Russia as represented by the people's commissaries. We are heart and soul with you. Are ready to organize revolutionary legions for Russia. Reply. Weinstein, Executive Committee of the Convention. 175 East Broadway."

"Smolny Institute, Petrograd—You have our unqualified faith and support. The whole colony is with you. Are ready to organize Red Guard for Russia. Americans will help. *Novy Mir*, A. Menshoy."

"Ferrer Association[26] is with you to the death. Are forming Red Guard to help defend the revolution. Leonard Abbot, Ferrer Association."

"Boris Rheinstein, Commissar of International Propaganda Russian Foreign Office, Petrograd—All American revolutionists aroused by German advance. Offer their services and their lives to the saving of Russian revolution and world freedom. Are organizing revolutionary army. Mass meetings, tremendous sentiment. Beg Russians to hold out for original peace formula. Louise Bryant."

"Maria Spiradonova, Chairman, Executive Committee, All Russian Peasants Soviets, Smolny Institute—All American revolutionists offer their sympathy and their lives to the Russian revolutionists in this hour of peril. In your fight against the invaders we are with you to the end. I will come back and fight with many American Socialists. Louise Bryant."

"Hail to the workers of Russia. We stand by you in your fight. The committee of 1,000 women."

"The Socialists of Greater New York view the German invasion with deep indignation as a blow to labor and democracy in all lands. We wish you success in revolutionary resistance to Russian as well as German imperialism. Help transmit our appeal to German and Austrian-Hungarian working classes to stop this outrage. We hold that on them now rests the greatest responsibility for success or failure of the world in the efforts for people's peace. Algernon Lee, acting secretary for city committee of Socialist party."

A message was sent by Lee to the Social Democratic party, Berne, Switzerland, the International Socialist Bureau, the Hague, Holland, and the Social Democratic Party at Dietz, Copenhagen, Denmark.

The message reads:

"Socialists of Greater New York ask you to help convey the message to working classes of Germany and Austria-Hungary as follows: We beg you vigorously to oppose your rulers' efforts to crush the Russian revolution. On you at this moment rests the responsibility for the success or failure of the world-wide efforts for a people's peace. The German invasion of Russia is a blow against labor and democracy in all lands."

The Women's Peace party of New York state, headed by Crystal Eastman, writes this:

"Please express to the Bolshevik government our firm belief in their courage, wisdom and ultimate triumph, and our horror at the brutal demands of German autocracy. Be assured that we will use all our strength toward bringing about official recognition of the Bolshevik government by our own. Crystal Eastman."

"The People's Council of America for Democratic Peace[27] representing 300 radical groups in 42 states has consistently stood for the Russian formula of 'no annexations, no indemnities and self-determination.' We urge you to make no other terms. Scott Nearing, James Maurer and Louis P. Lochner."

"National conference of members and representatives of labor, Socialists and radical movements in meeting in New York reaffirm Russian program and calls on the proletariat of the world to stand firm to the end for its realization. Louis P. Lochner, Secretary."

"Appreciating the courageous idealism of the Russian people the officers of the Fellowship of Reconciliation of the United States of America send greeting in this hour of darkness. Believing that the brotherhood as revealed by Jesus is the essential basis of true human society, we join with you in the confident expectation of its final triumph in political and social democracy among all peoples. Gilbert Beaves, 118 East 28th street."

"Revolutionary committee. With our lives and our last breath the Mother Earth groups[28] are with you in your fight. M. E. Fitzgerald."

"Socialist Propaganda League has unqualified faith in you. Have started Red Guard for service in Russia. Great enthusiasm among American workers. Your cause is ours. Cable instructions. Can League help any other way? Fraina, Rutgers and Mrs. Rovitch. 1572 Madison avenue."

"You have our wholehearted faith and support. Ready to organize and send you international revolutionary army from America. Rose Baron, International Social Revolutionary Group, 219 Second avenue."

——*New York* Evening Call, *February 28, 1918.*

18. THE PROMISE OF GREAT RUSSIA

In the following article, Meyer London, Socialist congressman from New York, attempted to shed light on various aspects of the Bolshevik revolution. Although London played down the revolutionary character of the movement in Russia—note his effort to compare the expropriation of land owned privately in Russia with the Homestead Act of 1862 which distributed 160 acres of the public domain to any one who settled on it—he did explain several aspects of the revolution.

by MEYER LONDON

There is a distressing lack of information about Russia. Not only is there an absence of knowledge of present events, which is bad enough, but there is a failure to grasp the meaning of those forces the working of which has resulted in the greatest change in modern history. . . .

One should not fear a return of the old regime.

The country is essentially democratic. There is alarm here over the demand for the redistribution of land. To the uninitiated it looks like old-fashioned agrarian rebellions. It is nothing of the sort. The principle of collective ownership of land is strong in the community life of the people. The village community owns the land in common today. The efforts made since 1905 to introduce private ownership in the village community have proven abortive.

While the theory of collective ownership of land is firmly embedded in the thought of the people, only 12 per cent of the land is owned collectively by the people, while 88 per cent is under individual ownership. Of this 88 per cent, one million square miles (640 million acres) was the property of the Tsar and his family. All this of course will go to the people. The problem of endowing the farmer with sufficient land to live on is a practical problem, not a dream of dreamers, but a mere application and extension of a principle strong in the lives of those who live by the work of their hands and in the sweat of their brows. Those who still reap the benefits of the old feudal system and who own millions of acres of land may not grasp the importance of it. To them the demands of the Russian peasant may mean bloodshed, violence and all sorts of horrors, but to the student of Russia it means only the next step to be taken in building Russia's future.

The program of the peasantry consists of two words, "land" and "liberty." This was the slogan of the Russian people for more than 60 years.

Russia's peasantry wants access to the land. Their demand is no more revolutionary than the American Homestead Law was revolutionary. The platform will now become a reality. It is only a question of method, of tactics. Russia's sacrifices will have been in vain unless the great masses of the people will gain access to the land.

Take the subject of woman suffrage. A smile goes over the face of the American who reads about the enfranchisement of women in Russia. He cannot get himself to understand how the Slav democracy, only a day old, seeks to outdo him, to outstrip republican France, to excel old England. How presumptuous, indeed.

But there is nothing peculiar about it. The emancipation of woman has been for more than two generations an accomplished fact in that strange land. The Russian woman was probably the first woman in the world to obtain the privilege of attending universities. She was the first to rebel against stifling conventionality. And then her part in the revolutionary movement.

The martyrology of that sad people abounds with the names of women. Out of a batch of 770 political prisoners during three months in one year, 158 were women.

The chief of the secret service reported to Alexander II in 1874 that in the most aristocratic families the women were the most dangerous revolutionists. Three of the women mentioned in that report are alive today and are shaping the course of the revolution, Vera Zasulich, Catherine Breshkovskaya and Vera Figner, who has survived 20 years of solitary confinement.

Women marched under convoy to Siberia and ascended the scaffold alongside of men. She did not claim superiority and no one dared to question her equality. The extension of the suffrage is but recognition of her share in the rejuvenation of a people.

The problem is not so simple when one approaches the industrial situation. Russia's industries are still underdeveloped. The efficiency which come from the organization and concentration of capital is unknown. While there is plenty of striving for industrial democracy, the necessary preliminary for democracy in industry is absent. There is no foundation upon which to build. The prerequisite of a highly organized capitalistic state is missing, and it will be up to Russia to show whether democracy in industry can be attained by the mere strong desire to be democratic. In any event, the barbarity which accompanied the growth of industry in other countries will be avoided. There will be no exploitation of women, no crushing of children, no suppressing of labor organizations, no class legislation by the money bag.

And if anybody had any doubt as to the genuineness of Russian democracy that doubt should be dispelled by Russia's attitude in the war. Hungry, exhausted and bleeding at every pore, Russia announced her readiness to support her allies. All she asked was the elimination of selfish designs and the proclamation of a higher code of international morality. What a pity that the Allies have not grasped the full import of her plea.

——The Ladies' Garment Worker, *February 1918, pp. 11–12.*

The Bolshevik Revolution   —Ryan Walker
                 New York *Evening Call*, January 11, 1918

19. BATTLE HYMN OF THE RUSSIAN REPUBLIC

Louis Untermeyer, the distinguished American Socialist poet, expressed in his poetry the widespread feeling that all progressives throughout the world should rally against the forces trying to crush the young Russian Socialist republic.

by LOUIS UNTERMEYER

God, give us strength these days—
  Burn us with one desire;
To smother this murderous blaze,
  Beat back these flames with fire.

Let us not weaken and fail
  Or spend ourselves in a shout;
Let our white passion prevail
  Till the terror is driven out.

Give us the power to fling
  Ourselves and our fury, employed
To blast and destroy this thing
  Lest Life itself be destroyed.

Friends in all lands, arise—
  Turn all these fires to shake
Against their refuge of lies;
  Force it to crumble and break.

Rise, ere it grows too late
  And we have not strength enough.
Sweep it down with our hate!
  Trample it with our love!

———The Ladies' Garment Worker, *February 1918, p. 12.*

20. RED GUARD GETS 500 RECRUITS

As soon as permission is forthcoming from Washington, an American Red Guard is expected to leave for revolutionary Russia, to help preserve the first Socialist revolution in the world.

Word is anxiously awaited today from President Wilson by about 500 "guards for the revolution" who have enlisted thus far, and by radicals of all shades throughout the city who, it is believed, will rally to the call to arms on revolutionary soil.

The organization of this army began last night at a most enthusiastic meeting held in Parkview Palace, 110th street and Fifth avenue, under the direction of the Socialist Propaganda League.

More than 3,000 Socialists packed the hall to the doors, and an equal number held an overflow meeting outside. Both meetings pledged "moral, spiritual and physical" support to the cause of the Russian revolution against German autocracy.

In answer to the call for volunteers at the close of the meeting, the Socialists surged toward the platform in cheering mass. At the call for funds there came a shower of bills, women throwing jewelry on the stage—rings, pins and earrings. The enthusiasm reached its height when a baby's ring was picked up from the platform. A handkerchief with a roll of bills was then thrown on the stage from the gallery, followed by a voice that said "all I keep is my subway ticket to get home." One worker pledged his wages from the moment of his enlistment to the time of going abroad with the American Red Guard.

The following telegram was sent to President Wilson, asking his permission to recruit a Red Guard for service including a cable to be sent to Russia:

"Two thousand workers and Socialists, in mass meeting assembled, request that you allow recruiting of an American Red Guard of men not subject to service under selective draft act, for military service in Russia against German imperialism. We also request that you allow transmission of the following cable to Council of People's Commissaries, Smolny Institute, Petrograd:

" 'Two thousand Socialists and workers in mass meeting assembled, send fraternal greetings and encouragement to revolutionary workers and peasants in heroic struggle against German imperialism. We have approved recruiting of an American Red Guard for active service in Russia. Long live the revolution!' "

The meeting was called to discuss the advisability of enlisting an American Red Guard for active military service in Russia, and was addressed by Louis C. Fraina, who presided; Arturo Giovannitti, André Tridon, Henry Jager, Gregory Weinstein of the *Novy Mir,* the Russian Socialist daily in this city, and A. Schwarzenfeld.

Tridon told the audience that a man who spoke to President Wilson two weeks ago told him that the President said he would be willing to recognize the Bolsheviki, but "I must be forced to do so by public opinion." Cheers, with cries of "we are public opinion," greeted this announcement.

All of the speakers insisted that what Russia suffers the workers of the world will suffer, but it remained for Giovannitti, the last speaker, to sound the keynote of the meeting by declaring that "a state of war now exists between the German empire and the proletariat of the world."

The speakers were unanimous in declaring that the Socialists and radicals in Germany, if they do not refuse to fight against the revolutionary workers and peasants of Russia, whose cause is their cause, should be branded as "outlaws" and "traitors" to the international Socialist movement.

Fraina, in a stirring address, declared that this demonstration is a tribute to solidarity of the workers for international brotherhood and a rebuke to the charges of "cowardice" and "traitorism" heaped upon the very men who are now offering their lives for their principle.

The American Red Guard and the thousands of sympathizers with it called upon the workers of Germany "to refuse to fight against the revolutionary workers and peasants of Russia, whose cause is their cause, and to sweep aside the infamous, imperialistic 'socialism' of Scheidemann and all the social patriots, and to rally around the standard of Karl Liebknecht and Rosa Luxemburg for the social revolution."

About 500 enlisted in the guard, and many others added their names after the meeting. The rings, it was said, will be auctioned off at a meeting in Madison Square Garden shortly.

——*New York* Evening Call, *March 1, 1918.*

21. CONGRESSMAN LONDON SCORES JAPAN'S PLAN TO INVADE SIBERIA

Reports that the Japanese, with Allied approval, were planning to seize Vladivostok and invade Siberia, reached the United States in early March 1918, and produced widespread protests. Meyer London, Socialist congressman from New York, introduced a resolution in Congress asking that Russia be left alone and that all intervention cease. Although London was critical of the Bol-sheviks for trying to achieve a social revolution "overnight," he pleaded for recognition of the Soviet government by the United States: "Why should we recognize the Tsar and then refuse to recognize a workingmen's government, mistaken though it may be in many ways." (New York Call, *March 4, 1918.) Congressman London's resolution was indorsed by Socialist branches in New York City. Shortly afterwards, on April 5, 1918, the Japanese landed two companies of marines in Vladivostok.*

Washington, March 5.—Saying that the invasion of Russian territory by Japanese troops would be just as criminal as the invasion of Belgium by the Germans, Socialist Congressman Meyer London of the 12th Congressional district of New York, which takes in a large part of the East Side, introduced a resolution calling upon Congress to use its influence with the foreign friendly powers to stop the sending of troops into Siberia.

The congressman in his resolution asks that Russia be let alone to work out its own destinies. The resolution reads:

"*Whereas* an insidious effort is being made by various unclean interests to suggest to the Japanese government that it take possession of Russian territory in the Orient; and

"*Whereas* such a step would be looked upon, not only by the people of agonized Russia, but by all liberal and liberty-loving elements throughout the world as an invasion of the rights of the Russian people; and

"*Whereas* the Russian people who have suffered the horrors of a long war under an inefficient and autocratic form of government, must, by all the principles of right conduct among nations, be left unmolested to work out their own destiny; therefore be it

"*Resolved,* by the Senate and House of Representatives of the United States of America in Congress assembled, that the Congress solemnly protest against any attempt to interfere with the management by the Russian people of their own affairs; and be it further

"*Resolved,* that the Congress further protests against all attempts to encourage any foreign power to take possession of Russian territory, whereas such an invasion would be on a par with the infamous attacks on Belgium and Serbia and the supposed peace inflicted upon the Russian people by brutal physical force."

——*New York* Evening Call, *March 5, 1918.*

22. PENNSYLVANIA SOCIALISTS GREET SOVIET

Reading, Pa., March 5.—The state convention of the Socialist party of Pennsylvania cabled the Russian Soviet at Petrograd and the International Socialist Bureau, the Hague. The message read:

"The Socialist party of Pennsylvania sends fraternal greetings to the Russian republic. Your achievement is our inspiration. Long live the workers' government and the international. Birch Wilson, Secretary."

The cablegram to the International Socialist Bureau read:

"The Socialist party of Pennsylvania asks you to convey this message to working classes of Germany and Austria. We beg you to vigorously oppose your rulers' efforts to crush the Russian revolution. The German invasion of Russia is a blow against labor and democracy in all lands. Join hands with the workers of Russia for a separate peace and international solidarity."

——*New York* Call, *March 6, 1918.*

23. NY SOCIALISTS PROTEST INVASION

WOODROW WILSON, PRESIDENT OF THE UNITED STATES:

The executive committee of the Socialist party of New York views with alarm the threatened invasion of Russian territory by autocratic Japan, considering it as an attempt to destroy the achievements of the Russian revolution and to subjugate a free people. The counter-revolutionary character of the Japanese invasion can only be compared with the military campaign against free Russia of Imperial Germany—both aiming to accomplish the same end. We indorse the resolution of Congressman Meyer London, and join him in the demand that the United States government protest against the imperialistic and reactionary designs of the Japanese government.

——*Executive Committee, Socialist Party, New York County, Julius Gerber, Executive Secretary. New York* Evening Call, *March 8, 1918.*

24. JAPAN'S INVASION OF RUSSIA

Reports come now that Japan is at last going to take an active part in the great world war outside of annexing new territory and selling munitions. Japan is to send an army to invade—

Germany? Austria? Turkey? Perish the thought. To invade—
Siberia, Russia's territory! . . .

The puzzle of Japan's invasion of Siberia remains unsolved,
except as it may be solved by the inference every intelligent
person may draw for himself.

In this connection an article in the *Wall Street Journal* as-
sumes special significance.

The article appeared in the issue of April 28, 1917, shortly
after the emancipation of Russia from Tsardom. The article,
entitled "The Russian Peril Still Faces Germany," discusses the
possibility of a separate peace between Russia and Germany. The
Wall Street Journal is no yellow and sensational paper catering
to the pennies of the great masses, but the organ of Big Business,
as its title clearly shows, and whose special mission is to keep Big
Business properly informed. Great weight must, therefore, be
given to the following words in the above named article: "We
understand from good sources that if the pledges of the Russian
people to remain faithful to the war for democracy and freedom
are broken, there is a power on the East of Russia ready to rise
and transfer the war peril from the West side of Russia to the
East."

The article continues: "If Russia yields to Germany she will
be quickly sliced up. The Teutons will take her Western part
and the Allies, headed by the Japanese, will invade from the
Pacific and carve Russia on the East as far as they desire."

The article concludes with the following geographical prediction: "Instead of Russia from the Baltic and the North Sea to
the Pacific and from the Arctic to Constantinople and the
Bosporus, Great Russia will be a contracted territory, regulated
on all sides by the Teutons, the Turks and the Japanese."

Russia fought bravely against a separate peace with Germany
and for a general and democratic peace. It was the Ukraine, playing into the hands of Germany and betraying Russia, who sought
and made a separate peace. Forced by Ukraine's treason, her own
physical exhaustion, and the abandonment by the other powers,
Russia, renewing her pledge of allegiance to the great cause of
true people's democracy, had no choice but to accept the terms
of the ruthless conqueror. It was no separate peace that Russia
made with Germany. The submission of an unarmed and
hungry man—whose cries for help are a call in the wilderness,
and whose sufferings and agonies are objects of mockery by
those who should come to his rescue—to a powerful highway-
man holding a pistol at his temple, cannot be called a "separate

peace" with the criminal. Brutal Germany had refused to grant helpless Russia even that "peace" which conquerors usually give to the vanquished. *Surrender* was not enough for Germany. She aimed at *crushing* Russia.

And now that Russia has signed Germany's "scrap of paper," her fate is still uncertain. The reason for it is clear. While Germany was anxiously seeking a separate peace with the Tsar's Russia she is in deathly fear of peace, separate or general, with democratic Russia, leaving the Revolution intact. Her commander has openly declared that Russia's "sickness" (revolution) if not "cured" (crushed) will infect other countries. Germany is more interested in defeating the revolution than in winning the war. With the war won, and the Russian revolution alive and active, the fruits of the victory will be lost to the rulers. The Teutonic peoples would follow the example of their great Slavic neighbor and send the Hohenzollerns and the Hapsburgs to join the Romanovs. But with the Russian revolution defeated, the rule of the autocrats receives a new lease of life. That is the meaning of the present German onslaught on Russia, which, though "peace" has been signed, may not yet be considered at an end.

In view of all the circumstances, we can draw but one conclusion from Japan's military expedition into Russia: To assist Germany in assassinating the Russian revolution.

————Advance, *official organ of the Amalgamated Clothing Workers of America, March 8, 1918.*

25. WILSON ASKED FOR RUSSIAN RELIEF SHIP

Support for the Bolshevik revolution also took the form of mobilizing relief for the Russian people. The appeal to President Wilson described below was rejected, and the Administration refused to permit a Russian relief ship to leave the United States.

Louise Bryant, talking on the Russian situation before a meeting of the 3d, 5th and 18th Assembly district branches of the Socialist party, brought home the suffering which revolutionary Russia is enduring in such a direct and forcible manner that a committee of Bolshevik relief was immediately formed for the purpose of sending food and clothing to Russia.

It was decided that a telegram be sent to President Wilson,

asking that a ship be set aside for this purpose and it is the intention of the committee to raise a fund to provide the cargo for such a ship.

The committee has its headquarters at 43 West 29th street. Here is an opportunity for the Socialists of America to demonstrate that they are with the people of Russia, with them not only in wordy sympathy but in an eminently practical fashion.

The following telegram was sent to President Wilson at the termination of the meeting:

"At a meeting of New York Socialists, addressed by an eyewitness of the Russian situation, a committee of Bolshevik relief was created and instructed to request that you set aside a ship for the purpose of carrying supplies of food and clothing to the Bolsheviks.

"An organization is being formed for the purpose of raising the necessary funds. May we count on the cooperation of the administration to carry out the plan?" Louis P. Lochner, chairman, F. C. Nixon, secretary.

——*New York* Call, *March 21, 1918.*

26. WON'T LET RED GUARD SAIL FOR RUSSIA

A second Soviet peace delegation, this time without Leon Trotsky, met with Germany at Brest-Litovsk in March 1918. The Germans now demanded control of the Ukraine, Finland, Poland, the Caucasus and great indemnities of Russian gold, wheat, oil, coal and minerals. This meant that one third of Russia's crop area, over half of her industrial strength, and 62,000,000 people would pass into German hands. Lenin informed Bruce Lockhart, British agent in Russia, that the Soviet government was ready to resist the Germans if the Allies would render it the necessary aid. He warned Lockhart, however, that the Bolsheviks would "not be made a cat's paw for the Allies." Likewise, Lenin sent a note through Colonel Raymond Robins, Assistant Chief of the American Red Cross Mission who was in the service of the Intelligence Division of the U.S. Army, to the U.S. government asking if the Soviet government could rely on the support of the United States, Great Britain and France in its struggle against Germany.

These inquiries brought no response from either the United

States or Great Britain. On March 24, 1918, the All-Russian Soviet Congress ratified the Brest-Litovsk Peace Treaty. The Congress declared: "Under present conditions, the Soviet Government of the Russian Republic, being left to its own forces, is unable to withstand the armed onrush of German imperialism, and is compelled for the sake of saving revolutionary Russia, to accept the conditions put before it."

Despite the news of the signing and ratification of the Brest-Litovsk Peace Treaty, Socialists who were organized in the American Red Guard were still anxious to leave for Russia, believing that it was only a temporary peace and that war would soon break out again between Germany and Russia. (For evidence that Robins' dispatch containing Lenin's note never reached Washington until the crisis was over, see George E. Kennan, Russia and the West: Under Lenin and Stalin, Boston, 1960, pp. 56–57.)

The war department has refused permission for the organization of an American Red Guard for service in Russia in defense of the revolution. In a letter to the chairman of the Red Guard meeting, Henry Jarney, Brigadier-General and Acting Assistant Chief-of-Staff, says:

"It is not the policy of the United States to encourage or permit the formation of distinctive brigades, regiments, battalions or other organizations composed exclusively or primarily of the members of any race, creed or political group. This policy will be adhered to whether the proposed unit is intended for service within the American army or with the armies of our allies.

"The natural ambition of American Socialists to assist in the cause of crushing German militarism is most praiseworthy. It can find adequate outlet through enlistment, in the regular army, by all men over the draft age who are otherwise eligible. Non-naturalized Socialists of draft age, who are regularly registered and called, can gain the same end by waiving their claims to exemption."

Commenting upon this answer, Louis C. Fraina, the chairman of the meeting, said yesterday:

"The answer to our request would be adequate, were it not for the fact that Socialists of revolutionary convictions are willing to fight only in the army of a Socialist republic. It may be pointed out that a Jewish battalion has been organized here for service in Palestine, and a Polish legion for service in France, apparently with the sanction of the government. Why not an American Red Guard for Russia? The Soviets, while accepting a temporary peace as a truce, are actively preparing for a revolutionary war. Imperialistic Germany and Socialist Russia cannot exist together in peace and the Bolsheviki are aware of this fact. Either Germany or Russia will break the peace. America has offered its aid in the event of war. This aid can be given in three ways—full and complete recognition of the Soviets as the only actual and legitimate government of Russia; the active and steady shipment of supplies for the new army now being organized, and allowing the formation and transportation of American Red Guards to Russia."

——*New York* Call, *March 27, 1918.*

27. THE SOUL OF THE RUSSIAN REVOLUTION

Eugene V. Debs, the leading American Socialist and frequent Socialist presidential candidate, wrote "The Soul of the Russian Revolution" especially for The Call *magazine.*

by EUGENE V. DEBS

The world stands amazed, astounded, awe-inspired, in the presence of Russia's stupendous historic achievement.

The Russian revolution is without precedent or parallel in history. Monumental in its glory, it stands alone. Behold its sublime majesty, catch its holy spirit and join in its thrilling, inspiring appeal to the oppressed of every land to rise in their might, shake off their fetters and proclaim their freedom to the world!

Russia! Russia! Thy very name thrills in our veins, throbs in our hearts and surges in our souls! Thou art, indeed, the land of miracles, and thy humble peasants and toilers stand forth the world's triumphant liberators!

Russia, domain of darkness, impenetrable, transformed in a flash into a land of living light!

Russia, the goddess of freedom incarnate, issuing her defiant challenge to the despotisms of all the world!

Think of the Ages Russia groaned in the agony of her travail, the deluge of blood and tears poured out in the long night of her persecution and exile, and the costly sacrifices laid by her daughters and sons upon the holy altar of freedom!

And now, as if by command of God himself, she rises from her bondage, stands erect in her supreme majesty, and breathes her benediction of peace and love upon the world.

The heart of Russia in this hour of her glorious resurrection is the heart of humanity disenthralled; the soul of her people, the real people, the only people—glows with altruistic fervor, throbs with international solidarity and appeals with infinite compassion to the spirit of worldwide brotherhood.

Not a trace of national selfishness has stained Russia's revolutionary regeneration. The Bolsheviki demanded nothing for themselves they did not demand in the same resolute spirit for the proletariat of all the world, and if history records the failure of their cause it will be to the eternal shame of those for whom these heroes offered up their lives and who suffered them to perish for the lack of sympathy and support.

But the Revolution will not, cannot, fail. It may not completely fulfill itself without reaction, but the mighty change that has been wrought is here to stay, and because of it every throne is tottering, every bourgeois sees the handwriting, and the old order throughout the world is being shaken to its foundations.

All the forces of the world's reaction, all its dynasties and despotisms, all its kingdoms and principalities, all its ruling, exploiting classes and their politicians, priests, professors and parasites of every breed—all these are pitted openly or covertly against the Russian revolution and conspiring together for the overthrow of the victorious Russian proletariat and the destruction of the new-born democracy.

But, whatever may be the fate of the revolution, its flaming soul is immortal and will flood the world with light and liberty and love.

———*New York* Call, *April 21, 1918.*

28. GREETINGS TO RUSSIAN ARTISTS

In April 1918, the National Institute of Arts and Letters, composed of American authors, artists and composers, sent greetings to fellow-artists in Russia.

We rejoice with you in the success of the recent revolution by which, once for all, a death-blow has been given to Russian autocracy by this courage, this devotedness and the wise moderation of the leaders of the people, insuring to your great country the blessings of representative government.

We congratulate you on this result, the more particularly because, like you, we are not merely practitioners of our several arts but citizens of the great world of idealism, which through the long and desperate contest for a free Russia, you have so nobly represented by your loyalty to the spirit of liberty.

With you we honor the names of those great writers and other artists no longer living who have contributed so largely to the result by their vision and their courage, and whose fame will forever be a cherished possession, not only of Russia, but of America and of all the rest of civilized mankind.

America welcomes your country to the family of the world's democracies. With one master stroke the leaders of the Russian people have made the greatest reinforcement of half a century to the cause of popular government. Your own contributions to this in sacrifice and wisdom are fortunate omens for the future of your country, and reassures us that only by the vigilance of the people can their rights be safeguarded against the intrigues of a reigning caste long entrenched in power and secrecy. We look forward to the time when your example in throwing off the yoke of tyranny shall inspire other nations with a like resolve.

At this moment, when America is enlisted with Russia and her intrepid allies in combating the last effort of autocracy to maintain its foothold against the tide of democratic aspiration, we extend to you the open hand of fellowship and pledge to you in the cause of human freedom and brotherhood, our sympathy, our faith and our utmost and unremitting cooperation.

——The Art World, *May 1918.*

29. CONFERENCE ENDORSES SOVIETS

The following report is important in illustrating support of the Bolshevik revolution by labor, radical and Socialist groups. The resolution protesting armed intervention in Siberia by the United States is significant in revealing that although it was not until August 16, 1918, that the first American detachments

*landed in Siberia, reactionary forces were already at work in early
May to achieve this goal. Wilson was under great British and
French pressure to support a Japanese invasion of Siberia and to
send an American force into Siberia. Although he resisted this
pressure for several months, Wilson did eventually consent to
send an American force.*

The three-day conference of labor, radical and Socialist groups
adjourned last night after having passed resolutions indorsing
"the revolutionary spirit of the labor and reconstruction program
of the Russian Soviets and the British Labour party."[29] The 216
delegates present represented 29 states, 16 trade unions, 20 locals
of the People's Council, 17 Socialist party branches and central
or local organizations of the Socialist Consumers' League, the
Young People's Socialist League, the Fabian Society, the Women's
Peace party, the National Civil Liberties Bureau (represented by
its entire executive board), the American Union Against Militarism, the Collegiate Anti-Militarist League, the League of Small
Nations, the American Liberties Defense Union, the Workmen's
Circle, the James Connolly Socialist Club, the League for Demo-
cratic Control, the Professional League and the New Thought
Society.

The text of the resolutions on the work of Russian Soviets
and the British Labour party is as follows:

"The second conference of labor, Socialist and radical movements declares that we are in full accord with the revolutionary
spirit of the labor and reconstruction program of the Russian
Soviets and the British Labour party. This conference feels it
incumbent upon American labor to adopt a plan embodying the
same revolutionary spirit in a form adapted to American conditions. . . ."

The resolution protesting against intervention in Siberia, as
presented by Mrs. Rose Pastor Stokes, and which was unanimously adopted, read:

"Whereas, daily efforts are being made by reactionary forces in
the United States in favor of armed intervention in Siberia by
the United States, and whereas in Finland and Ukraine and in
other parts of Russia it has been shown that the Bolshevik forces
are the only organized opposition in Russia to German imperialism; and whereas, the forces which have cooperated with German
militarism to crush the revolutionary democracy of Russia
appear to be the same forces which are working for Siberian

intervention, therefore, be it resolved, that this assembly emphatically condemns such policy of armed intervention in Siberia."

———*New York* Evening Call, *May 6, 1918.*

30. A DREAM NO LONGER

Abraham Cahan, editor of the Jewish Daily Forward, *the most widely read Yiddish language newspaper in the United States, had been among the few Socialists who refused to endorse the party's enthusiastic support of the Bolshevik revolution. But when Cahan learned that the Bolshevik government was erecting a statue of Karl Marx in Moscow, he urged that every Socialist critic of the Bolsheviks, "should forget his former feelings and become inspired with affection and enthusiasm for them." Cahan's "affection and enthusiasm" lasted until 1922 when he began to feature anti-Soviet articles.*

by ABRAHAM CAHAN

Some days have passed since we published the special telegram from our Petrograd correspondent, telling us, among other things, that the Bolshevik government had erected a monument to Karl Marx in Moscow. Some days have passed and that statement won't leave my mind.

Whatever I say, whatever I do, the picture is continually thrusting itself upon my imagination: a statue of Karl Marx in the very heart of the Kremlin, in the very heart of that section of Moscow "sacred" to the palaces and temples of the Tsars.

A statue of Karl Marx in the Kremlin! A monument to the father of the Socialist movement in the "holy of holies" of Russian darkness and Russian despotism! It sounds incredible, but it is true nevertheless. It is a gorgeous piece of historical reality.

Those who are not familiar with Russia and her history will scarcely realize to the full what it means. The Kremlin was the most important, the most inviolable, the most awe-inspiring spot in the Russia of the Tsars. There it was where the despotic rulers were crowned ever since Moscow became Moscow. Every inch of the ground in the Kremlin was sacred ground. The remains of the old Tsars lie there. The throne of the Tsars stands there. The oldest and greatest churches and the most gigantic church bells are there. And now behold—a statue of Karl Marx stands there.

What has been one of our golden dreams has become an inspiring actuality.

It seems to me that in view of that glorious monument to Marx which now stands in the Kremlin the most bitter opponent of the Bolsheviki among our comrades should forget his former feelings and become inspired with affection and enthusiasm for them.

The First of May festival was combined in Moscow with the celebration of Karl Marx's hundredth birthday. It was the Socialist government of Russia that celebrated the two events. A national holiday was made of it. Workingmen marched through the streets, and with them the ministers and all other officials now residing in Moscow.

Ah; what a joy it would have been for us comrades of New York to participate in that pageant!

Truly, it reads like a story of the coming of the Messiah.

How, then, can one bear the Bolsheviki a grudge? How can one experience anything like a hostile feeling against them?

We have criticized them; some of their utterances often irritate us; but who can help rejoicing in the triumph? Who can help going into ecstasy over the Socialist spirit which they have enthroned in the country, which they now rule.

The antagonists of the Bolsheviki are continually endeavoring to show that it will be impossible for them to retain their power. The present writer has remarked on more occasions than one that there is nothing in the program and aspirations of the Bolsheviki; that nothing, in fact, is impossible these days. And now, as one visualizes that monument to Karl Marx, as it rears its venerable head in the Kremlin, one's heart swells with an ardent wish, with a prayer, that their victory should prove to be a lasting victory and that the exalted figure of Marx should forever remain standing in the Kremlin.

Try to picture the Bolsheviki driven from power and the monument to Karl Marx dashed to the ground—can a real Socialist afford to wish for such a day?

Our cherished dream has come true.

If 15 years ago, some one had depicted Tsar Nicholas as an inmate of a Siberian prison, while a Socialist government is erecting a monument to Karl Marx, he would have been set down for a madman, yet this is exactly what has taken place; and with this vision for a hard tangible fact, the hope of seeing Socialism established all over the world is no longer a piece of remote idealism but something on the threshold of realization.

When the Bolsheviki had brought about their revolution, the present writer was one of those who criticized them adversely. He acclaimed as well as criticized them, in fact. But since then there have been so many changes; so many great events have taken place. We are living at a time so eventful that a single day is often more pregnant with epoch-making occurrences than is a quarter of a century in ordinary times. Circumstances are altering cases so rapidly that what was white yesterday may be black today and what is black today may become white in 24 hours. Where is the sense then in assailing the Bolsheviki with the same arguments which were advanced against them seven months ago? Indeed, such arguments sound like the words of an old calendar.

At the end of seven months we see the Bolsheviki not weaker as has been predicted, but much stronger than they were, stronger in their grip upon the country and stronger as a moral force. Many of their sworn enemies, even among capitalists, have since been fascinated by them. How, then, are we Socialists to tell?

Is it not about time for all of us to cast off our former bitterness and venom? Is it not about time to clear our hearts of all factional pique, fix our mind's eye upon the monument to Karl Marx as it stands in Moscow and wish our victorious comrades in Russia further success and happiness?

—Jewish Daily Forward, *May 17, 1918.* (*An English translation was published in the New York* Evening Call, *May 30, 1918.*)

31. A NEW PAGE IN HISTORY

by Morris Hillquit

... I am safe in saying that for the historian of the future, the revolution in Russia will be of greater importance than the entire war. The war will pass some day; it cannot last forever. Conditions in the world will be readjusted. But the fact that one of the greatest countries in the world has broken away from the old capitalistic moorings, has once and for all turned a new page in history, a page of the domination, of the control, of the rule of the people, instead of ruler, the fact that this country has broken all past traditions, all past prejudices, the fact that it has created a living idea for the workers of all countries to follow—that cannot pass without the most vital effect upon the whole world.

——*Address to Convention,* Report and Proceedings, Fourteenth Convention of the International Ladies' Garment Workers' Union, Boston, Mass., *May 20 to June 1, 1918,* p. 142.

32. ACW AND ILGWU SUPPORT REVOLUTION

While the top officials of the American Federation of Labor, led by President Samuel Gompers, opposed the Bolshevik revolution, important trade unions hailed the Soviet government and rallied to its defense. Taking the lead in this activity were the Amalgamated Clothing Workers of America and the International Ladies' Garment Workers' Union, many of whose members were Socialists.

"The sentiment among our people is all one way," declared Joseph Schlossberg, general secretary of the Amalgamated Clothing Workers. "They are opposed to any interference in Russia's internal affairs and believe intervention in Siberia or Russia would spell disaster.

"They are heartily in favor of recognition of the Soviet republic on the part of our government. The interest in Russian affairs among our members is intense. Many of them have been citizens of Russia in the past, and they are familiar with conditions there and know what the revolution means to the great mass of the Russian people."

Other officers of the Amalgamated, in referring to the enthusiasm for recognition among the membership, cited a resolution for recognition that was passed at the recent convention of the union amidst tremendous enthusiasm. The great demonstration in favor of this resolution on the part of the delegates made it plain that it reflected the sentiment of the 100,000 workers in the organization.

The resolution reads:

"*Whereas* the Russian people have emancipated themselves from the tyranny of tsardom and established a free people's republic, *be it*

"*Resolved,* That we hail with joy free Russia and send to her our most fraternal greetings. We realize the tremendous difficulties that are now in the way of the Russian people in the working out of order and national prosperity. Those difficulties are but natural for a great nation just freed from autocracy, freed at a time when the world is in such a state of universal upheaval as the present. We do not wish to enter into a consideration of the merits of the several parties in Russia, but we rejoice in the fact that the Russian nation is free, and are confident that it will successfully work out its own salvation. It is our fervent hope that our own country and all other civilized nations will come to the assistance of free Russia by recognizing the Russian people's Soviet government, and giving the Russian people all aid in working out their own destinies."

It was pointed out today that the recent International Ladies' Garment Workers' Union convention also reflected this enthusiasm for the Russian revolution and the formation of a workers' republic in Russia. An official report unanimously passed at the convention hailed the revolution as "a great event which has had a vital and far-reaching effect upon the fate of human civilization and the progress of the labor movement." In summing up the progress of the revolution from a bourgeois overturn, "A program of substituting one Romanov for another," to a real workers' republic, the report greeted the present regime in Russia as "the first truly democratic Socialist republic." The report concluded:

"The members of the International Ladies' Garment Workers' Union will follow the struggles of their brothers in Russia with immense interest and sympathy, not only because many are linked to them by ties of kinship and sentiments, but also because the fate of the first great working class republic in the world cannot but be a matter of prime concern to organized and progressive workers of all countries."

> ———*New York* Evening Call, *June 6, 1918.* (*The text of the resolution adopted by the Amalgamated Clothing Workers appears in the union's* Documentary History, *1916–1918, p. 259, and that of the resolution adopted by the ILGWU in* Report and Proceedings, Fourteenth Convention of the International Ladies' Garment

Workers' Union, Boston, Mass., *May 20 to June 1, 1918,*
pp. 42–43.)

33. THE SOVIET

*The Messenger, a Socialist Negro monthly edited by A. Philip
Randolph and Chandler Owen and described as "the only Radical Negro magazine in the world," consistently defended the
Bolshevik revolution. The following editorials are typical of its
position.*

The Soviet is, doubtless, the most hated, the most loved and
most misunderstood political institution in the world today. The
Russian people love it; the capitalists of all countries hate it.
Most people don't understand it because the channels through
which they get their information are controlled by its enemies,
the capitalists.

The Soviet government resembles the elements in our American democracy which are the most stable and strong. The Soviet
organization rests upon local self-governing bodies, like the
famous New England town meetings. These local self-governing
bodies are comprised of the peasants and working men of local
communities. These local bodies send delegates to the All
Russian Assembly of Soviet Delegates, which must meet every
three months, sometimes more frequently. This All Russian
Assembly of Soviet Delegates, in turn, elects a central executive
committee of about 250 members. This executive committee is
the legislative body of the Russian people.

This central committee elects what are called "Commissioners
of the People," who are similar to cabinet officers in England,
France and Italy and the President and Cabinet officers in the
United States. These "Commissioners of the People" are always
responsible to the legislative body which has chosen them.

Where, then, is the ground for the cry of disorder and anarchy
in Russia? Nothing can be more orderly or more stable in a
democracy than this!

Here the representatives of the Russian people are both selected and elected by them. Whereas in all capitalists' countries
the representatives are selected by the capitalists and elected by
the people.

Of course, the capitalists maintain that anarchy exists in Russia, because the discarded and discredited Romanovs and their ilk no longer rob, exploit, pillage and plunder 180 millions of Russian peasants.

The ruling class in Germany, England, France and America are in a state of consternation and despair, lest the clock of democracy be striking the high noon of the reign of the ruling class in their countries, too.

Order! Who calls for order in Russia? "Let him who is without sin cast the first stone." By order, do we mean a state in which life, property, liberty and the pursuit of happiness are safe? If so, have we order in America, where over 280 Negroes have been lynched since the war began; where free speech, free press and free assemblage no longer exist; where 1,200 IWW miners were torn from their families in Bisbee, Arizona, packed in cattle cars, and deported away into an hapless desert by capitalist thugs and gunmen;[30] where men are being imprisoned because they dare to quote the Declaration of Independence or a passage from the New Freedom by President Woodrow Wilson; where the Supreme Court, by a decision of 5 to 4, declared the child labor law unconstitutional?[31] Can England make a motion in "the Parliament of the world" for order, who has held her heel of oppression upon the neck of Ireland for over 800 years, and whose hand is red and reeking with blood of India and other underdeveloped peoples?

After the revolution of 1789, France was chaotic for years and changed governments constantly and rapidly, swinging from a republic to a monarchy.

Germany only became an organized nation in 1871. The North German Confederacy welded with the sword, the recalcitant duchies, monarchies and principalities into a stable affair. And yet the "Zabern affair"[32] is a fact of common knowledge to every student of world politics.

As for the Negro, neither property, life, liberty nor the pursuit of happiness, which by the way, is only possible by the possession of the former, is secure in the Southern section of these United States.

The Messenger denies the right to every capitalist hypocrite in Christendom to speak to the motion of order on the Soviet of Russia. Long Live the Soviet!

——The Messenger, *May–June 1918.*

34. BOLSHEVISM AND WORLD DEMOCRACY

Bolshevism is the Banquo's ghost to the Macbeth capitalists of the world, whether they inhabit Germany, England, America or Japan. It is a foreword of a true world democracy. The Soviets represent the needs and aims of the masses.

Bolshevism has already defied the imperialist vultures to lay their cards of secret diplomacy on the table of justice before the high court of world opinion. It has led the world in making a concrete application of the principle of self-determination of smaller nationalities.

* * *

A sound and just economic, political and social program of reconstruction is gradually being adopted.

Bolshevism is not yet one year old in Russia. Russia is still at war with a great nation, and is virtually without help from her former allies. One hundred and eighty-seven millions of people have been delivered from the autocracy of the Tsar—a people 85 per cent of whom are illiterate.

Bolshevism has given these people a new hope, a new promise, a new ideal—economic and political freedom!

Will Bolshevism succeed? The tories of England and America asked the same question about the American people after the revolution of 1776. The Bourbons of France doubted the power of the French people to exist without the rule of the aristocracy—after the revolution of 1789. Governments are living organisms which have structure and function and are governed by the laws of growth. Hence, the Russian people must be helped, not hindered; they are still young.

——The Messenger, *May–June 1918.*

35. NEW BODY DEMANDS JUSTICE FOR RUSSIA

Announcement is made of the formation of the Russian Soviet Recognition League, an organization formed of individuals and societies interested in securing justice for Russia and aiding in the rehabilitation of that country under the Soviets.

The League will work for the recognition of the Soviet government. It holds that recognition by the United States would speedily result in the establishment of a working understanding between America and the Soviet republic and be the most effective way of combating German penetration in Russia. . . .

Alexander Trachtenberg, editor of the *American Labor Year Book,* has been chosen temporary chairman. . . . "The idea of the League grew up almost spontaneously," declared Trachtenberg today. "A great demand has arisen, particularly among the Americans of Russian blood, and those of Slavic descent generally, that an organization be formed to present the case for the Soviets, counteract counter-revolutionary propaganda which serves only the interests of Germany, and show the logical reasons for recognition. Virtually all Russian factions in this country, except the reactionaries and Germanophiles, are now united on realizing the need for recognition."

The League was formed as the result of a number of conferences in which members of various Russian groups in this city took part. Conferences were also held with officers of some of the Russian commissions, now in this country, who were sent here at the beginning of the Kerensky regime. Most of these Russians have refused to follow "Ambassador" Bakhmetev in his counter-revolutionary activities, are firmly opposed to the idea of allied intervention in Russia's internal affairs, and are entirely sympathetic to the idea of recognition of the Soviet government as the only power supported by the Russian people today.

Many well-known Americans interested in the welfare of Russia are interested in the formation of the League. A list of names will be published later.

The big drive engineered by Russian counter-revolutionists and other reactionary forces here to attempt to involve the United States in schemes for intervention in Siberia and the recognition of a "Siberian Republic" to be declared by the Cossack Colonel [Gregori] Semyonev and his handful of yellow battalions, roused Russian sympathizers here to the necessity of forming an organization to present the case of the Russian people. The intervention schemes apparently have collapsed[33] and the friends of democracy in Russia are convinced that the time is ripe to press the case for the recognition of the Soviet Republic.

———*New York* Evening Call, *June 4, 1918.*

36. LEAGUE FOR RECOGNITION OF SOVIETS

by ALEXANDER TRACHTENBERG

. . . No impartial student of the Russian conditions can deny the following facts:

1. The Russian Soviets have the support of the vast majority of the people. This support is not passive only, as has been asserted by those favoring an allied intervention. The Russian peasants, who constitute an overwhelming majority of the Russian people, are fully conscious of the fact that any force that could overthrow the Soviets would at once proceed to deprive them of the lands which they have expropriated during the revolution. For this reason they are ardently supporting the Soviets. Whether we like it or not, the fact remains that the peasants are bent upon keeping the nationalized land they have taken. Expropriation is an accomplished fact, and the readjustment of the financial disruption caused by the invalidation of land investments must be done on some other basis than the return to the "status quo ante" in Russia.

2. The Russian Soviet Government earnestly and with apparent success is establishing order and stabilized conditions in Russia.

3. If assured that the Allies, for the time being at least, will not try at any cost to unmake the social revolution in Russia, the Soviet Government obviously is willing and anxious to enter into friendly relations with the Allies and willing to readjust its foreign relations and its policy in general, in as far as it can be done without destroying the fundamental principle of the Russian revolution, in harmony with the most vital interests of the Allies.

4. The Soviet Government is wide awake to the necessity of forcible resistance to the German penetration into Russia. However skeptically many persons may seem to regard the efforts of Trotsky to raise a revolutionary army against Germany, the fact remains that such an army is being raised. If the effort is encouraged by sincere support on the part of the Allies, Russia will become a formidable factor in the struggle against German imperialism—even granting that the re-entrance of Russia in the war will take place only in the interest of the revolution.

5. A great part of the Russian middle class and intellectuals realize that the Soviet Government has come to stay. They are

re-entering the service of the Government in ever increasing numbers. The same thing is taking place among Russians in the United States who have been opposed to the Soviets. Only a small number of irreconcilables, mostly those financially affected by the expropriation of land, or their agents, have not yet resigned to their fate, and would be willing to risk hundreds of Allied and Russian lives, as well as the whole future of democracy, if only that they could get back their former possessions.

No close observer of the Russian conditions can deny these facts. They are supported by testimony of most of the Americans who have recently returned from Russia. The Russian and the Scandinavian press bear strong witness to our contentions.

Yet the American press seems to publish reports, which eliminate all bright sides of the Russian situation and do not stop at misrepresentations in order to paint a picture of complete chaos in Russia.

Every friend of Russia, every person interested in justice and truth, everyone who desires the downfall of German imperialism and understands the great role which Russia may play in this, should be interested in bringing the true facts about Russia to the American public. Until the present time sinister interests have flooded the American press with distortions and lies. A bogus "Russian Information Bureau," run under the auspices of "Ambassador" Bakhmetev in the interests of counter-revolution has been instrumental in spreading this campaign.

The Russian Soviet Recognition League has been organized to conduct meetings, to furnish the press with true reports about the doings of the Soviet Government of Russia, and to urge official recognition of the Soviet Government.

We invite you, members of the Amalgamated, if you are interested in our undertaking and are willing to do your share toward bringing about a better understanding with Russia, to support us in our work, morally and materially. We need your cooperation in every way.

——Advance, *June 11, 1918.*

37. "RECOGNIZE SOVIETS!" 15,000 CRY

Although the secret plans for Allied intervention in Russia did not come out into the open until August 1918, friends of

Soviet Russia tried to stave off the planned intervention through mass protest meetings.

"Block Intervention!"

"Recognize the Soviet Government of Russia."

These were the two demands cheered and urged by 15,000 Russian and American Bolshevist sympathizers in Madison Square Garden. The demands were voiced in diverse languages, but all languages are alike when it comes to the words "proletariat" and "revolution." . . .

Promptly at 8 o'clock Alexander Trachtenberg, who was exiled from Russia by the Tsar for his part in the revolution of 1905–06, opened the meeting, and after a short address introduced Norman Thomas, who was warmly received. The first big moment in the meeting was reached when Thomas, after reviewing the Russian situation, declared:

"There is only one thing this government can do—recognize the Soviets."

The audience rose as one man, cheering and waving flags, hats and handkerchiefs. . . . "Recognize the Soviets! Recognize the Soviets!" they cried, and that was the keynote of the meeting. Every subsequent speaker made it the "burden of his song," and even now the cry has reached Washington, and tomorrow it will be heard in every capital in the world. . . . So fervid were the appeals and demands made by the speakers and echoed by the cheering mass, that the resolutions urging the recognition of the Soviet government in Russia and the blocking of intervention read by Alexander Trachtenberg, chairman, were almost drowned in a roar of unanimous approval. . . .

The resolutions follow:

"*Whereas,* the federated republic of Russia and its government of the workers' and peasants' Soviets is the only organ of actual governmental authority in Russia in accordance with the will of the millions of Russian toiling masses, and resolutely supported by them;

"*Whereas* this republic, the guardian and the hope of the loftiest ideals of the toiling masses, is in grave danger of destruction at the hands of German junkers in the West and Japanese and other interventionists in the East;

"*Whereas* plans of invasion in Siberia, originated with and nursed by reactionary tendencies all over the world, and by representatives of former privileged classes of Russia, can bring nothing but internal confusion in Russia;

"*Whereas* such an intervention will, by its very logic, lead to further annexations of Russian territory on the part of the German oppressors;

"*Whereas* intervention will undoubtedly evoke bitter resistance on the part of the Russian people and thus hamper the work of reconstruction and rehabilitation energetically carried on by the Soviet government;

"*Whereas* intervention would create a gulf of hatred and bitterness between the Russian people and the United States;

"*Whereas* an invasion would hamper the organized resistance to German militarism, which is being successfully planned and organized by the Soviet government; *be it*

"*Resolved,* that we, 15,000 men and women, Americans, Russians, Finns, Lithuanians, Letts, Ukranians, Poles and Esthonians, in a meeting assembled in Madison Square garden in New York urge the government of the United States to recognize the government of the Russian Soviets as the government reflecting the will and the ideals of the Russian people; *be it further*

"*Resolved,* that we most emphatically protest against the treacherous campaign in the interest of armed intervention in Russian affairs carried on in the United States by various imperialistic elements of several deposed tsaristic regimes, and other discredited reactionary elements of Russia. This campaign only plays in the hands of German imperialism, and is supported by enemies of democracy, justice and freedom."

———*New York* Evening Call, *June 12, 1918.*

38. RECOGNIZE RUSSIA

John Reed's defense of the Soviet policy in signing the Brest-Litovsk Treaty came at a time when even radicals and liberals in the United States were upset by Russia's capitulation, believing that the defeat of Germany was a revolutionary duty. Reed fully supported Lenin's decision to sign the harsh treaty, explained why it was necessary, and urged recognition of the Soviet government by the Allies as the best way to defeat Germany.

by JOHN REED

The capitalist press of the Allied countries is loud in its indignation against the so-called "Russian betrayal" at Brest-Litovsk.

At the same time, however, it is full of excuses for the peace treaty signed by Rumania with the Central Powers on March 5, 1918; and even justifies the action of the bourgeoisie of Finland and Ukraine in calling upon German troops to fight their own countrymen.

Yet the Russo-German peace treaty was as much a matter of military necessity as the Rumanian treaty. The Russian army was demoralized and exhausted; Russian economic life had broken down. For all this the Bolsheviki are not to blame. Have we forgotten how the Government of the Tsar deliberately disorganized the economic machinery of the country, allowed the transportation system to go to smash, and deprived the army not only of arms but even of food—in order to force a separate peace with the Germans? The newspapers were full of these things at the time.

Then came the Provisional Government, which was an unworkable compromise between the Socialists and the party of the bourgeoisie. This regime was unable, at first, to accomplish any reorganization of the national life. Even the breadlines instituted under the Imperial Government were never done away with. The soldiers themselves, if they could have received proper support from the country, would have remained in the trenches *to defend the country;* it was their voice and the voice of the Russian masses which had proclaimed, "No annexation, no indemnities, and the right of self-determination of peoples," and they would have defended those terms. But under the pressure of the Allied Governments, an offensive was commenced in Galicia, and in that act the majority of the Russian troops refused to participate.

After this the bourgeois wing of the Government bent all its efforts to the destruction of the Revolution, continuing the process begun by the Tsar, and even conniving, it is generally believed, at the fall of Riga, in order to strengthen discipline in the ranks of the Army. Under their systematic campaign to starve the workers by closing the factories, to break down the Soviets by wrecking the transportation and supply system, and to crush the soldiers' committees by diverting food and arms from the front, Russia was brought into a complete disintegration. The saving of Russia was the Bolshevik revolution. If that had not happened, the German army would now be garrisoning Moscow and Petrograd.

At Brest the Russians were not supported by the Allies, and

for that reason were forced to accept the German terms. Not only that, but they are wholly abandoned now, and by the pressure of Japan in Siberia, greatly weakened in the heroic struggle they are carrying on against the armed might of the Central Powers.

For the Russian Soviet Government is at war with Germany—has been at war with Germany since last summer. It stands to reason that this is so. The Soviet ruling powers are Socialists, and as such, enemies of capitalism, and most of all, enemies of the German Imperial system, the arch-exponent of militant capitalism. They have been fighting Germany with the strongest weapon in the world—propaganda—the only weapon against which the sword is ultimately powerless. This propaganda, not only among the German troops, but also in the interior of the country, is remarkably successful. Austria is ready to crack open because of it, and during the Brest-Litovsk negotiations the entire eastern front of the German troops was permeated with it to such an extent that the invading force into Russia had to be made up largely of volunteers from the western front. As for the war-prisoners in Russia, they are deeply infected by Bolshevism, and many thousands of them are enrolled in the ranks of the Russian Red Army against their own peoples.

The Red Army is rapidly being organized—as Lenin says, "not for defense of nationalistic interests, or Allied aims . . . but to defend the world's Socialism." It is a compact little well-drilled force, composed of volunteers, not from the old Russian army, but from the untouched reserves of young revolutionary workers and peasants.

According to figures in possession of the United States Government, there are present more than *eight hundred and fifty thousand* German and Austrian troops now engaged in pacifying Ukraine—a country not half as revolutionary as Great Russia, and without any Red Army. The latest moves of German diplomacy indicate that the Imperial Government is not at all anxious to attempt the military invasion of Soviet Russia.

But just as the Soviet Government considers the German Imperial Government its worst enemy, so Germany well knows that Soviet Russia on her flank is mortal to her military autocracy. By every means, by commercial and financial pressure, by capturing the food-supplying countries of the South, Germany is attempting to destroy the Soviets. At the time of the advance into Russia, Prince Leopold of Bavaria, in an army order, said, "Our aim is not annexation . . . but the restoration of order and *suppression of anarchy threatening to infect Europe.*" And if this "restoration of order and suppression of anarchy" can be accomplished by Japanese intervention, so much the better for Germany. For Germany fears not military force; she fears not a Japanese army in Siberia, nor a bourgeois republic in Russia— whose power of propaganda among German troops would be as limited as that of the French Republic. Soviet propaganda, incredibly contagious, is the only thing that Germany fears. Allied recognition of the value of Soviet propaganda would be a blow at Germany.

At the present moment, however, most of the Allied Governments seem to be acting on their theory that it is more important to defeat the Russian Soviets than to defeat Germany. In the Brooklyn *Eagle* the American Consul at Helsingfors, Mr. Hayes, is quoted as praising the Germans for having restored order in Finland. . . . And the movement for Japanese intervention in Siberia is actuated as much by the motive of restoring "law and order" in Russia, as by the rather farfetched excuse of combating "German influence."

The Soviet Government of Russia is there to stay; it is based on the almost universal will of the Russian masses. At the present moment it is being attacked on one side by the Germans, and on the other side by all sorts of bourgeois and reactionary movements based on the Japanese in Siberia. The threat of active, serious Japanese intervention, besides, hangs over it like a storm-cloud. When Central Russia was famine-stricken in the past, food could be got either in Ukraine or in Siberia. Now the Germans have the Ukraine, and counter-revolutionary hordes are over-running Siberia. Russia is being starved from both sides. Its ability to make war on Germany is crippled by this and by the possible necessity of making war upon Japan.

Recognition of the Soviet Government by the Allies will immediately put an end to the menace of counter-revolution in Siberia, and strengthen immeasurably the Soviet power against Germany.

Make no mistake, however. Soviet Russia will not re-enter the war as an ally of the Allies; it will defend itself against the capitalist world. But Germany is the nearest, worst, and most active capitalist menace. The time has come for the Allied governments to decide whether their hatred is greater for German militarism or Russian Bolshevism.

——The Liberator, *July 1918.*

39. NY STATE SP ENDORSES SOVIETS

The following resolution was passed by the convention of the Socialist party of New York State:

The Russian revolution since last November has assumed the form of a Soviet government, the natural and inevitable form in Russia, which expresses the will and aspirations of the masses of the people. In spite of counter-revolutionary plots, the hostility of all foreign governments and the general economic disorganization inherited from the old regime and accentuated by the war, the Soviet government has lasted for nearly eight months and progressed in the colossal task of social and economic reconstruction.

We greet with joy and confidence the Russian Soviet Socialist Federated Republic, the first Socialist republic in the world.

We denounce the treacherous attitude of the German and Austrian majority Socialists, who did not tear from the hands of their imperialist masters the brutal treaty of Brest-Litovsk, imposed on the Russian workers and peasants by military force. We call upon the workers throughout the world to insist that the people of Ukraina, Finland and the Russian border provinces, now under the heel of junkerdom, must receive freedom and self-determination.

We denounce equally all attempts on the part of any government to invade Russia by force and overthrow the government of the Russian people. We denounce the counter-revolutionary plots being conducted by reactionary Russian emigres in every capital in the world, which are being supported and stimulated by predatory capitalist interests, greedy to loot Russia.

We protest against the continued isolation of Socialist Russia. We call upon all true believers in democracy in the United States to join with us in urging our government to recogize the Russian Soviet republic, and to cooperate with and assist it and the Russian people disinterestedly, to the end that the democratic forces in the world may be strengthened and heartened, and autocracy, junkerism and imperialism be banished from the world forever.

We call upon our representative in Congress, Meyer London, to introduce a resolution in Congress urging the speedy recognition of the Soviet government by the government of the United States.

Resolved, that a copy of this resolution be sent to the President of the United States, the Speaker of the House of Representatives, the President of the Senate, and Meyer London.

——*New York* Evening Call, *July 1, 1918.*

40. AMERICA'S COURSE IN RUSSIA'S CRISIS

President Wilson is about to make the greatest decision of his whole career. He is about to place his hand on the pivot of the whole world's future. He is about to enter Russia. Let us, therefore, get clearly into our heads the one prime fact about Russia. The fact is not Lenin. That fact is not the Bolsheviki. The prime fact about Russia is the Soviets.

Most of us in America do not believe in Lenin; most of us do not believe in the Bolsheviki. Very well. But it is absolutely necessary for us to believe in the Soviets. The strength of our belief in the Soviet is the strength of our chance of success in Russia.

The Soviet is the soul of Russia—and more. From each village in Russia we see delegations going to the provincial Soviet. From each provincial Soviet we see delegates going to the all-Russian congress of Soviets. Starting with being the dreaming soul of Russia, the Soviet has become its communicating nervous system and its deciding brain.

True, the Soviets are not completely democratic. They exclude the capitalists. This exclusion is wrong. But let us be practical. The capitalists of Russia are very few. They and all their friends and associates are not 5 per cent of the population. Even if they were admitted to the Soviets, they would be overwhelmingly outvoted. The Soviets, in action, would remain what they are. They are Russia. . . .

Let us saturate ourselves with one prime fact. The Russian republic is precisely what it says it is. It is a republic of Soviets, and in the mouth of every American the word Soviet must become a word of friendship, a word of comradeship, a word of great hope for a great, irresistible alliance against Berlin.

What the president must offer Russia to win Russia is a loyal America. We are that America. Let us be loyal.

——*Editorial, Chicago* Daily News, *July 2, 1918.*

41. ON BEHALF OF RUSSIA

In his "Open Letter to America," published in The New Republic *and reprinted as a pamphlet, Arthur Ransome, correspondent in Soviet Russia for the London* Daily News, *described the real character of the February revolution, the nature of the Provisional government and the Soviet, the Constituent Assembly, peace negotiations between Russia and Germany, and the Soviet government and the Allies. In his preface and conclusion, selections from which are published below, Ransome told why he made this appeal to America.*

by ARTHUR RANSOME

Every day brings a ship,
Every ship brings a word;
Well for those who have no fear,
Looking seaward well assured
That the word the vessel brings
Is the word they wish to hear.

Emerson wrote the poem I have stolen for a headpiece for this letter, and Emerson wrote the best commentary on that poem: "If there is any period one would desire to be born in—is it not the age of Revolution; when the old and the new stand side by side, and admit of being compared; when the energies of all men are searched by fear and by hope; when the historic glories of the old can be compensated by the rich possibilities of the new era? This time, like all times, is a very good one, if we but know what to do with it." Revolution divides men by character far more sharply than they are divided by war. Those whom the Gods love take youth of their hearts and throw themselves gladly on that side, even if, clear sighted, they perceive that the fires of revolution will burn up perhaps the very things that, for themselves, they hold most dear. Those others, wise, circumspect, foolish with the folly of wisdom, refrain, and are burned up none the less. It is the same with nations, and I send this pamphlet to America because America supported the French Revolution when England condemned it, and because now also America seems to me to look toward Russia with better will to understand, with less suspicion, without the easy cynicism that prepares the disaster at which it is afterwards ready to smile.

Why?   —*The Liberator,* March 1919

Not that I think all this is due to some special virtue in America. I have no doubt it is due to geographical and economic conditions. America is further from this bloody cockpit of Europe, for one thing. For another, even rich Americans dependent for their full pockets on the continuance of the present capitalist system, can wholeheartedly admire the story of the Bolshevik adventure, and even wish for its success, without fearing any serious damage to the edifice in which they live. Or it may be, that, knowing so little about America, I let myself think too well of it. Perhaps there too men go about repeating easy lies, poisoning the wells of truth from simple lack of attention to the hygiene of the mind. . . .

No one contends that the Bolsheviks are angels. I ask only that men shall look through the fog of libel that surrounds them and see that the ideal for which they are struggling, in the only way in which they can struggle, is among those lights which every man of young and honest heart sees before him somewhere on the road, and not among those other lights from which he resolutely turns away. These men who have made the Soviet government in Russia, if they must fail, will fail with clean shields and clean hearts, having striven for an ideal which will live beyond them. Even if they fail, they will nonetheless have written a page of history more daring than any other which I can remember in the story of the human race. They are writing it amid showers of mud from all the meaner spirits in their country, in yours and in my own. But, when the thing is over, and their enemies have triumphed, the mud will vanish like black magic at noon, and that page will be as white as the snows of Russia, and the writing on it as bright as the gold domes that I used to see glittering in the sun when I looked from my windows in Petrograd.

And when in after years men read that page they will judge your country and mine, your race and mine, by the help or hindrance they gave to the writing of it.

———The New Republic, *July 27, 1918.*

42. ROSE PASTOR STOKES DEFENDS REVOLUTION

A left-wing Socialist who was tried by the government for writing a letter to a newspaper charging that " the government is

*for the profiteers" and sentenced to ten years' imprisonment,
Rose Pastor Stokes frequently defended the Bolshevik revolution.*

Ninety-one thousand and forty-five working men and women
were represented at the opening of the conference of the Liberty
Defense Union at Webster Hall. . . .

The following organizations were represented: The Consumers' League of Greater New York; the Amalgamated Ladies'
Garment Cutters' Union, Local 10; the Hebrew Butchers' Workers' Union; the Trade Union League of Greater New York, and
numerous branches of the Workmen's Circle. . . .

Rose Pastor Stokes, in her speech, declared:

"There is no nation in the world today striving more passion-
ately for the ideal of the brotherhood of man than Russia in
revolt against privilege and exploitation. The press of the
plutocracy points to the violence accompanying the great Russian revolution as an excuse for interfering with the divine out-
come, as if any fundamental justice was ever established except
through sacrifice accompanied by some measure of violence.

"As if Russia could have been expected to wave a fairy wand
over the heads of the self-interested and greedy elements, who
must first lose their power to do harm, in order that the people
might win the victory for justice and humanity. Any great war,
civil or otherwise, is worth waging if the issue is greater human
freedom and greater equality. And such measure of human
liberty is being fought for in that glorious Russian revolution,
as makes every struggle for liberty waged in the past pale into
insignificance.

"That is why, indeed, the American and allied imperialists are
for intervention. And that is why, too, they would stop our
mouths with their legal dust, so that they may have their way
with Russia also, without effective protest.

"They know that the liberty arising in Russia will spread the
light of her torch over the whole world, and the dark night of
the capitalist regime will be dispelled. They know that a new
order must result if Russia is permitted to stand: Land for all,
industry for all, security and equality of opportunity for all—
an end to exploitation and an end of the wars between nations,
that is why those who have battened on the blood and tears and
miseries of the people from time immemorial, itch to destroy
Socialist Russia—the hope of the world—the desapir of
capitalism."

——*New York* Evening Call, *August 1, 1918.*

43. ACTION IN SIBERIA

On August 2, 1918, British troops landed at Archangel. That same day Major General William S. Graves of the U.S. Army, commander of the 8th Division at Camp Fremont, Palo Alto, California, was summoned to a conference with Secretary of War Newton D. Baker. General Graves was informed that the War Department had selected him to take command of an expedition of American troops which was to leave immediately for Siberia. The decision, General Graves learned, had been reached on July 5, 1918, and the purpose of the military action in Russia was ostensibly "only to help the Czecho-Slovaks consolidate their forces and get into successful co-operation with their Slavic kinsmen." (See *William S. Graves,* American Siberian Adventure, *1918–1920.*)

At first the Allied governments explained that they had landed troops in Murmansk and Archangel in the spring and summer of 1918 because it was necessary to prevent supplies from falling into the hands of the Germans. Later they used the excuse that their troops were in Siberia to help Czechoslovakian forces withdraw from Russia. There were in Russia about 50,000 Czechoslovakian soldiers who had deserted from the Austro-Hungarian Army to the Russian lines before the revolution. They had fought with the Russians against the Austro-German forces, and after the fall of Kerensky, the Soviet government had agreed, at the request of the Allies, to transport them from Kiev to Vladivostok with the intention of their sailing for France. The Czechoslovakian troops, however, involved themselves in hostilities against the Soviets, and became the center of counter-revolutionary organization. The Czechs refused to surrender their arms to the Soviet authorities and, under reactionary commanders, began to seize a number of towns, overthrew the local Soviets and established anti-Soviet administrations. Encouraged by American agents and even more by the French and British, the Czechs fought side by side with the Whites against the Bolsheviks, staged a coup in Vladivostok and set up an anti-Soviet government in that city.

With the excuse that the Allied troops were coming to save the Czechs from unprovoked attack by Red Army troops and by German war prisoners armed by the Bolsheviks, the Allied governments intervened in Russia. (George F. Kennan maintains that Wilson's decision to send troops to Siberia was based on a misunderstanding of the role being played by the Czechs.) British, French, Japanese and American troops landed in Vladivostok. The action caused wide protests in the United States.

The State Department announced on August 3 the plan for joint American-Japanese military intervention in Siberia and for armed allied intervention by way of the Murmansk coast. The *Call* has withheld comment on this announcement, in the hope that a clearer statement of the purpose of these expeditions would be made. Apparently none is forthcoming. Meanwhile the capitalist newspapers that have been shouting for months for an invasion of Russia and the overthrow of the government of the Russian people by the allies by force have acclaimed the intervention plan with enthusiasm. . . .

In the note of the State Department there is no mention of the Soviet government of Russia. It is as if that government had never existed, and the story of the past 10 months of the risen people of Russia, a story that will thrill the heart of humanity for generations to come, had been completely wiped out. Yet the Soviet power is not only an inspiration for the future. It is the great vital present-day fact in Russia. According to reputable newspaper correspondents who came through Siberia from Moscow in May with the Red Cross mission, that power was firmly established everywhere. The mission traveled on a note of safe conduct signed by Premier Lenin, and that paper was respected by each local authority in Siberia as thoroughly as a note from President Wilson would be respected in this country.

The *Call* does not believe that an uninvited invasion of any country by foreign powers, however small its forces and however unavowedly benevolent its purpose, will be welcomed by the invaded inhabitants. We should not welcome an invasion of the United States by a foreign army led by the Angel Gabriel, and we have no suspicion that the masses of the Russian people are greatly different in psychology from any other people in this respect. We believe that an invading foreign force, even led by angels, could not avoid interference in the domestic affairs of the invaded nation. We do not see how intervention in Russia that disregards the government of the Russian people can be productive of anything but strife and turmoil, and inevitable armed clashes with the population that will lead to a real sympathetic invasion. That prospect, which surely cannot serve any military purpose in the war against Germany, we do not contemplate with enthusiasm.

For many months the kept capitalist press in America, in common with similar organs in the allied countries and the central powers, has been filled with a mass of lies about Russia. The groups of reactionary Russian émigrés in every great capital have been clamoring their scandalous recriminations against free Russia. Apparently all the tremendous forces of reaction in the world have been in conspiracy to overthrow the newly won democracy in Russia which they so hate and dread. We have tried not to be dismayed by this persistent chorus of lies, and through it all we have kept in mind the one great word about Russia, a word uttered by the responsible spokesmen of the American democracy.

"The treatment accorded Russia by her sister nations in the months to come," said Woodrow Wilson in his solemn message to Congress on January 8, [on the "Fourteen Points"] "will be the acid test of their good will, of their comprehension of her needs as distinguished from their own interests, and of their intelligent and unselfish sympathy."

It has been our deep and heartfelt prayer that the United States might stand this acid test.

——*Editorial, New York* Evening Call, *August 9, 1918.*

44. PROCLAMATION ON RUSSIA

Since the French Revolution established a new high mark of political liberty in the world, there has been no other advance in democratic progress and social justice comparable to the Russian Revolution. The Russian people have cast behind them three centuries of Tsarist oppression. They have established an advanced form of democracy—a Socialist government—based on co-operative effort for the common good. They have cast aside the false idols of secret diplomacy and imperialism and are abolishing exploitation of every kind. Economically and socially, as well as politically, the Russian Socialist Federated Soviet Republic is a government of the workers, by the workers and for the workers.

The French people, a century and a quarter ago, found all nations turned against them because of their ideals of political liberty. The Russian people are facing a similar experience because of their ideals of economic freedom. The forces of capitalism and reaction throughout the world are determined to crush the newly won freedom of the Russian workers. They are working with the remnants of the old regime and the wealthy bourgeois exiles for the overthrow of the Soviet government, and for the restoration of the rule of feudalism and imperialism in Russia.

German imperialism, recognizing democratic Russia as its worst enemy, has attempted to crush Russia from the West. It has wrested from Russia by brute force, under the legal form of a brigand's peace, the Russian border provinces, and the great territory of the Ukraine, against the will of their peoples.

Imperialists in the countries at war with Germany have adopted an attitude toward Russia similar to that of the Prussian junkers. They have been demanding an invasion of Russia from the east and north and the crushing of the Soviet Republic by Allied armies.

We denounce the schemes of these imperialists to use the Czecho-Slovaks as a counter-revolutionary force, used against the declared will of the Czecho-Slovaks themselves.

We denounce as utterly incompatible with any principle of democracy or international decency any and all plans of invasion. Such action can only result in throwing Russia into a bloody struggle of which German imperialism will be quick to take advantage. We believe that such an invasion would outrage every principle of justice and international law and make a re-arrangement of friendly international relations very difficult.

The representatives of Russian junkerdom in the Allied capitals are now fomenting plots for counter-revolution in Russia. They know that a reactionary government in Russia, such as they desire, could maintain itself only with the aid of German bayonets, as do now the reactionary governments in Finland and Ukraine. We urge the United States government not to assist these enemies of democracy and freedom.

We protest against the continued isolation of the Soviet Government of Russia, which is being held incommunicado by the governments of the world.

We call upon the workers throughout the world to aid the Russian people in their struggle for freedom.

We call upon all true believers in democracy in the United States to join with us in urging our government to recognize the Russian Soviet Republic. In spite of the hostility of the most powerful forces, it has endured for ten months, successfully performing the great task of reconstructing the social and economic life of Russia. The Socialist Party of America declares itself in accord with Revolutionary Russia and urges our government and our people to co-operate with it and to assist it to the end that democratic forces of the world may be victorious and autocracy and imperialism banished forever.

> ———*Adopted by Conference of State Secretaries and Socialist Party Officials, August 10–12, 1918. Published in the* Special Official Bulletin, *September 17, 1918, copy in Duke University Library.* See also *New York* Call, *August 14, 1918.*

45. RUSSIA AND THE INTERVENTION

From the beginning *The Nation,* as its readers know, has been opposed to military intervention of any sort in Russia. That opposition has not been based upon any extravagant notions regarding the aims or accomplishments of the Russian revolution, nor upon an overweening fondness for the principles or methods of the Bolsheviki, nor yet upon the imputation to the United States or the allies of selfish or ignoble motives. We have realized to the full the gravity of the German menace and the desirability of enlisting Russia on the side of the allies if Russia is to fight at all. Our opposition to armed intervention, regardless of whether the force be large or small, has had quite different grounds. We have from the first believed, and still believe, that the whole truth about Russia has not been told, that important facts unfavorable to the allied view have been deliberately withheld, and that both the nature and work of the Soviet government have been in important respects systematically misrepresented and discredited. More than that, we have felt that the appearance of an armed force in Russia, no matter with what professions of high purpose it might be heralded, was not only likely to help rather than hinder the German designs, but was almost certain to arouse, in large sections of the Russian people, feelings of deep and lasting resentment at the coercion to which the country was henceforth to be subjected.

The resort to military intervention is all the more regrettable because, as it seems to us, an opportunity for helping Russia in other more useful and sounder ways has in the meantime been lost. What Russia has needed for months past is the sympathy and forbearance of the governments which were once its friends. Its effort to reconstruct its society upon a democratic basis, novel and groping as some of those attempts apparently have been, have merited some better form of recognition than cold and critical neglect. The humiliating peace of Brest-Litovsk need never have been made had not the allies and the United States, with amazing blindness, turned a deaf ear to the Russian appeal to be represented in the conference. The rehabilitation of Russian industry, agriculture and commerce, without which Russia could not hope to regain a place among the nations, might at any time have been begun, and with small likelihood of thereby replenishing Germany's exhausted stores to any appreciable extent, if only the allies had permitted foreign trade to be resumed. And even if the economic revival had been small, the supplies of food and clothing needed to cope with widespread hunger and nakedness, and the medical resources necessary to combat epidemic disease, might still have been introduced with beneficent results had not the American Red Cross folded its arms. This much at least a Christian civilization might have done without calling to its aid a single soldier.

If the Czecho-Slovaks turn out to be more concerned to win some political advantage for themselves or appropriate some portion of Russian territory than to fight the central powers on the Eastern or Western fronts, their spectacular career as a distinct force should be terminated without delay. There ought certainly to be no time lost in repairing and equipping the railways, reopening factories, restoring foreign and domestic commerce, distributing food and other necessaries, checking typhus and cholera, and opening the schools and the universities.

There are powerful influences ready to restore Kerensky and others equally ready to keep him from power at any cost. A cunningly contrived division of Russia into several states is a very real danger. All this, with international intrigues and secret schemes of every sort, the allied powers must resist if through their efforts Russia is to be free. The world waits for the first example in history of a great nation upon which the fortunes of war have brought evil days, restored to liberty, health and power without force or fraud, by the unselfish help of a group of sister states. And while this good work goes on, let us have the truth, the whole truth and nothing but the truth about Russia.

——The Nation, *August 24, 1918.*

46. "I PLEAD GUILTY TO THE CHARGE"

On June 29, 1918, Eugene V. Debs was indicted for violating the Espionage Act during an anti-war speech he delivered in Canton, Ohio, on June 16. In his speech to the jury, Debs defended the Bolshevik revolution. He was found guilty, sentenced to ten years in prison, and remained imprisoned from April 1919 to December 1921. In 1920, while still in prison, he received 901,000 votes for President of the United States, running on the Socialist ticket.

From Speech by EUGENE V. DEBS

I have been accused of expressing sympathy for the Bolsheviks of Russia. I plead guilty to the charge. I have read a great deal about the Bolsheviks of Russia that is not true. I happen to know of my own knowledge that they have been grossly misrepresented by the press of this country. Who are these much-maligned revolutionists of Russia? For years they had been the victims of a brutal Tsar. They and their antecedents were sent to Siberia, lashed with a knout, if they even dreamed of freedom. At last the hour struck for a great change. The revolution came. The Tsar was overthrown and his infamous regime ended. What followed? The common people of Russia came into power, the peasants, the toilers, the soldiers, and they proceeded as best they could to establish a government of the people.

It may be that the much-despised Bolsheviks may fail at last, but let me say to you that they have written a chapter of glorious history. It will stand to their eternal credit. Their leaders are now denounced as criminals and outlaws. Let me remind you that there was a time when George Washington, who is now revered as the father of his country, was denounced as a disloyalist, when Sam Adams, who is known to us as the father of the American Revolution, was condemned as an incendiary, and Patrick Henry, who delivered that inspired and inspiring oration that aroused the colonists, was condemned as a traitor.

They were misunderstood at the time. They stood true to themselves, and they won an immortality of gratitude and glory.
——*New York* Call, *September 12, 1918.*

47. RUSSIAN POLICY

On September 1, 1918, General Graves arrived in Vladivostok to take over command of the American Expeditionary Force in Siberia which consisted of approximately 8,000 soldiers. Although General Graves tried to adhere to the policy of "non-interference with the internal affairs of Russia," Americans did engage in battle with Red Army detachments.

There was one disappointing feature in President Wilson's great speech—he told us nothing about his Russian policy.[34] So far as the country as a whole is concerned, it is entirely in the dark as to what is going on. Only one thing is clear, and that is that *The Nation* was well within the truth a few weeks ago when we wrote that our war with Russia had begun. Thus we read of American troops occupying Shoushough, Tulgoisk, and Seltzo in the advance toward Kotlas. The dispatches have all the familiar phraseology. They tell, of course, of "enemy atrocities," of "undoubtedly large enemy casualties," of sinking "enemy gunboats," etc., etc. Thus the "friendly intervention" takes on all the marks of ordinary hostilities. How can the plain Russian be expected to differentiate? May he not say to us, that is all very well to dissemble our love, but why do we kick him downstairs—to say nothing of our artillery and machine guns? Those who object to any criticism of our policy aver that if the critics only knew the facts they would write and speak differently. They may well be true. But if it is so why should we not be told the facts? The President is opposed to secret diplomacy; why should we be kept in ignorance as to his reasons for proceeding into Russia? It does not help to give out documents of doubtful authenticity alleging that Trotsky and Lenin are in German pay;[35] particularly as some of the European correspondents declare that, despite the atrocities committed by the Reds which our government has so eloquently portrayed, the Bolsheviki are stronger than ever.
——The Nation, *September 29, 1918.*

48. THE TRUTH

by NORMAN THOMAS

The truth is that Russia is now in process of working out the most significant social experiment since the French Revolution. In the Soviet form of government she has made a unique contribution to the organization of the political state. But that is the smaller part of the story. Her great task is that she is striving to secure economic democracy as a basis for the development of mankind. If her revolutionary emphasis has been over much on economic changes we must remember how desperately the great masses of the dispossessed have suffered not only in body but in mind and soul at the hands of the owners of the earth. Surely that unique spiritual quality of Russia which found noble expression in Tolstoy and Dostoevsky is not dead, and on the basis of economic liberation, it will yet build a new and glorious structure of humanity.

——The World Tomorrow, *September 1918.*

49. POLICING RUSSIA

As we predicted, the war correspondents are now putting out feelers suggesting that, even if Germany withdraws from Russia, the allied forces will have to increase their forces there, in order to maintain "law and order." It is even expressly stated that the withdrawal of the Teutons will be the signal for uprisings and unrest, which we must be ready to "police."

Perhaps our armies should also "police" Belgium, because its people might want to arise and take the power when their oppressors are driven out. Strange that no one suggests it. Why is it only in Russia that the rule of the Teutons is considered a beneficent protection of the people against disorder?

Certainly Russia will revolt when the iron heel is withdrawn. Certainly her people will rise to power, even over the heads of those business men of hers who have incorporated in Germany in order to protect their property by international law from the demands of their workers. But why is it our job to handle this revolt—we who declare for self-determination of peoples?

——*Seattle* Union Record, *November 5, 1918.*

50. GREETINGS TO RUSSIAN COMRADES

by EUGENE V. DEBS

Comrades of the Russian Soviet and the Bolshevik Republic: We salute and honor you on this first anniversary of your great revolutionary triumph, the greatest in point of historic significance and far-reaching influence in the annals of the race. You have set the star of hope for all the world in the eastern skies. You have suffered untold persecution, exile and misery and you have shed your blood freely all these years in the great struggle for emancipation, not only of your own oppressed people, but the oppressed of all the earth. On this historic anniversary we extend our proletarian hand to you from all directions and across the spaces and assure you of our loyalty and our love.

The chief glory of your revolutionary triumph is that you have preserved inviolate the fundamental principles of international Socialism and refused to compromise. It will be to your everlasting honor that you would rather have seen the Revolution perish and the Soviet with it than to prostitute either one by betraying the workers to alleged progressive reforms which would mean to them an extension of their servitude under a fresh aggregation of exploiters and parasites.

You, Russian Comrades of the Soviets and of the Bolsheviks you represent, are resolved that for once in history the working class which fights the battles, sheds its blood and makes all other sacrifices to achieve a revolution, shall itself receive and enjoy the full fruitage of such a revolution; that it shall not allow itself to be used, as dumb driven cattle, to install some intermediate class into power and perpetuate its own slavery and degradation.

On this anniversary-day we pledge you, brave and unflinching comrades of the Soviet Republic, not only to protest against our government meddling with your affairs and interfering with your plans, but to summon to your aid all the progressive forces of our proletariat and render you freely all assistance in our power.

We pledge you, moreover, as we grasp your hands in comradely congratulations on this eventful day, to strive with all our energy to emulate your inspiring example by abolishing our imperialistic capitalism, driving our plutocratic exploiters and oppressors from power and establishing the working class republic, the Commonwealth of Comrades.

——One Year of Revolution, *a Socialist party pamphlet, November 7, 1918.*

51. THE BOLSHEVIK BIRTHDAY

by VICTOR BERGER

One year ago, today a giant was born. On November 7, 1917, the Soviet republic was established in Russia.

Solomon said: "There is nothing new under the sun." Solomon did not live to see an industrial democracy. The Soviet government is something really new under the sun. For the first time in the history of this poor old world the working people took the reins in their hands. The new Russian government is the first real democracy.

Around the giant's cradle storms beat and tempests howled. Kerensky's government had left everything in confusion. More than that, generations of tsarism has impoverished and ruined Russia. Bolsheviki quickly got things into running order. The Kaiser thought he saw an opportunity to snatch a slice of Russian territory from the weak young government and crush the rising tide of Bolshevism. But the young government was not so weak as he thought. He has been obliged to withdraw his troops from Russia. The allied governments also sent troops to "help" Russia. They imagined that the Russians would seize the opportunity to throw off the hated Bolsheviki rule and flock to their standard. The Russians did not flock. Evidently they did not hate the Bolsheviki.

No, the Russian people love the Soviets. They are the Soviets. Here is a government of the people, by the people, for the people in actual fact. Here is a political and industrial democracy. How long the Soviet republic can survive against the opposition of a capitalist world nobody can guess. But the fact remains that it has lived one year in spite of the hatred of every other government in the world. That it has survived in fact in the face of all attacks proved it has satisfied its own people. It has fitted their immediate needs. It has maintained their interests, and they are with it.

Whatever may happen later on, an industrial democracy, under the most adverse circumstances, has survived for one whole

year. That mighty fact alone is enough to terrify all the autocrats.
That is the reason why November 7 is a great day in the list
of our unhappy planet.

——*Milwaukee* Leader, *November 7, 1918.*

52. MANY CHEER ANNIVERSARY OF REVOLUTION

November 7, 1918, the first anniversary of the Bolshevik tri-
umph, was celebrated at a series of meetings, and in editorials
and articles. These celebrations were heightened by startling
events in Europe. Mass peace demonstrations swept Germany.
German sailors mutinied at Kiel, killed their officers and hoisted
the Red Flag. On November 9, the Kaiser abdicated and the
Social-Democrats took over the government. On November 11,
the armistice was signed, and fighting ceased. The First World
War was over.

Thousands of clamoring New Yorkers were turned away from
the doors at the chain of great mass meetings held in Manhattan,
Bronx and Brooklyn to celebrate the first anniversary of the
Russian Soviet republic.

To cheering crowds in Hunts Point Palace, Bronx; New Star
Casino, Harlem; Brooklyn Labor Lyceum, Williamsburg, and
Brownsville Labor Lyceum, Albert Rhys Williams, John Reed,
Scott Nearing, Max Eastman, Santeri Nuorteva and others re-
counted the achievements of the Bolsheviki and urged the Ameri-
can workers to redouble their efforts for industrial freedom.

From the New Star Casino audience the following message was
adopted to be forwarded by cable to the Russian government:

"We, working men and women of New York City, in mass
meetings assembled, send hearty greetings to the Russian Soviet
republic. We congratulate our Russian Comrades on their wonderful achievements, and pledge our hearts and lives to follow
their noble example and establish in our own country a free
working class."

All the speakers affirmed that the revolution in Germany, of
which the news had just reached the city, was directly the out-
come of the pioneer working class revolution of the Bolsheviki.

Scott Nearing roused his hearers to the highest enthusiasm of
the evening when, after picturing the control which the indus-

trial masters of America are to gain during the next few years under the domination of the Republican party, he said:

"When the American working class comes face to face with that condition, it will send to the citizens of the Russian republic the only message they care to hear from us, and that is that we have made the same answer to our tories that they have made to the tories of Russia.

"President Wilson has gone as far as he can with his program because of a system that is absolutely opposed to a working class control. He will now be brushed aside. That is what the Republican victory means. It means a Republican president in 1920.[36] It means that Weeks, Penrose, Lodge, Roosevelt and their kind will be in control. Lodge will be chairman of the Senate foreign relations committee, possibly before the peace treaty is ready to be signed, and his committee will have power to accept or reject it. The Republican party will control the policy of reconstruction.

"That is exactly as it should be. The political structure of a nation should reflect its industrial organization. Under the domination of a set of despots, bourbons and tories, such as no other country possessed, our political structure will exactly reflect our industrial structure. We'll have no more camouflage."

Nuorteva at the close of a brilliant speech outlining the influence of the revolutionary Russian Soviet government on the working class of Bulgaria, Austria and Germany, said: "In that sign the world will be won. In that sign only will the world receive real peace and happiness."

Nuorteva, referring to the widespread talk as to the foreign flags that would make their way to Berlin, said:

"The first flag of the real enemies of German imperialism to reach Berlin was the flag of the Russian Soviet government. Around that flag, flying at the Russian embassy, the forces of German revolutionists flocked. To that flag Karl Liebknecht came when he was let out of prison.[37] There the plans were laid that led to what we are reading of today."

John Reed, complaining that he had been attacked by a bourgeois neutral disease, the Spanish influenza, thrilled the crowds with reports of the first days of the triumph of the Bolsheviki and branded as lies the reports of massacres and disorders in Russia.

Ella Reeve Bloor was chairman of the New Star Casino meeting, and told of being in Budapest during a great working class demonstration some years ago. Hearing hoarse cries, she asked the meaning and was told it was the workers demanding the votes. She said her informant could not believe her when she said that the American working class had the vote, but used it to elect their economic masters to power.

Williams did not arrive at the Casino till nearly midnight.

Other speakers to address the audiences in the various halls were Louis C. Fraina, Benjamin Gitlow, N. I. Hourwich, Sen. Katayama, Ludwig Lore, A. Philip Randolph, A. I. Shiplacoff, Joseph A. Whitehorn and Gregory Weinstein.

——*New York* Call, *November 8, 1918.*

53. ONE YEAR OF RED RUSSIA

One year ago November 7 the Bolsheviki came into power in Russia. They gained their power by the votes of the people (not all the people, but according to competent observers, 90 per cent of the people voting through the Soviets). They have retained their power for a year in spite of minor armed revolts, in spite of German invasion, in spite of allied invasion.

They have given the people a government which has proved successful enough to make the workers vote for them again and again. For in Russia political representation is not something which happens once a year, or once in four years. The delegates to the governing body are constantly subject to recall, as informally as a union meeting often can recall its delegates to the Central Labor Council. And no news has yet come which points to the lessening of Bolshevik popularity among the workers.

On the contrary, after the allied forces had been in military possession of Vladivostok for a month, a municipal election in that city showed a big majority for the Bolsheviki over the moderate Socialists and the Cadets combined. In the face of a "government" in Archangel, approved by the allied forces, containing only one Socialist, the population gave a big majority to the Socialists.

The Bolsheviki have given Russia a government attractive enough to excite the desires of the workers in all the countries nearest to them. We see little nations of Austria breaking into a flame of Bolshevism which, in spite of our ignorant newspapers, is not anarchism, but a very rigid Marxian Socialism. We see even China called to account by the allies because she refused to put down governors "sympathetic to the Bolsheviki."

The Bolsheviki have given Russia a government so stable that competent observers of all kinds say it never can be overthrown, except by foreign occupation and force of arms, a government so orderly that, even in the midst of a revolution, Professor Albert Ross traveled 20,000 miles in Russia and "never saw a blow struck," but, "instead of agitation and tumult, found habit still the lord of life."

The Bolsheviki have been accused of every crime under the sun. They have been accused primarily of selling out their people to the Germans. And yet report after report comes from Russia to the effect that it was the Tsar's regime which betrayed 7,000,000 Russians to death in pre-arranged slaughter; that even now it is the business group, the capitalists of Russia, who hope and plot for a German invasion to introduce "law and order" with an iron hand; that peace was inevitable when the allies would give the starving Russians no help, although the Bolsheviki offered their strength to fight, if the allies would supply help and munitions.

The Soviet government of Russia, lied about and opposed, set out, even without help, to overthrow the autocracy of the central empires by the only weapon left them—propaganda. And how successful they have been in this the many revolutions in Austria, following one year after Lenin became premier, are the best evidence.

——*Seattle* Union Record, *November 12, 1918.*

54. THE FIRST AND SECOND REVOLUTIONS

by JOHN REED

The important thing to remember about Russia is that there have been two revolutions there since March 1917, and that these two revolutions are absolutely different in character, and are fighting for control.

The first revolution was a revolution against the Tsar. The Tsar and his blood-stained government was overthrown. A new government was established—a republican government, a bourgeois republic, in which the capitalists and the employers of labor governed instead of the nobility.

The government was changed but that was all. The peasants didn't get control over the land. The workers didn't get control over the factories. It was simply a political revolution, not an economic revolution; the rights of the Tsars and the nobles had been destroyed, and in their place was established the rights of the capitalists. The workers had no industrial rights; they were still wage-slaves, still an oppressed class.

Then started a new revolution—an economic revolution against the capitalists and the employers of labor. The workers and the peasants had organized into Soviets, Councils of Workers and Peasants, in which no capitalist or owner of property could become a member. These Soviets decided on November 7, 1917, that they would become the government of workers and peasants; and that the capitalists, the owners of industry, should have absolutely no share in the government. All men and women should become useful workers; if any person was not a useful worker, he was a parasite, and as such should have no share in the government. The capitalist republic became a republic of the workers.

The capitalist republic, such as Russia under Kerensky, gives the people political democracy—that is, you have a right to vote in politics; but you have no right to vote in the shops where you work, you have no industrial democracy. . . . Political fraud. . . .

The Soviet government is the real democracy. The peasants get together in the villages, the workers in their factories, and elect delegates to the local Soviet. Every three months these local Soviets elect delegates to the All-Russian Congress of Soviets, which meets in Moscow. It elects the members of the Council of People's Commissars, the executive organ of the government, and a Central Committee which sits permanently in Moscow during the period elapsing between sessions of the All-Russian Congress. Lenin and Trotsky and others, including the Central Commission, make a report; if their work has been satisfactory, they are reelected, if not, they are thrown out and new persons elected in their place.

Is this despotism? It is the real democracy, it is the workers themselves making the government. By means of such a government the workers are able to realize freedom, industrial democracy and the control of their own lives in their own way. . . .

The Soviet government is the government of workers; everything that is done is done in the interests of the workers. It is a worker's republic, not a republic of landlords and capitalists and the sweaters of labor. And that is the kind of society that must be established in every nation, by means of Socialism—the world for the workers.

——*Revolutionary Age, November 18, 1918.*

55. NOVEMBER SEVENTH, 1918

In the following address celebrating the first anniversary of the Bolshevik revolution, Max Eastman, editor of The Liberator, *denounced the so-called Sisson documents, purporting to prove that Lenin and other Soviet leaders were in the pay of the German high command and that the Bolsheviks were really German agents. The documents consisted of supposed letters from the German general staff, correspondence between Bolshevik leaders, orders on banks and reports of telephone conversations, all said to reveal the direct connection between the Germans and the Bolsheviks. They had been originally offered for sale by White Russians to the British Secret Service, but had been rejected as crude forgeries. They were purchased for $25,000 in Petrograd by Edgar Sisson, a State Department official and President Wilson's special representative in Russia, who brought them to Washington. The State Department would not accept the documents as proof of the allegation that the Bolsheviks were German agents, but President Wilson personally authorized the official publication of the documents. They were distributed by George Creel, chairman of the Committee of Public Information, a U.S. government agency, who claimed that they were genuine.*

The documents were immediately denounced as fraudulent not only by Socialists like Santeri Nuorteva, John Reed and Max Eastman, but also by liberal newspapers and magazines such as the New York Evening Post *and* The Nation. *The* Post *observed: "The plain fact is that some of the most important charges and documents brought forward by Mr. Sisson were published in Paris months ago and have, on the whole, been discredited." (Sept. 17, 1918.)*[38]

by Max Eastman

Comrades and friends, this meeting is called to celebrate two of the greatest events in all the history of mankind. It is the anniversary of the achievement of social revolution in the Empire of Russia, and it is the date of the dawn of social revolution in the Empire of Germany. Today the German fleet is in the hands of the revolutionary working class, and the red flag flies at Kiel. Tomorrow the army. Then Berlin and the old empire!

And we are not only met to celebrate the establishment of the Socialist republics, but we are met to demand that the capitalist republic of the United States keep its hands off these republics.

The war is over now, and there is no excuse left. We want our soldiers who are invading the territory of the Russian Soviets under the command of a Japanese general, in order to make the world safe for English, French, American and Japanese capital, called off.

And we want our army of libellers and scandalmongers, who are vilifying the name of the Russian Soviets throughout the width of the world, under the command of an unreliable yellow journalist, George Creel, called off.

George Creel boasts that he has the full backing of the United States Government in sending out documents purporting to prove that the leaders of the Russian Soviets are pro-German agents and traitors to democracy. But what is there in the behavior of the United States Government since this war began to show that it knows how to estimate the character and motives of revolutionary Socialists?

George Creel had also the full backing of the United States Government in sending out documents purporting to prove that the leaders of the Socialist party and the IWW in this country were pro-German agents and traitors to democracy. I read one of these documents, and I know that it was the deliberate lie of the man who wrote it. What reason is there for Socialists to believe better of the Sisson documents? They prove that the United States Government has the same opinion of Lenin and Trotsky that it has of Eugene V. Debs and Bill Haywood, and that is all they prove, and the opinion rests upon the same basis of fact, namely, that these men were loyal in the utmost extremity to the interests of the international working class.

When the Sisson documents fell rather flat, a more plausible scheme was devised for discrediting the government of Russia. A bloody and indiscriminate "Reign of Terror" was devised, and Lenin and Trotsky were denounced throughout the nations of the world as outlaws and wholesale murderers. This scheme is more plausible because it rests upon a certain basis of fact. It is no doubt true that a number of people have been officially put to death for conspiracy to overthrow the Soviet Government and assassinate its leaders. A report through Amsterdam, giving the official organ of the Bolshevik Government as its authority, says that the exact number since August is 68.

It is also no doubt true that a number of people have been unofficially put to death by mobs of the Russian people for the same crime, although we are assured by the British envoy, Lockhart, that Lenin is using every effort to bring such things to an end.

Sometimes when I read the New York papers I am almost convinced that they may be taking as many lives over there in this way as one in every four days. And one in every four days is the number of people that are lynched, burned, tortured or strangled to death by mobs in the United States as a regular routine part of our civilization in times of peace.

Whatever reign of terror exists in Russia today, and whatever extreme measures may have been taken by the Russian Government to protect itself against conspiracies, are the direct inevitable result of the invasion of Russia by foreign armies—an invasion whose commonly expressed purpose is to stir up among the Russian classes conspiracies to overthrow that Government.

I want you to imagine what would happen in this country if an imperial Kaiserdom was invading our territory from the south, and five imperial republics were sending expeditionary forces down through Canada, all of them opposed to our form of government, all with the open purpose of overthrowing it, and if at the same time thousands of seditious Americans were plotting to assassinate the President and dynamite the Houses of Congress. Would not Woodrow Wilson declare martial law all over this land in a hurry, and would not its execution be more prompt than discriminate? And martial law is the respectable name for a reign of terror.

If they give Eugene Debs ten years in the penitentiary for intellectually disagreeing with the policies of President Wilson on a public platform, what would they give Theodore Roosevelt if they caught him in a back cellar in Washington with a bomb in his pocket for the assassination of the President, and a knife to stick in the bowels of the Postmaster General? That is exactly the situation in Russia. I venture to say that considering the comparative seriousness of the crimes being committed, there is a more unscrupulous reign of terror in this country at this moment than there is in Russia.

Withdraw the invading armies and leave the Russian people free to develop their own destiny as they must, and not one-millionth part of the blood will be shed by them in the cause of liberty that these armies are shedding now in the cause of capitalism.

I understand that they maintain in the District Attorney's office and the courts that it is unlawful to denounce the invasion of Russia by Woodrow Wilson. I maintain that it is unlawful for Woodrow Wilson to invade Russia. Just before I came here I was regaling myself with that delightful old romance, the Constitution of the United States. And I notice that the constitution locates the power to declare war in the representatives of the people. And it nowhere delegates to the executive branch of the Government the right to ship citizens out of the country, and half way round the earth, to wage war on a foreign power *without* a declaration of war by the representatives of the people. I am told by a distinguished lawyer in this community that President Wilson is waging his own private and personal war on the Government of Russia, in direct violation of the spirit, and even of the letter, of the United States Constitution.

There is one thing that this war has done in this country—it has killed the Constitution. It has deeply destroyed the force and honor of its provisions which guaranteed liberty and the rights of man. And what are we going to do about this? Are we going to try to pump new life and new blood and meaning of liberty into that old document? We are going to leave it lying among the honorable dead, and go forward to the day of power when we will establish a new constitution with new life and a new meaning of liberty. And the essential principle of that constitution, as of the constitution of Russia, will be this, that no man or woman is a citizen entitled to vote, who does not live upon the income of his own labor.

A hundred years ago throughout the countries that were called democratic there was a *property qualification* for the franchise. Only those men could vote who lived, in part at least, upon the profits of capital. With the growth of the conditions of democracy that system was broken down, and by the end of the last century almost all men, and even women, were entitled to vote, both those who lived upon the wages of labor and those who lived upon the profits of capital. And now the next step— the twentieth century—there has been established in Russia a *labor qualification* for the franchise, and only those men and women are entitled to vote who *do not* live upon the profits of capital, but live by the actual service of their hands and brains.

In that change of sovereignty is expressed and ensured the death of all caste and privilege and the birth of industrial democracy—the greatest revolution and creative political act in the history of mankind. . . .

——The Liberator, *December 1918.*

56. THE SISSON DOCUMENTS

Although George Creel accused the New York Evening Post *of having given "aid and comfort to the enemies of the United States" for daring to question the authenticity of the Sisson documents (New York* Evening Post, *Oct. 12, 1918), he was forced to agree to have them examined by impartial scholars. Creel asked the National Board for Historical Research to appoint a committee of experts to investigate the documents. When it was revealed that Professor Samuel Harper of the University of Chicago was one of the committee of three selected—the other two were J. Franklin Jameson and Archibold Cary Coolidge—there was considerable doubt expressed that a disinterested investigation would take place. For Harper was widely known as a supporter of the Administration's interventionist Russian policy. When Harper and Jameson, after only a week's study of the documents—Coolidge took no part in the investigation—reported that most of them were clearly genuine and that there was nothing in the others "that positively excludes the notion of their being genuine," there was an outcry that the report had been written to order in response to Administration pressure.*[39]

The report on the authenticity of the so-called Sisson documents, signed by Dr. J. Franklin Jameson and Professor Samuel N. Harper, and scattered broadcast by the committee on public information through the press and in a pamphlet edition of the documents themselves, not only calls for stern rebuke from every American historical scholar who values the good name of his profession, but fairly justify a congressional investigation of the conduct of Mr. Creel and his committee in the whole affair. Had Mr. Creel refused to submit his documents to Dr. Jameson and Professor Harper, or even rejected their report after it was prepared, he would have been blameless and would have scored a point for his committee; but, having accepted the report and included it in his official edition of the documents, he must share the odium which the transaction casts upon the good name of the government and the integrity of American historical scholarship.

Mr. Creel's first step was altogether creditable. Having in mind the attacks which have been made, particularly by the New York *Evening Post*, upon the creditability of the Sisson documents, he requested the national board of historical service, a self-constituted body of historical students formed early in the war to assist the government in such ways as might offer, to appoint a committee to pass upon the authenticity of the papers. The board appointed as such committee Dr. Jameson and Professor Harper. Dr. Jameson is a historical scholar of international reputation, director of the department of historical research in the Carnegie Institution at Washington, and editor of the *American Historical Review*. A higher authority in the treatment of historical documents could hardly have been chosen, and there was every reason to anticipate a judicial decision in any report to which he affixed his name.

The selection of Professor Harper, on the other hand, was amazing. Professor Harper, is, indeed professor of the Russian language and institutions in the University of Chicago, and presumably is able to read the Sisson documents in the original and to pass upon the accuracy of the English translations. A more unfit person in other respects, however, could hardly have been found in academic circles. Professor Harper is an open opponent of the Bolshevik government. He is on record in print as accepting the authenticity of the Sisson documents. He is, or was, a member of the Russian information bureau at New York, a propagandist agency established and maintained by Mr. Bakhmetev, the so-called Russian ambassador; and a member also of the American-Russian League, an organization believed to be very friendly to Mr. Bakhmetev and to intervention in Russia. Had a paid attorney for the anti-Soviet forces in this country been employed to pass judgment upon the authenticity of the documents purporting to show a corrupt connection between Lenin and Trotsky and the German government, the choice could not have been worse.

The report is such as the followers of Mr. Bakhmetev and the enemies of Soviet Russia might have desired. Mr. Creel submitted the documents to the committee. Mr. Sisson "detailed . . . with all apparent candor" his connection with them, and "several officials" at Washington kindly contributed "other pertinent and valuable information." If any one outside of official and prejudiced circles was invited to testify, the fact does not appear from the report. On the basis of this sham investigation the committee "have no hesitation in declaring that we see no reason to doubt the genuineness or authenticity" of the first 53 documents; that two others are perhaps derived, at one or two removes, from actual documents, and that of the remainder, while their genuineness cannot be positively affirmed, there is "little in any of them that makes it doubtful." Of the many criticsms of the documents, only those of the *Evening Post,* and a part only of them, are dealt with, and "most of them fall away," we are told, when it is remembered that the more important documents are written in Russian (not an entirely unknown language, it may be observed), and when the difference between the old style and new style Russian calendar is regarded. A number of the strongest substantive criticisms voiced in the editorial columns of the *Evening Post* and in letters of various correspondents are passed over altogether; no attempt is made to meet the weighty objections brought against the credibility of some of the documents by the *Petit Parisien* and the *New Europe* months ago,[40] and more recently by the New York *Call;* the source of the documents, if it was ever traced by the committee beyond Mr. Sisson's story, is not revealed, and the statements of the alleged fact in the documents themselves are passed over with only one or two unimportant allusions.

If two German historians had made a report of this flimsy and superficial sort on a highly controversial matter in which the reputation of the German government for truthfulness and fair dealing was involved, would Dr. Jameson and Professor Harper have accepted it as a scholarly performance? Must the reputation of American scholars go by the board as a part of the wreckage of war?

——The Nation, *November 23, 1918.*

Gompers
—WILLLAM GROPPER
The Liberator, August 1919

"Before we help Russia, we must
kill the Bolsheviki!"
—WILLIAM GROPPER
The Liberator, March 1919

Clemenceau: "But where will you get the troops?"
Lenin: "I'll use yours."

The Liberator, February 1920

—ROBERT MINOR

THE SECOND YEAR

November 1918 to November 1919

1. NO INTERVENTION IN RUSSIA

By the autumn of 1918, there were more than 7,000 British troops in northern Siberia. In addition, 7,000 British and French officers, technicians and soldiers were with Admiral Alexander Vassilievitch Kolchak, an ex-tsarist naval commander who had come from Japan to organize an anti-Soviet army in Siberia. There were also 1,500 Italians assisting the British and French, and 8,000 American soldiers under General Graves' command. Finally, over 70,000 Japanese soldiers were in Siberia. The Allied troops fought alongside the counter-revolutionary White Armies led by Admiral Kolchak and General Anton Denikin against the Red Army, while the Allies blockaded Russia's ports, hoping thereby to starve its people into submission.

As the following documents reveal, this brutal, undeclared war against Soviet Russia produced vigorous protests in the United States and repeated calls for the end of the intervention. There rose a popular demand, echoed in Congress, that American soldiers be withdrawn from Russia.

Now that Germany is beaten and prostrate, the most immediate need of the allied nations is a new policy toward Russia. The existing policy of armed intervention was originally justified as an answer to German penetration in Russia, and as an attempt with Russian assistance to restore the eastern front. These explanations are ceasing to have any meaning. German influence is no longer penetrating Russia. Russian revolutionary influence is penetrating Germany. Intervention did not succeed in restoring the eastern front, because it met with Russian resistance, rather than with Russian help. If, under such circumstances, the allied troops remain in Russia, it can be only for one purpose—a purpose similar to that which kept German troops in the Ukraine, Lithuania and the Baltic provinces. It will mean that the allied governments have decided to overthrow the Soviet government in Russia and establish in its place a government more to their liking. If this is their decision, the sooner they communicate it to the world the better. It is not a decision in which the government of the United States can participate without abandoning the whole spirit and method of its past attitude toward revolutionary countries, and for this reason we hope and trust it will not be taken. The policy of intervention in Russia could be carried out only by an enormous military force, which would be obliged to overcome the most stubborn and embittered resistance on the part of the ruling political faction. Under existing circumstances it would be a dangerous and, perhaps, disastrous adventure for any free nation, or group of free nations, which undertake it.

In putting an estimate on the material and moral costs of intervention, American public opinion should attach due weight to a new fact of the utmost importance. The military collapse of Germany, accompanied, as it has been, by a political revolution, has strengthened Bolshevism in Russia. The ordinary Russian will consider the breakdown of German morale and the appearance of revolutionary committees in Germany as a sufficient proof of the final efficacy of Bolshevist propaganda. Bolshevism did not thrive, as so many people in this country erroneously imagine, on the friendship of Germany. It thrived on the hostility of Germany. Just before the final downfall, the German government drove the Bolshevik representative out of the country, because it feared him as an instigator of revolutionary agitation. Bolshevism will not be weakened by the fall of the government with which it signed the Brest-Litovsk treaty. But it will obtain a substantial increase in prestige as a consequence of the advent of the revolutionary proletariat in Austria-Hungary and Germany. Its adherents will have some excuse for thinking themselves justified by events and they will be confirmed in their fanatical determination to fight it out. They will, consequently, be able to command the support of a larger percentage of the Russian people than they could two months ago, and they can put up a stouter resistance to an army of occupation. If this

account of the fundamental fact is true, it would be well to extri-
cate the Czecho-Slovaks in the neighborhood of Samara without
any delay and to abandon further intervention. . . .

——The New Republic, *November 16, 1918.*

2. ST. LOUIS MEETING PETITIONS WILSON

St. Louis, Nov. 30.—At a meeting held in this city under the
direction of the Socialist party, which was attended by more
than 2,500 people, according to the capitalist press reports,[1]
resolutions were unanimously adopted demanding the immediate
withdrawal of troops from Russian territory. The resolution
read:

President Woodrow Wilson, in public addresses and statements, has repeatedly made the solemn declaration: "We will
stand by Russia." The statement has the approval of all fair-
minded American men and women, and the Socialist party
approvingly repeats the declaration: "We will stand by revolutionary Russia."

However, the time has come to demand a plain and unambig-
uous answer to this question: "Is our Washington government
at war with the Russian Workers' Soviet republic?"

The reports from the Murmansk coast and from Vladivostok
would indicate that the troops our United States government
sent to help revolutionary Russia and "to stand by Russia" are
fighting the great Russian Soviet republic. This would mean
nothing less than a state of war between the greatest and oldest
republic of the new world and the young Soviet republic of
Russia.

Allied statesmen tried to explain and justify the policy of
armed intervention in Russia as an answer to German military
penetration in Russia and as an attempt with Russian help to
restore the eastern battlefront.

These explanations are ceasing to have any meaning. The
great German revolution chased the kaiser and his ruling hench-
men out of the country. German militarism, junker rule and
autocracy are out of commission.

Allied military intervention in Russia failed to restore the
eastern front, but has caused indignation and resistance on the
part of the Russian people.

Therefore, be it resolved by this public mass meeting of Socialists and other citizens, that we condemn efforts to overthrow the Workers' Soviet government under the pretense of helping Russia;

Resolved, That we still believe in the justice and fairness of President Wilson's declaration: "We will stand by Russia," which to us means nothing less than to stand by the Russian Workers' Soviet republic;

Resolved, That we demand the immediate withdrawal of American troops from Russian territory, to permit the Russian people to establish such government as to them will seem best for their safety and happiness.

——*New York* Call, *December 1, 1918.*

3. AFFAIRS IN RUSSIA

On December 12, 1918, Senator Hiram Johnson of California, formerly Progressive governor of that state, introduced in the Senate a resolution calling on the State and War Departments for a frank statement of U.S. government policy in Russia and American troop operations in that country. In a speech on the resolution, Senator Johnson declared that, in spite of disavowals by the government of any intention to intervene in Russia, reports in the press indicated that a state of war existed. Yet no public official or member of Congress appeared to know what the government's policy was.

During the course of his lengthy speech, Senator Johnson raised a list of questions to which, he declared, the American people had the right to demand answers. Two of his questions were:

"Is it true that the Soviet government offered to the American government a basis of cooperation, economic and military, and sought the help of the American government to prevent ratification of the shameful treaty of Brest, and that the American government never replied to this offer?"

"Is it true that the Russian Soviet government offered a program for making America the most favored foreign nation in trade and commerce and involving the control by the allies of all those supplies most desired by the Central Powers?"[2]

The text of Johnson's resolution and excerpts from his speech follow:

The Resolution

Whereas in August 1918, United States soldiers were sent to Vladivostok and Murmansk and Archangel, and in public announcement by the State Department armed intervention in Russia was distinctly disavowed; and

Whereas the State Department for the United States then declared, "In taking this action the Government of the United States wishes to announce to the people of Russia in the most public and solemn manner that it contemplates no interference with the political sovereignty of Russia, no intervention in her internal affairs—not even in the local affairs of the limited areas which her military force may be obliged to occupy—and no impairment of her territorial integrity, either now or hereafter, but what we are about to do has as its single and only object the rendering of such aid as shall be acceptable to the Russian people themselves in their endeavors to regain control of their own affairs, their own territory, and their destiny"; and

Whereas, since the arrival of United States troops in Russia, press dispatches have recounted skirmishes and battles between them and Russian soldiers, the taking and retaking of Russian towns, and various incidents indicating a state of war; and

Whereas Congress has not declared war upon Russia and is without information as to the conditions existing between our soldiers and Russian soldiers;

Therefore be it resolved, First, that the Secretary of State be, and is hereby, directed to send to the Senate, if not incompatible with the public interest, all data, documents and information showing or bearing upon our present relations with Russia as to peace or war, so that the Senate and the nation may know why and for what purpose our soldiers are in Russia and what is the policy of the Government in reference to Russia.

Second, that the Secretary of War be, and is hereby, directed, if not incompatible with the public interest, to advise the Senate of the number of United States soldiers in Russia and their location, and of their operations, together with any lists of casualties which they may have suffered.

From Speech by SENATOR HIRAM JOHNSON

In this day, when intolerant newspapers imperatively demand immediate and complete indorsement of prevailing opinion, it is a dangerous and a delicate thing to speak of Russia, or to inquire concerning our activities there. . . .

Some of us for some months desired to inquire into existing

relations between the United States and Russia. We have recognized that in the Russian situation most tremendous and vital issues are involved. Free discussion of the question has been hitherto impossible, because of its complex relationship to a greater problem, the world war. While the war was on and Germany yet a menace to civilization, we thought it inappropriate to demand information or to discuss what might have been deemed mistakes or indiscretions. But now Germany has been beaten, and German militarism has been crushed. The President in repeating to Congress the armistice terms declared: "Thus the war has ended"; and on December 2 again stated this fact, and further said that the armistice was in effect a complete submission of the enemy, that the central empires knew themselves beaten and their very empires were in liquidation. The demands of the military situation, therefore, no longer require silence. The war is over. We have won. The enemy empires are in liquidation.

With the authoritative utterances of the President no reason exists why we should not know the position of the United States in respect to Russia, the activities of the Army in that country, and the purposes of our Government. Not to endeavor to inform ourselves is timidity and cowardice. And it is because no Senator with whom I have talked, no public official of whom I have inquired, knows, because, indeed, we do not know, and our people do not know, what we do or what we seek in Russia or what our ultimate purpose is, that I present my resolution and these remarks.

I am quite aware that the most respectful, modest, and hesitating inquiry upon the subject of Russia will be met with the accusations of Bolshevism; that a mere purpose of seeking information will be denounced as sympathy with anarchy; that a demand that American boys shall not be sacrificed to the rigors of a Russian winter and conflict with a desperate people will be termed a defense of international agitators and of the "red flag." I understand full well that the peculiar intolerance which has been fostered in the past few months, the state of mind deliberately cultivated which has sought to bully and to terrorize either mild objector or seeker for information will look askance at one so lost as to ask the facts concerning Russia and our participation in its affairs. But those of us who are neither Bolsheviki nor in sympathy with Bolshevism of course would be unfit to sit here if we feared to pursue a legitimate inquiry within the sphere of our duties. . . .

The situation which now confronts us in Russia is no longer a mere isolated flame in a discordered land; it is something far greater and something far more important. Let in the light on the Russian situation and let our people know the facts. We have been told each day for a year past that the Soviet government is about to fall, that the wretched and corrupt leaders of the Bolsheviki are in flight. I read this again only yesterday. My desire is, and it is our right as well, whether the Soviet government exists or is overthrown, whether Bolshevism is yet in power or another order has taken its place, to know the activities of our own and our nation's policy. . . .

Wrong, injustice, cruelty and tyranny made Russia the natural breeding place of Bolshevism. During the recent years of the world's great advance, Russia remained the Russia of old. Every cry for progress, for education, for freedom, for political reform was there called revolution and was met by the knout, the prison, Siberia, and execution. Ninety-three per cent of the population of that great unknown country were composed of peasants and workmen. A scant seven per cent, constituting the privileged class, were the only ones who could receive official favor, hold positions of power, or commissions in the army.

Ninety-three per cent were ever cold and hungry and under the lash. Seven per cent were God's anointed and alone were permitted in God's sunlight. These 93 per cent, fighting and dying in the armies of the Empire, conceived the idea of fighting and, if need be, dying for themselves, and they broke through the centuries of darkness and stood, by revolution, for a moment in the glare of the sunlight of freedom. . . .

What is the policy of our nation toward Russia? Are we now engaged in destroying Bolshevism? If we are, what have we decided shall take its place? Are we again to put the Romanovs upon the throne? Is there a single faction, is there a single individual, we intend to put in power after we have waded through blood to Moscow and Petrograd? When we have buried our dead of cold, of privation, and of fatigue, and those who were slain in battle, are we, with the American flag flying in the streets of the Russian capital, to set up one kind of government as against another kind, one set of men as against another, or one man who comes out of the old regime? I ask these questions in the utmost good faith. I do not know our policy, and I know no other man who knows our policy. I do know that we are killing Russians, and they, when they can, are killing ours, and that this we are doing upon Russian soil. Is it presumptuous upon the part of one in this Chamber to ask why we are slaughtering Russians and why do we sacrifice our own blood? I warn you of the policy, which God forbid this nation ever should enter upon, of endeavoring to impose by military force upon the various peoples of the earth the kind of government we desire for them and that they do not desire for themselves. We have broken one nation which started to impress its will upon others by ruthless militarism. Its fate is the warning to every nation of the world that military force shall not impose one nation's will upon another.

We will hear very much in the days to come about "stabilizing" governments. And the "stabilization" will always be by hostile invasion and overpowering military forces. I want none of this for America. I want these boys who now wear our uniform in Europe, just as soon as our obligations to the peace treaty will permit, to return to their homes. I want them given the opportunity to make their own careers, to live their lives in their own way, to have their firesides, and their families, and their loved ones, and to be simple American citizens. I want no policy in our Republic of subjugating or subduing nations or peoples who do not think as we do. . . .

———Congressional Record, *Vol. 57, Part I, pp. 342–46.*

4. WITHDRAW FROM RUSSIA

. . . . We have neither a national nor an international interest which today legitimately sanctions the presence of our troops on Russian soil. It is false to our traditions to be fighting a workingman's republic, even if we do not approve of its form or its manners. It is not in accordance with any doctrine of American national policy for us to be engaged in crushing a revolution or in crucifying the hopes and aspirations of a great and mighty people. It is really difficult to believe that this is the same country which in Washington's time almost had a civil war because this government refused to intervene in the French Revolution on behalf of the revolutionists.[3] And not even the most severe critics of the present leaders of the Soviet government have said one-tenth as bitter things as were said of Robespierre and Marat in their day. No; to help crush a revolution is not in accordance with the real American tradition.

For that reason we demand of our government that our troops now in Russia be immediately withdrawn. We are asking no more than British labor and French labor and Italian labor have already officially demanded of their governments. We are asking no more than President Wilson has again and again promised to the Russian people. We have fought for freedom and, as the President has said, the undictated development of all peoples. We demand that Russia have her fair chance at that freedom and self-development, and that if we are in no position to direct or guide the actions of other nations with respect to her, we at least shall leave her free to work out her own destiny. Let a war which has not been declared by the nation we are fighting, or by ourselves, cease. And let those representatives of Russia who speak for the majority of the Russian people and not for interested cliques of intriguers have a voice and a hearing at the Peace Conference.

We demand that freedom of communication with Russia be at once restored, and that the whole truth be permitted to appear without let or hindrance in our periodicals; that the motives back of intervention, be they either political or economic or what not, be given to the American people in order that they may have full knowledge and may of themselves determine whether or not they are willing to back up the present intervention in Russia and what is the logical activity implied by that intervention. We demand that the open diplomacy for which the President has declared be practiced with respect to Russia. We demand, in a single word, the truth. We have lived for the last year in a poisonous atmosphere of lies and slander and intrigue and double-dealing. As Americans who honestly believe that we speak for the sober second thought of this country, and for those who have no organ of publicity or appeal, we demand that once and for all the clean wind of the truth be allowed to sweep away the false conceptions and interested propaganda which have infected the country. We demand of our government a clear formulation and simple, honest statement of its Russian policy. We demand that that policy be based on the facts and not on lies, that that policy be American, and American alone.

——Dial, *December 14, 1918.*

5. ONE SENATOR SPEAKS OUT

In supporting Senator Johnson's resolution, the New York Call *pointed to the real reason for Allied intervention in Russia: the plans of "international imperialism . . . to divide up Russia and exploit the fragments for their private profit." Russian timber, coal, gold, and oil were the targets as well as recapture of mines, mills, factories, railroads and other industrial enterprises nationalized by the Soviet government. Finally, international capitalists were bent on reversing the action of the Soviet government in repudiating the foreign debts incurred by the tsarist regime.*

It is a bit encouraging to note that, of the 500 representatives of the American people in Congress, one, at least, has had the courage to ask why the United States is maintaining armies in active service in Russia. Senator Hiram Johnson of California has put this question. He has introduced a resolution calling upon the state department to explain and clarify our government's Russian policy, and requesting the war department to give the number and disposition of our troops in Russia, and what operations they are engaged in.

It is to be hoped that the whole Russian situation will thus be dragged into the sunlight. Senator Johnson will meet with determined opposition from powerful interests of international imperialism, which are planning to divide up Russia and exploit the fragments for their private profit. He will face a bitter warfare on the part of the reactionist Russia émigrés, the big landholders and capitalists now gathered in Washington, and in every European capital, who seek to reestablish a crushing tyranny over the Russian people with the aid of foreign bayonets. He will be attacked in the press, the pulpit, the university stadium. If he is a weakling, he will succumb to these attacks, and the black fog will again envelop Russia. If he is a fighter, and will force the foreign relations committee to conduct a thorough investigation, the American people will, beyond doubt, experience a startling reversal of opinion about Soviet Russia.

There are available no lack of unbiased American witnesses who can testify that the leaders of the Soviet government are not a handful of German-led and fanatical terrorists. These witnesses, though they will not agree with the Soviet program, surely will pay tribute to its high idealism. Such available witnesses are numerous American correspondents who have lived in Soviet Russia, and who have no axes to grind, and the members of the American Red Cross mission to Russia. There is, particularly, Colonel Raymond Robins of the mission, who was in closest touch with the Soviet government for many months. Theodore Roosevelt now confirms the fact that Colonel Robins thought the Soviet government worthy of recognition, and urged recognition in his official report.[4] But neither Colonel Robins nor any of his colleagues, nor any of the unbiased newspaper correspondents, is quoted in our newspapers which catch up so eagerly columns of drivel from every tsarist adventurer who comes to our shores.

It is high time we had the truth about Russia. Unless we get the truth, and the whole truth, very soon, we may find ourselves involved in an alien adventure which will bring upon us nothing but dishonor, and which may well turn the coming of peace into a mockery.

The sixth of President Wilson's 14 essential points for a just peace reads:[5]

"The evacuation of all Russian territory and such a settlement of all questions affecting Russia as will secure the best and freest cooperation of the other nations of the world in obtaining for her an unhampered and unembarrassed opportunity for the independent determination of her own political development and national policy, and assure her a sincere welcome into the society of free nations under institutions of her own choosing."

It is time to turn away from dark phantoms of the past in Russia and acknowledge present-day realities there. It is time for the application of President Wilson's sixth point.

———*New York* Call, *December 15, 1918.*

6. JOHNSON'S DEMAND FOR INFORMATION

Senator Johnson's outspoken demand for information regarding the administration's Russian policy comes at a favorable moment. There are many signs that American public opinion is becoming a good deal concerned over the whole Russian imbroglio, and that it is ill-disposed to be put off much longer with silence, or evasion, or half-truths. To be sure, the press dispatches about Russia continue to be as fragmentary as ever, and the partisans of the Kerensky regime, or any regime at all save the present one, go on denouncing the Bolsheviki and clamoring for military action. The American public has long since ceased to believe, however, that any of the great news agencies is telling the whole truth about Russia, and it is rapidly taking the measure of the special pleaders who talk the language of intervention and force. Meantime, the texts of a good many important Russian documents are being published, and the number of enlightening books and magazine articles by writers who know Russia from within is steadily increasing. The light is breaking, be it ever so dimly. When, accordingly, Senator Johnson demands the reasons for the maintenance of American troops in a country which has done us no wrong and against which we have not declared war, and asks a long list of "is it true?" questions about our diplomatic dealings with Russia, he speaks to a public which is eager and anxious to hear.

——The Nation, *December 21, 1918.*

7. FACTS VS. PRESS REPORTS

by ALBERT RHYS WILLIAMS

. . . Every peasant who falls before the Allied guns in defense of the Soviet only roots more deeply the loyalties to this institution. The Soviet is only silenced. It is not destroyed. It goes underground and becomes an object of religious devotion. The aggressive, capable and younger elements—those who will make the future of the country—are centered in the Soviet.

What is the basis of this loyalty to the Soviet? The Soviet is a simple state apparatus which the workers and peasants can understand—a logical development of the war. It is so natural that when the first revolution came along, destroying the old order, the Soviets spontaneously sprang up in every city, village and shop through the length and breadth of Russia. It has given to the peasants land, and to the workmen control of the factories. But more than that it has given the people freedom, a sense of human worth and an instrument through which they can work out their own ends. In the Soviets the masses have tasted power and the ownership of government. They feel that the Soviets have made good. Toward the mistakes and failures of the Soviets they take the same attitude that a man takes toward his own mistakes and failures—a very lenient one.

Attempts to touch the masses by attributing corruption to the Soviet leaders will only discredit those who attempt it. These tactics were tried in July and August 1917, when documents were produced against the leaders. The verdict of the people was "not guilty," and a stampede of the masses to the Bolsheviki followed.

There are two alternative logical policies for Central Russia:

1. The Allies should throw in enough troops to smash utterly the Soviets and keep them smashed and replace them with some authority like the monarchy or the Zemstovs and the Duma, supported by foreign bayonets. That will produce a surface quiet at any rate, but it will also produce such an atmosphere of class antagonism that no real organization of society can be effected. It will meet the constant conspiracy of the aggressive and younger elements of Russia and the sabotage of a part of the peasants and all of the workers. (On the railroads of Russia, the Central Council elected by all the railroad men is composed of 28 Bolsheviks, 10 Left Social Revolutionists and only 4 of the Right parties.) This sabotage is in evidence now in Siberia, though it is not a Soviet stronghold. Just as soon as the foreign troops are withdrawn, the revolution will be repeated. The workmen and peasants will reestablish their own state apparatus, the one which has been tested, tried and approved by them—the Government of the Soviets.

2. The other logical position is to recognize the Central Russian Soviet Republic as the *de facto* government or to leave it alone and let it work out its own destinies. The Left parties have not merely indulged in destructive orgies. They have made large and effective contributions to constructive enterprises. Anyhow if they cannot organize Russia, they will necessarily give way to the Right Moderate policies. But there is no catastrophic upheaval involved in this change as in the other policy.

——The New Solidarity, *Chicago, December 21, 1918.*

8. JUSTICE TO RUSSIA

. . . . We ask the withdrawal, as rapidly as physical conditions permit, of all American troops from Vladivostok and northern and southern Russia and, meanwhile, the complete cessation of hostilities. We ask that the plans announced for a military expedition into the Ukraine be abandoned. We ask the recognition of the Soviet government and, as the immediate consequence of such action, negotiations leading to the establishment of commercial relations with Russia. We ask that diplomatic and other accredited agents of the Soviet government be received, and that Boris Bakhmetev, the so-called Russian ambassador, be deprived of the diplomatic and financial privileges now accorded him. We ask that all unfriendly propaganda carried on by the government of the United States or any of its branches immediately cease. We ask that the government of the United States bring pressure upon the Allies to abandon their present policy in Russia and secure, under threat, if need be, of complete dissociation from their plans, the withdrawal of all Allied troops. We ask that representatives of the Soviet government be admitted to the peace conference.[6] We ask the prompt dispatch, in cooperation with the Soviet government, of food and clothing and necessary industrial and agricultural machinery for sale or free distribution. We ask these things for the Russian revolution and the starving people of Russia; but even more, we ask these things in order that the United States may, for its own sake, share in righting an intolerable wrong, that no man in this war shall have died for empty words and worthless phrases, and that from this time forth the world may be made forever safe for hopeful experiments and new adventures in democracy.

——The Nation, *January 4, 1919.*

9. "EVERY DROP OF BLOOD IN
MY VEINS IS BOLSHEVIK"

by EUGENE V. DEBS

Some people are against the Bolsheviki. They don't know what it is. That's the reason they are against it. Every worker who is against the Bolsheviki stands in his own light, spits in his own face. There are other people against the Bolsheviki. And if they were for the Bolsheviki I would be against them. It is because they are against them that I am for them. Every drop of blood in my veins is Bolshevik.

There is not a plutocrat in America who is not for "democracy," the kind that keeps him a plute and you a slave. There is not a plutocrat in America who is not against the kind of democracy which abolishes slavery and makes all men free. That's the Russian kind.

——*From speech at Cleveland, Ohio, January 5, 1919, The Ohio Socialist, January 8, 1919.*

10. AFFAIRS IN RUSSIA

On January 7, 1919, Senator Robert M. La Follette, former Progressive Governor of Wisconsin, delivered his first speech in Congress on the Russian question. He charged that fear of truth was behind the campaign of slander being heaped upon the Soviet government by the American press, and demanded that U.S. troops be withdrawn immediately from Russia, or their presence there be explained to the satisfaction of the American people.

by SENATOR ROBERT M. LA FOLLETTE

Whatever comes to the American people through the censored channels of the press regarding the Soviet government of Russia ought to be subjected to pretty careful scrutiny before it is accepted as stating the whole truth. The great organized wealth of all the established governments of the world at this time fears above all things on earth the principles attempted to be established by the Soviet government of Russia. So long as the news channels are censored it is not to be expected that there shall be permitted to reach the ears of the masses of the people of the world anything approaching the truth with respect to that government or what is taking place in Russia at this time. . . .

I say of this Soviet government, of which we know so little; if it is the sort of government that 130 or 140 million people of Russia want, that is their business and not ours, nor the business of any other government on earth and, whatever the pretext, no government should intrude itself into their affairs.

Disorder and bloodshed have accompanied every revolution of history. We ourselves passed through a period that one of the great historians has devoted a chapter to, entitled "Anarchy." From the day of the fall of the Bastille, France was drenched in blood. The bloodier a revolution the stronger the evidence that there has preceded it oppression unspeakable. The law of action and reaction is the same, not only in physics but in the affairs of men. . . .

I would not, when the war was on, raise any question here or elsewhere concerning the presence of troops in Russia; and yet, under the recognized rules of international law the question might well have been raised. Russia at that time had withdrawn from the war. Other nations at war, for their own advantage, under international law, had no right to take possession of Russian territory, occupy it, and make it a base of operations; but everybody, in the presence of the awful catastrophe which had come upon the world, felt that at that stage matters should take their course.

But, Mr. President, the war is ended. There can be no pretext that the troops of the United States on Russian soil today are fighting anybody but the Russian people. Under what rules of international law, tell me, can the military forces of the United States engage in killing in Russia without our Government being held to indemnify the Government of Russia and the people of Russia? This nation and our troops are protected there by no declaration of war. There have been no grounds presented to this Congress, and I venture to say that no grounds can be presented, upon which a declaration of war could be predicated against the Russian people and the de facto Russian Government. But battles are fought, American blood is shed, Russians are killed on Russian soil. Evidently . . . desperate fighting is going on there continually. We have no more lawful right to maintain an army for aggressive warfare—for such is the character of the operation shown by the dispatches—in Russia than we have in China or Japan or any other country. I am most anxious to hear our right in that respect stated and defined, not in general terms, not in phrases that relate to something that occurred or is supposed to have occurred many months ago, when we were at war with Germany, and about which there never has been a syllable of proof furnished excepting the "Sisson papers," over which the slime of chicane and falsification and fraud and forgery is plainly manifest.

When my constituents appeal to me, as they do daily, to explain why their boys, having entered the service of their country to fight the declared enemy of their country, are retained in remote parts of the earth to wage a war not against the common enemy, but against a people with whom we are at peace, I have no answer.

But, sir, those citizens of Wisconsin and of every other State who are asking that question have made the most supreme sacrifice for their country, and they are entitled to an answer. I am aware, Mr. President, that these are troubled times. We should proceed with caution and with no more precipitation than the terrible exigencies of the situation require, but in my judgment the time has come when an explanation is due from the administration concerning its purpose in keeping our soldiers in Russia. It is due that we should know by what right they are there and for what purpose they are engaged in prosecuting war. . . .

It is no answer to say that the Government of Russia at the present time is unstable or that it is corrupt or that it is unjust. That we do not like the government of a country is no reason for making war upon it. There is no reason at this time for us either to support or oppose the present Soviet Government of Russia. It may be as bad as its enemies claim or as idealistic as its friends declare. That has nothing to do with the question.

Why should we either condemn or defend the Russian form of government? In the first place we know next to nothing about it, and we are not likely to know much about it while the present censorship continues. We do know, however, from our knowledge of the Russian people gained long before the present war, that they are a great, idealistic, hard-working and liberty-loving people who struggled for many years against one of the worst and most tyrannical governments that ever cursed any country. Yet, sir, these are the people that, so far as we can judge, have organized and are upholding by a great majority the present Soviet Government. These facts respecting the Russian people should not make anyone hesitate to believe the fantastic tales respecting the present Government of Russia.

But aside from all that, whether the Russian Government is good or bad according to our standards it is not for us to attempt to overthrow it. We have enough to do at present right here in the United States and are likely to have, for some time to come, in making living conditions more tolerable and in restoring peace and prosperity and self-government to our own people. The first step in that process is to withdraw our soldiers from Russia or explain their presence there to the satisfaction of the people of this country.

——Congressional Record, *vol. 57, Part 2, pp. 1102–03.*

11. JOHNSON BREAKS WITH GOP ON RUSSIA

by FELIX MORLEY, *Staff Correspondent*

Washington, Jan. 7.—Senator Hiram Johnson of California today said flatly he would fight to the end against the policy of armed intervention in Russia by American troops.

He made this statement in conversation with the *Call* correspondent. "Already," said Senator Johnson, "I have told Lodge and Knox that I will not follow the Republican lead in this matter."[7]

On Johnson's desk are stacks and piles of letters from the plain people of America. In simple and often unlettered language, they one and all thank him for what he has had the courage to say regarding the withdrawal of American troops from Russia. One that he read me is from a young wife in a Middle Western state whose husband is at Archangel.

"I had a letter from John the other day," this letter said. "Things don't seem right. He says it's awful cold and the country's all a marsh. He went to fight the Kaiser and not the Russians. The papers said the war was over, and it seems as though the married men anyway ought to be allowed to come home. Our business isn't paid up and things are going to smash without him. If he isn't home by the middle of next month, I don't know what will happen."

It is for such as these that Senator Johnson is waging his single-handed fight, not for political capital, with the Republican national committee.

"Isn't it plain," he said this morning, walking up and down the floor of his office and driving his points home with a clenched fist against the palm of his open hand, "isn't it plain that if, without observing the Constitution, or going through prescribed forms, wars may be fought by this republic upon the whim of a single individual or an administration's *ipse dixit,** that a most dangerous and menacing precedent has been established. . . ."

He looked out of the window to where the winter sun touched the crown of the Statue of Liberty on the white dome of the Capitol.

"There's one explanation for it though," he said, turning suddenly.

"And that is?" I asked.

* Latin. Literally, "he himself has said"; hence, an arbitrary decision.

"We're getting too terribly militaristic."

Only the adjective he used was not "terribly," but a shorter, crisper one of just four letters.

——*New York* Call, *January 8, 1919.*

12. TRUTH ABOUT RUSSIA COMMITTEE FORMED

The anti-Soviet campaign in the United States reached such heights by the beginning of 1919 that it became almost impossible to obtain factual reports on true conditions in Russia either because such reports were suppressed or ignored in most commercial newspapers. This deplorable situation led to the formation of the Truth About Russia Committee by a group of liberal Americans—publishers, educators, lawyers and social workers. In announcing the committee's formation, the following statement was issued.

The Truth About Russia Committee has been formed as an American movement to inquire into the Russian situation on non-partisan grounds, without prejudice or ulterior motives, to collect and distribute authentic information regarding the progress of events in Russia, especially with respect to documentary material now in existence in America, to review in a spirit of constructive criticism the Russian policy pursued by America and the Entente Allies since the first revolution in the spring of 1917, and in general to attempt to present to American public opinion as accurate a picture as it is possible to obtain of the present status of the Russian revolution.

The American people are entitled to know the true facts and all of the facts bearing on the Russian situation. This situation, in its social and economic, as well as in its political aspects, constitutes the most important single problem which confronts the peace conference at Paris. It unquestionably is destined to be the dominating factor in the rearrangement of world affairs.

The American people already are becoming deeply disturbed, because they feel that they have not been given the truth about Russia. The committee which has been formed in the name of this demand proposes to go about its work earnestly and candidly, in an effort to cut through the fabric of misrepresentation which has been woven around the Russian situation by propagandists and interested parties and to get at the heart of what really has happened in Russia and what is now going on.

Signed ALBERT BONI, ALVIN JOHNSON, HENRY R. MUSSEY, ALBERT J. NOCK, WILLIAM MCDONALD, PAUL U. KELLOGG, MARTYN JOHNSON, HAROLD STEARNS, ROBERT MORSE LOVETT, FRANK P. WALSH, JANE ADDAMS, GILSON GARDNER, J. A. H. HOPKINS, ALAN MACCURDY, AMOS PINCHOT, GEORGE P. WEST, and LINCOLN CONCORD, director.

——*New York* Call, *January 28, 1919.*

13. WITHDRAW U.S. TROOPS FROM RUSSIA

Meeting in Chicago, the National Executive Committee of the Socialist party again called for withdrawal of all American troops from Russia and recognition of the Soviet government by the United States.

The Socialist party again protests against the use of troops in Russia and demands the immediate withdrawal of allied and American armies from that country. The Soviet government of Russia is so far the greatest achievement in the establishment of working class governments in the history of the world. It should not only be permitted to develop unhindered, but should receive the encouragement and support of the workers in all countries.

Russia has been cut off from communication with the outside world. It has been interned by a barrier of censorship and boycotted by nations professing to be democratic. Plots, counter-revolutions, intrigue, wholesale lying by a mercenary press, and invasion of territory have not shaken the affection of the Russian masses for the Soviet government. No other government in all history has survived such tests of stability.

Despite these facts, press accounts report from day to day the co-operation of allied troops with old Tsarist generals for the restoration of order in Russia. The German armies invaded Russia with the same cry for their justification. Thousands of Russian workers and peasants were killed in this enterprise at the same time that we are assured that the United States is not at war with Russia.

While this program proceeds, Russian representatives of the old Tsarist regime carry on their reactionary propaganda here for the overthrow of the Soviet government. Some of them frankly state that the property of the former landed junkers is to be restored, thus reducing the peasants to their former servitude. Monarchist generals and black reactionaries conduct this propaganda in the United States while the friends of the Russian masses and their government are denied a hearing.

This is a reversal of all American traditions. This country has always claimed to be an asylum for the oppressed and refugees of all nations, not as a field for the activities of foreign reactionaries.

Castro, the Venezuelan dictator, was not permitted to plot in this country for the return of his dictatorship. The assassin, Huerta, attempting a similar coup in Mexico from this country, died a prisoner of the United States government.[8]

In 1800, the masses of this country turned the Federalist party out of office for its lack of sympathy for the French Revolution.[9] On the other hand, Kosciusko, the Polish revolutionist, and other exiles, were always welcomed in this country.

Today, the reactionaries propose to bayonet and starve the Russian Revolution. This shameless proposal means a reversal of the historic attitude of the American people. It would make us the jailor of refugees, and the partners of imperialists and mercenaries.

In January 1918, President Wilson said, "The evacuation of all Russian territory and such a settlement of all questions affecting Russia as will secure the best and freest cooperation of the other nations of the world in obtaining for her an unhampered and unembarrassed opportunity for the independent determination of her own political development and national policy, and assure her of a sincere welcome in the society of free nations under institutions of her own choosing; and more than a welcome, assistance also of every kind that she may need and may herself desire. The treatment accorded Russia by her sister nations in the months to come will be the acid test of their good will, of their comprehension of her needs as distinguished from their own interests, and of their intelligent and unselfish sympathy."

Why should American soldiers be used to recover the gold of British, French and American bankers, loaned to the former Tsar to pay his hangmen?[10]

Why should American boys shed their blood to restore the monarchy or recover the losses of the former ruling classes of Russia?

Withdraw the troops from Russia! Abolish the censorship which prevents real news and encourages wholesale lying about Russia. Refuse to cooperate with the Kolchak, the Semyonevs, the Denikines and other monarchists of the old bloody regime. Recognize the Russian Soviet Republic.

We demand this in the name of democracy, in the interest of world peace, in the interest of the Russian workers and in the name of international decency and fair play.

——The Ohio Socialist, *January 29, 1919.*

14. THE DAY OF THE PEOPLE

by Eugene V. Debs

Upon his release from the Kaiser's bastille—the doors of which were torn from their hinges by the proletarian revolution— Karl Liebnecht, heroic leader of the rising hosts, exclaimed: "The Day of the People has arrived!" It was a magnificent challenge to the Junkers and an inspiring battle-cry to the aroused workers. . . .

In the struggle in Russia the revolution has thus far triumphed for the reason that it has not compromised. The career of Kerensky was cut short when he attempted to turn the revolutionary tide into reactionary bourgeois channels.

Lenin and Trotsky were the men of the hour and under their fearless, incorruptible and uncompromising leadership the Russian proletariat has held the fort against the combined assaults of all the ruling powers of earth. It is a magnificent spectacle. It stirs the heart of every revolutionist, and it challenges the admiration of the world. . . .

So far as the Russian proletariat is concerned, the day of the people has arrived, and they are fighting and dying as only heroes and martyrs can fight and die to usher in the day of the people not only in Russia but in all nations of the globe. . . .

Who are the people? The people are the working class, the lower class, the robbed. The oppressed, the impoverished, the great majority of the earth.

They and those who sympathize with them are *The People* and they who exploit the working class, and the mercenaries and menials who aid and abet the exploiters are the enemies of the people. . . .

In Russia and Germany our valiant comrades are leading the proletarian revolution, which knows no race, no color, no sex, and boundary lines. They are setting the heroic example of a world-wide emulation. Let us, like them, scorn and repudiate the cowardly compromisers within our own ranks, challenge and defy the robber-class power, and fight it out on that line to victory or death!

From the crown of my head to the soles of my feet I am Bolshevik, and proud of it.

"The Day of the People has arrived!"

———*The Class Struggle, vol. III, February 1919, pp. 1–4.*

15. "NATIONALIZATION OF WOMEN" A HOAX

On September 19, 1918, a U.S. Senate subcommittee, with Senator Lee S. Overman as chairman, was appointed to investigate brewing and liquor interests and German propaganda. After the end of the war, the committee turned its attention to Bolshevism, and a parade of anti-Soviet witnesses appeared before it. A common point emphasized by these witnesses was that the Bolsheviks instituted free love. Testifying before the committee, Roger T. Simmons, former representative in Russia of the Department of Commerce, charged that the "Anarchist Soviet" had issued a decree declaring women the property of the nation. Simmons read the alleged decree to the Overman committee.

Jerome Davis, a YMCA worker who was in Russia from April 1916 to November 1918, challenged the authenticity of Simmons' testimony, in a statement to The New York Times,

The Public, a liberal weekly, describing itself as a "Journal of Democracy," condemned the entire "free love" campaign and tried to introduce a note of reason.

by JEROME DAVIS

I am absolutely opposed to the Bolsheviki, but I believe that it never pays to make charges that are untrue. Because a great deal of the evidence presented seems to be an attack on President Wilson's policy of withdrawing our troops from Russia and of treating with all factions of the Russian people, perhaps it is worth while to call attention to one false report. Mr. Simmons charges, as reported in the *Times* of February 18, that the Saratov Soviet nationalized women on March 15.

It so happens that I was in the city of Samara, not far from Saratov, shortly after the decree which Mr. Simmons read was published. In order to ascertain the truth of this decree, I went to the headquarters of the anarchists in Samara and asked if such a decree had been published. They denied absolutely that any anarchist group had ever published such a decree and stated that the decree had been published by the rich, who were trying to discredit them. Soon after this they published a handbill denying the decree read by Mr. Simmons and stated that it was prepared by counter-revolutionary elements. I have a copy of this decree in my possession.

Soon after this, one of the wealthy men in the town admitted to me that the decree nationalizing women had been prepared as a joke by some of the rich young men of the town. The second decree, purporting to come from the city of Vladimir, I never heard of. It may be true, but I am certain that no responsible leader of the Bolsheviki, such as Lenin or Chicherin, would ever approve of the nationalization of women. Whenever I mentioned to a Soviet man this decree I was told that it was too ridiculous to talk about.

To let lies about the Bolsheviki pass unnoticed will only tend to discredit those things which are really bad about Bolshevism. Because unauthentic statements, such as that of the nationalization of women by the Saratov Soviet, seem to be an attack on President Wilson's Russian policy, I think they ought to be corrected.

————The New York Times, *February 23, 1919.*

16. FAIR PLAY FOR RUSSIA

One fact in regard to Russia has been established beyond a doubt: the false reports coming out of that unhappy country are matched by the misrepresentations from the outside. It has long been apparent from the contradictions in the reports from Russia that some of them must necessarily be false. But it is now evident that critics in this country who pretend to interpret events are guilty of gross unfairness. *The New York Times* has played up sensational reports in a way that conveys a wrong impression of the situation. On the 18th the New York *Tribune* had a display heading on the front page, reading, "Soviet Plan of Forced Free Love; Two Decrees for Nationalization of Women Given to Overman Committee; Children State Owned." And the *Globe* of the same day devoted its leading editorial to exploiting this, together with similar reports, as evidence of the depravity of the Bolsheviki.

Many persons read only the headlines of long dispatches, others are not discriminating and lack technical knowledge or specific information that would enable them to judge the importance of these alleged decrees, even if taken as reported. Russia is a large country, both in area and population. The decrees in question that have been so eagerly exploited come from two cities, and those not of the first class. It might have been said at one time that the United States was a free-love nation because of the Oneida community,[11] or that it was a bigamist nation because of the Mormons in Utah,[12] or a lawless nation because it lynched an average of 100 persons annually for 20 years, or a nation of savages because mobs burnt men alive at the stake. If the Russian press were to play up these things as the *Times, Tribune, Globe* and other newspapers have exploited the things that are a discredit to Russia, the people there might easily think us all that our most conservative-minded think the Russians.

The things that are now written with such assurance appear really to have no more basis of fact than the reports that have appeared from time to time during the past year, when we were told that the tottering government of the Bolsheviki would fall in a few days, that industry was at a standstill and food in the cities gone; that starvation would annihilate government and people in a few weeks; that a handful of Allied troops entering the country from the north or from the east would be welcomed with open arms and serve as a nucleus for a great army. But these things have not happened, and since they evidently were false, there is no knowing how many of the others are false.

Not only is this bad reporting and senseless comment evil in their effects as regards Russia, but they tend to discredit the press in other respects. The people are dependent upon the press for information and news. Whatever discredits its reliability will weaken the faith of the people in it and render them the more ready victims of adventurers and demagogues. Russia is entitled to fair play and a free field. If we cannot help, we should do as little as possible to hinder.

———The Public, *Chicago, March 1, 1919.*

17. OUR TROOPS HAVE NO BUSINESS
IN RUSSIA: BRING THEM HOME

William Randolph Hearst's New York American *in an editorial reflected the widespread sentiment for withdrawal of troops from Russia.*

Private John Przybviski, a soldier of the 339th Infantry, who has just been invalided home from Russia, tells a vivid story of the terrible conditions under which our soldiers are marching and fighting in the Russian winter. Among other things, he says:

"No man not a native can stand the climate. When we were there it was cold and wet and unhealthy. We would march a day wet to the skin, and then have to sleep in our wet clothing. Under the conditions we faced it was terrible. The cold and damp got into our joints, and we contracted rheumatism and other ills. Everything was bad, but the marching was terrible; in places we would sink in above our knees; the mud would pull the boots right off our feet, and then it was a case of push ahead in your stocking feet. But shoes were poor protection at best. After a few strides they were full of slush.

"I am glad that we were able to get home again alive."

This soldier's description of the suffering endured by our boys in Russia makes painful reading.

It is all the more painful when we reflect that the United States troops have no business in Russia. There is no reason why they should go to Russia. There is no reason why they should try to interfere with the internal government of Russia. There is no reason why they should try to impose the ideas of France or the ideas of England upon the democracy of Russia. There is no explanation of their being in Russia except that they are there to try to collect the money which some of our big financiers loaned to Russia.

But for whatever purpose they are there, they have no legal or constitutional authority for being there. And whatever power is keeping them there is violating the Constitution of the United States and outraging the people's government in the United States.

If this Congress were not a lot of whipped and frightened children they would exert their power and assert their authority and refuse appropriations for maintaining troops unconstitutionally and illegally and unwarrantably in Russia.

If the Democratic party in Congress had any regard for true democracy, any consideration for the will of the people, any disposition to consider the welfare of the people, they would take the necessary steps to bring these American troops home at once. . . .

——*New York* American, *February 27, 1919.*

18. THE REAL RUSSIAN QUESTION

. . . The feeling is growing that, no matter what the Russians believe, it is their right to practice their creeds without foreign dictation. This invokes a principle to which democracies must subscribe. Let the Russians alone, but by all means find out what they are about, since the idea which dominates them is no respecter of national boundaries. . . . We cannot strike an idea with a sword, even if we lunge in the dark. Fallacy is invulnerable to every foe but wisdom, and wisdom does not grow impatient, malicious or angry. The very rabidness of the hostility to Russia is the proof of its folly. If we are to be strong opponents of dangerous doctrines, we must be able to refute them quietly.

——The Nation, *March 15, 1919.*

19. THE MAN FROM RUSSIA

On January 2, 1919, the Soviet government appointed Ludwig C. A. K. Martens as the first "Representative of the People's Commissariat for Foreign Affairs in the United States of America." Thus, even though American troops were invading Russia in an undeclared war, the Soviet government still wanted recognition from and friendship with the United States. Martens took up his duties on March 18, 1919, and sought to establish trade and diplomatic relations with the United States.

The *Call* gives hearty greetings to the first representative in the United States from the 150,000,000 people of the Russian Socialist Federal Soviet Republic, L. C. A. K. Martens. We wish him all success in opening commercial intercourse between the American and the Russian people. His appearance is a happy augury. . . .

The mild-mannered Russian engineering expert and business representative of the famous Demidorff Iron and Steel Works, who has appeared here as envoy from the Russian government is a startling contrast to the wild-eyed, wild-haired Bolshevik caveman with the torch and knife, as portrayed in picture and story in our hysterical press. It appears that his mission here is not to blow up the Capitol, inaugurate "a bloody revolution," overthrow the government and nationalize our sisters and wives, but to try to lift the blockade and arrange for the purchase of American products, some $200,000,000 worth to start with, for cash, and more to come after satisfactory concessional arrangements can be made.

It is a question whether we have enough horse sense left in America to go after this business with the 150,000,000 customers of Soviet Russia. British commercial agents are already on the ground in Russia, ready to skim the cream of the trade, but our newspapers and magazines that are supposedly devoted to American business interests, are still filled with pages of drivel and tommyrot about Russia and are advocating great armed invasions to shoot down the largest possible number of these customers. Have our "paytriotic" societies, volunteer snooping organizations, "intelligence" officials and Overman committees, ably assisted by the propaganda of tsarist émigrés and that of astute foreign diplomats anxious to keep Americans out of Russian trade, so steeped our population in their silly defamations that it will be impossible to think straight and act straight about Russia? We shall presently see. . . .

———*New York* Call, *March 21, 1919.*

20. LABOR PARTY DEMANDS RECOGNITION

In November 1918, delegates to the Chicago Federation of Labor adopted a resolution, introduced by John Fitzpatrick, the Federation's president, favoring the formation of a Labor party for the next mayoralty election to be held in Chicago, April 1919. Soon after the Labor party was organized, it adopted a resolution calling for recognition of Soviet Russia.

Chicago, March 28—A demand that the United States government recognize the Lenin-Trotsky Soviet government of Russia was made by the executive committee of the new Chicago Labor party today.

In resolutions the party officials asked that troops be withdrawn from Russia as soon as physical conditions permit and that this be followed immediately by establishment of commercial relations with Russia.

"We further ask that diplomatic and other accredited agents of the Soviet government be received," said the resolutions, "and ask early dispatch, in cooperation with the Soviet government, of food and clothing and necessary industrial and agricultural machinery by sale or free distribution."

The committee met immediately on receipt of reports that the Russian Soviet government again had asked recognition.

"Whereas, the great people of Russia are struggling with the hardest problem a nation has ever faced," the resolution said, "we see with wonder a spectacle of nations calling themselves democracies picking up their weapons and trying to destroy that young faith with arms and lies and starvation."

Excuse for an eastern front disappeared with the armistice, the resolution declared, and the duty of chasing Germans out of Russia disappeared at the same time.

The resolution asks that the United States persuade the Allies, under threat, if necessary of "complete disassociation from their plans," to withdraw all troops and admit Russian delegates to the peace conferences.

These things are asked, the resolution continues, "for the Russian revolution and starving people of Russia"; but even more for the righting of "an intolerable wrong."

Copies of the resolution were ordered sent to Illinois Senators and Congressmen and to the Department of State.

——*By United Press, in the New York* Call, *March 29, 1919.*

21. THE RED TERROR

by NORMAN THOMAS

The so-called Red Terror in all its worst excesses has not cost the lives of a tithe—nay of a thousandth part, of the unnumbered conscripts who were slaughtered in that vast holocaust we call the European war. What terror can compare with the long terror of the trenches? When therefore the supporter of war— who is the average man—condemns the Bolsheviki he must, if he is just, show that the violence of Bolshevism is at least as cruel, as wanton and as unnecessary as the violence of militarism. . . . I make bold to say that there has been comparatively little Red Terror under Bolshevik rule (as distinct from the violence due to the original confusion of revolution). Whatever violence there has been was in most cases provoked by the terrorism of counter-revolutionists or by the fear of foreign military intervention.

——The World Tomorrow, *March 1919.*

22. AT ARCHANGEL

By the spring of 1919 reports began to appear in the press that American soldiers in Russia were displaying little enthusiasm for the anti-Soviet military campaign. They were openly asking why they should be fighting in Russia when the war was supposedly over. The American 339th Infantry refused to obey orders, and mutinies broke out.

The reported refusal of American troops on the Archangel front to continue aggressive operations against the Russians is a development anticipated for some time by those who have followed closely the course of events in northern Russia. It indicates that American boys in uniform do not differ essentially from French or Canadian or Greek boys in uniform. When their country drafted them, they left their homes obediently to go forth to fight against German autocracy and the German military machine. Their present task, however, bears no relation whatever to the purpose for which they were drafted. It is six months since the armistice with Germany was signed, and under the circumstances, it is not unnatural that they should object to being kept in an arctic wilderness fighting Russian workingmen and peasants who are defending their homes and their country. The fact that these Americans are fighting under an alien command doubtless has not added to their satisfaction. It is noted that the Associated Press report from Archangel says that the officers share the feeling of the men.

"No American in Archangel," says the report pathetically, "is in a position to tell them what they are fighting for." It is, indeed, a bitter thing for every lover of American liberty to realize that 5,000 American boys are kept fighting in this remote arctic region for secret reasons wholly unexplained.

——*New York* Call, *April 12, 1919.*

23. SOVIET CITIZENSHIP

by Scott Nearing

The Russian Constitution in its present form was adopted on July 18, 1918. It provides for economic citizenship in the same sense that the American Constitution provides for political citizenship.

This is well illustrated in the provision for the franchise. All men and women, irrespective of religion and nationality, who have completed their eighteenth year may vote, provided they have acquired "a means of living through labor that is productive and useful to society, and also persons engaged in housekeeping, which enables the former to do productive work." Soldiers and sailors may also vote, as may citizens who have lost their capacity to work. Following this provision is a statement of those who may not vote nor be voted for. Included in this list are, "Persons who employ hired labor in order to obtain from it an increase in profits; persons who have an income without doing any work, such as interest from capital, receipts from property, etc." The right to vote and to hold office in Russia is thus limited to those who perform a service that is productive and useful to society. Economic parasitism is banned by the fundamental law of Russian society.

The Russian Constitution goes further. Section 18 provides that "The Russian Socialist Federated Soviet Republic considers work the duty of every citizen of the Republic, and proclaims as its motto: 'He shall not eat who does not work.'" In Section 3 there is the following provision: "Universal obligation to work is introduced for the purpose of eliminating the parasitic strata of society and organizing the economic life of the country."

The workers of Russia living in the 20th century and reflecting the spirit of its civilization, have formulated a basis for economic citizenship. They are convinced that men cannot be

free until society is built on the fundamental right of the
worker and of the work his labor creates.
                                ——Advance, *April 18, 1919.*

24. RUSSIAN REVOLUTION MUST GO ON!

*On May 25, 1919, under the auspices of the People's Council
of America for Democratic Peace, 10,000 people met in New
York's Madison Square Garden to demand justice for Russia.
"At times," reported the People's Council in its account of the
meeting, "it was difficult for the speakers to resume their dis-
course, for the audience carried off by some particularly elo-
quent passage, would rise to their feet, cheer, wave handkerchiefs,
throw their hat in the air and for minutes at a time continue to
applaud."*

Last night's meeting at Madison Square Garden to demand
justice for Soviet Russia made the following demands on the
government of the United States:

That the blockade against Soviet Russia be lifted;

That Russia be allowed, "unhampered, to determine her own
fate";

That all American troops now in Russia be recalled, and that
enlistments for service in Russia, now being called for, be can-
celled;

That the American government refuse to recognize directly or
indirectly any counter-revolution, or any government representing the former monarchist elements in Russia.

In opening the meeting, Chairman Frederic C. Howe, United
States Commissioner of Immigration, declared: "There are many
reasons for this meeting. There is the hunger, the suffering and
the cry for food of millions of innocent men, women and
children who are starving from one end of Russia to the other.
There are the generations of American sympathy to the Russian
people in their struggle to be free from the tyranny of the old
regime. There is recognition for the millions of Russians who
gave their lives under faithless Russian leaders of the war. Then
there is the right of any people to work out their own destiny in
its own way without interference by any outside power. This

right was inscribed in every line of American participation in the war. . . .

"Revolutionary Russia wants only peace. She alone of the powers is ready to scrap all militarism and end all wars. She wants to devote her attention to other things.

"Russia, too, accepts without reservation the Magna Charta of peace with which America entered the war. She has ended secret diplomacy and opened her archives to the world. She freed Persia and declared that she would not accept Constantinople from anyone but the Turks themselves. She has declared for an applied self-determination of peoples, and said to her peoples 'you can govern yourselves as you like, even in your smallest local affairs.' Russia has spoken across the seas and accepted our ideals of peace. She has sent them to the heart of Germany. According to [General] Ludendorff, it was the Russian propaganda back of the German lines that broke the power of Germany. It bred revolution and resulted in the dethronement of the Kaiser and the military caste.

"Russia is the problem of problems of the world. She contains one-third of the population of Europe. She is seething with something new that cannot be quenched by arms. It can only be overthrown by ideas. To attempt to police Russia in the interest of reaction means a continuation of wars and possibly the complete destruction of the European world. It may be by war, it may be by revolution, it may be by disease and pestilence bred of hunger, and the emancipation of the people."

Commissioner Howe then introduced the first speaker, Dr. John Haynes Holmes, pastor of the Church of the Messiah, who said in part: "I am here to ask that the Russian people be left alone to work out their own destiny in their own way. I am here to plead that the Russian people, with whom I have no quarrel, be given sympathy and help in preserving the victories which they have so heroically achieved. I am here to demand, in your name and my own, that the revolution be not delayed. . . .

"It may be well to consider for a moment what are the reasons offered in justification of this hostile interference with the happy progress of the Russian revolution. These are all summed up in the word 'Bolsheviki.' The Allies, forsooth, would save the revolution from the ruthless hands of those who are leading it to betrayal and death.

"Thus it is alleged that the Bolsheviki are pro-German, that they represent the success of the pro-German propaganda in

The Sailing of the Buford

The Liberator, February 1920

—BOARDMAN ROBINSON

Russia! Of all the great fairy tales of the world, the most marvellous ever written, may I say, is that of the life and work of pro-German propaganda. If you happened to believe that Moses meant what he said in his commandment, 'Thou shalt not kill,' and that Jesus was serious when he declared, 'Love your enemies,' it was pro-German propaganda. If you went on strike for wages enough to meet the extortions of war profiteers, it was pro-German propaganda. If your wife's grandmother died on the day you were supposed to be at the office to sell Liberty bonds, it was pro-German propaganda. And so when a great revolution broke out in Russia, and the people began to use it for their own emancipation, and that of the proletariat the world around, it was again pro-German propaganda.

"It is true that the Bolsheviki didn't trust the Allies—how could they after reading the secret treaties, and who that has read the recent treaty of peace drawn up in Paris, will not say that the Bolsheviki were right from the beginning? But this distrustful attitude toward the Allies does not mean that the Bolsheviki were pro-German. No greater lie was ever forged in a professional publicity office—and that is saying a good deal! The Bolsheviki and all other Russian revolutionists hated the German autocracy, and labored unceasingly for its overthrow. And, what is more, they labored successfully. For when all the truth is told, it will be known that it was not [General] Foch in the west, but Lenin in the east, who broke German morale and thus destroyed the power of German arms.

"Again, it is said that the Allies must interfere in Russia, because the Bolsheviki do not represent the Russian people. Who says that they do not represent the Russian people? Is it America, with her strangle-hold on Costa Rica, San Domingo and Nicaragua? Is it France, which has just seized the Saar Valley, with its German population? Is it Japan, which saps the life-blood of Korea, and robs China of the 40,000,000 people in the Shantung peninsula? Or it is, perhaps, England, with her 300 years record of popular government in Ireland? What evidence is there that the Bolsheviki do not represent the Russians? I will stake my life on the fact that they represent more of the Russian people than the Tsar and the Grand Dukes ever did—and I have yet to hear that any one of our western democracies ever proposed to compass their overthrow by intervention! If it is true that the Bolsheviki do not represent the Russian people, then there is one thing, and one thing only, to be done—and that is, to leave the people alone—to leave them free from outside interference, to work out their own destinies and put in office a party which more nearly represents them than those who now hold the seats of power. If a free people do not like a government, they can themselves be trusted to destroy it. . . .

"What we need in this whole business of our relation to Russia is a little plain, every-day honesty. The Allied states, and many of the people in the Allied countries, are hostile to the revolution, not because of anything that the Bolsheviki have or have not done. Bolshevism is simply a convenient piece of camouflage. The real fact is that a genuine, thoroughgoing economic and political revolution has gotten started in Russia, and we recognize that if this revolution succeeds, it means the doom of every capitalistic system in the world. Our capitalists know that they have either got to destroy this revolution or the revolution will destroy them. The people of Russia have come into their own— our leaders know that other peoples elsewhere will come into their own as well, if these Russians be not punished with terror and enslaved again with chains.

"The revolution must be saved! Saved first because the Russian people want it, have sacrificed for it, are sacrificing for it now! Saved secondly because the world, brought to the brink of destruction by the madness of capitalism, can alone be saved by some new discovery of democracy! Be not deceived by subordinate and insignificant side issues. . . . The Russian revolution, I say again, must be saved! And this means what? Let me conclude with the program for which I trust this vast assemblage of American citizens will stand this night. It is the program laid down on January 4, 1918, by President Wilson, in the sixth of his 14 points:

" 'The evacuation of all Russian territory, and such a settlement of all questions affecting Russia as will secure the best and freest co-operation of the other nations of the world in obtaining for her an unhampered and unembarrassed opportunity for the independent determination of her own political development and national policy, and assures her of a sincere welcome into the society of free nations under institutions of her own choosing, and more than a welcome, assistance also of every kind that she may herself desire. The treatment accorded Russia by her sister nations in the months to come will be the acid test of their good will, of their comprehension of her needs as distinguished from their own interests, and of their intelligent and unselfish sympathy.' "

"This program the President has failed to make good. We must now make it good for him or in spite of him."

Rabbi Judah L. Magnes followed Dr. Holmes, and said in part: "We are here to ask our government to stop the war it is waging against Russia. We ask that the blockade be lifted, and that instead of sending British gunboats into the Baltic now freed of its winter's ice, food ships be sent in, in order to free the millions of Russia's peoples from their long winter of starvation. We ask that our troops be withdrawn, in fact as well as in name, from the Murmansk and the Archangel and Siberian fronts, and that no more troops be recruited for service in the war against Russia, whatever be the pretext. We ask that no further funds and no more munitions, poison gasses and flame-throwers among them, be sent to the aid of the counter-revolutionary forces under Kolchak and Denikin, whom Lloyd George unctuously calls 'our friends,' and we ask that an end be put to the propaganda emanating from the State Department on behalf of the recognition of the Tsarist counter-revolutionaries.

"We ask that self-determination be given to the people of Russia in accordance with the promises made to them over and over again by the President of the United States.

"We ask that the text of the three peace offers made by Lenin since the armistice of November 1918, be made public in order that the American people may know and judge their terms. We ask that a halt be called to hostilities on every Russian front, and that the opportunity be given so that the peoples of every Russian region may freely dispose of their own destinies. . . .

"What the Allied governments are afraid of is not the Red Terror, nor the force of Bolshevik bayonets, but the power of the Soviet idea, the victorious march of a new and better social order. They think that by cold-bloodedly and piously starving hundreds of thousands of men and women and children, by disrupting the productive processes of Russia, by creating unemployment and a spirit of dissatisfaction, they can convince all the world that Soviet Russia is inefficient, cruel, hopeless. They think that by establishing a series of barrier states under the political mandate, and financial and military tutelage of the Big Three or the Big Four or the Big Five they can encircle Soviet Russia with a *cordon sanitaire* in the mad belief that thus new ideas may be isolated and may be kept from infecting the organism of Western Europe and America.

"The same thought was expressed at Brest-Litovsk by Prince Leopold of Bavaria who was the military commander of the Kaiser on the eastern front, when he said: 'Russia is trying to contaminate all the countries of the world with a moral infection. We must fight against the disorder inoculated by Trotsky and defend outraged liberty. Germany is fortunate in being the incarnation of the sentiments of other order-loving peoples.'[13] Thus the Kaiserists and Junkerists of Germany and the Kaiserists and Junkerists of the Entente meet on common ground—in the endeavor to prevent, by all means in their power, the great radical changes that men will bring about in the world, the co-operative state, the rule of justice and of mercy, the freeing of the poor and the slaves, the production of wealth for all, and the exaltation of mind and spirit and the soul. Prince Leopold and Kolchak, Lloyd George and Clemenceau and Orlando and Makino and Wilson—whatever be their names—they are all of one mold, children of a dying generation, men who did their best in accordance with the old ways, but who are lacking in faith that the new world actually would come.

"These men, who seek to govern by fiat, by compromise, by phrase-making, by barter and exchange of living organisms and of pulsating ideals, who hold themselves responsible in the last analysis, not to the peoples, whose names they take in vain, but to the powerful capitalists of the earth. All of these men and all of their armies cannot keep back the onrushing flood of freeing, cleansing ideas which are refreshing the hearts and minds of men, and which are making the face of the earth a greener, sweeter, lovelier place to look upon."

Lincoln Colcord, an editor of *The Nation,* spoke next: "If there is one factor which could be pointed out to show that our policy toward Russia has not been truly American, I would say that that policy has not been based upon an investigation of the facts. It has been based almost wholly upon opinion. . . .

"Ladies and gentlemen, as an American in the tenth generation, I protest against a foreign policy based wholly upon prejudiced opinion! There has not been in the whole atmosphere of this administration, in the whole machinery of the State Department, the slightest inclination sincerely to get at the facts in Russia, and find out what was going on, and base a policy on facts as they lay on the ground. Not for a moment! Not the slightest inclination! But, having made up their mind after the Bolshevist revolution that Lenin and Trotsky were tottering, and were about to fall at any moment, they have based their policy upon that decision from that time, and every effort of their machinery has been exerted to maintain that policy. No wonder we stand today face to face with chaos! . . ."

The final speech of the evening was delivered by Amos Pinchot who spoke as follows: "Russia has lost 7,000,000 people through the war, fighting for a great ideal, a democratic, non-imperialist peace. The Russians were willing to go on fighting for liberty forever, if it was to be a fight for liberty. Just as they are now ready to fight forever for liberty and against the Kolchak army, backed, be it understood, not by the United States or the people of the United States, but by a Democratic administration that dares illegally, illogically and wickedly to keep American soldiers in Russia to fight for the return to power of the old tsarist regime. . . .

"Today the American people believe in Russia. They believe in the Soviet government. And yet the Democratic administration is backing that murderous and fraudulent patchwork of unrelated parts, which we call the Kolchak government, in fighting the Russian people and starving them by an airtight food blockade.

"The New York *Globe,* whether accurately or not, intimates that 200,000 people a month are being starved to death by our blockade. Do the American people understand the enormity of the crime which we allow our government to participate in? If we starved to death two or three children in a cage in City Hall Park, then the American Defense Society would object. . . . But to starve to death thousands of Russian children each day— for children are the first to sicken by the attack of hunger—seems a very proper course for a humane and Christian government to take. Are they not the children of the inhuman Bolsheviki?

"And why is this appalling and criminal blockade maintained against 120,000,000 Russians? Why the only excuse the government can give is that we do not approve of their form of government and economic institutions. Mr. Wilson certainly could not claim, even if it were a fact that interference in Russia was for the purpose of saving non-Soviet Russia from Soviet rule, when he has just acquiesced—Mr. Wilson has easily become history's foremost acquiescer—in handing over 36,000,000 people on the Shantung peninsula to their hereditary enemies, the Japanese.

"But more remarkable than the fact of our blockading on account of political and economic doctrines, 120 million people with whom we are not at war, is the government's defense of its action. For it solemnly assures us that only a small minority of these 120 million people are adherents of the political and economic program on account of which we are starving them.

"Of course, undeceived America is quite well aware that the blockade and the rest of the attempt to put the tsarist element back in power does not flow from benevolence, disguised or otherwise, or from stupidity, disguised or otherwise. It springs from the fact that by the peace treaty the world is to be made over on the basis of imperialism and economic slavery. Metternich saw—as far back as 1820 when he proclaimed the doctrine of the Right of Intervention (originally laid down in the Congress at Aix La Chapelle in 1818) in order to crush the revolutions in Piedmont and Italy—that an autocratic government cannot live next door to a free nation."[14]

Resolutions Adopted at the Mass Meeting

This mass of citizens, assembled at the Madison Square Garden, this 25th day of May 1919, congratulates the people of Russia upon having thus far maintained a successful revolution against the powers of reaction in the face of terrific obstacles interposed from within and without, and sends greetings of sympathy and solidarity to the people of Russia and to the Federated Soviet Republic.

Further, this mass meeting demands:

1. That in the interests of humanity the economic blockade against the Russian people, which is costing hundreds of thousands of innocent lives be lifted;

2. That Russia be afforded the opportunity to determine her own fate, unhampered and "under institutions of her own choosing";

3. That, as a token of our good faith, all American troops stationed in Russia be recalled forthwith, and enlistments for service in Russia, now being called for, be canceled;

4. That the American Government refuse to recognize, directly or indirectly, any counter-revolution or any governments representing the former monarchistic elements which, under the guise of "liberating" our sister republic, are now attempting to set at naught the will of the Russian people.

——*New York* Call, *May 26, 1919;* and Justice to Russia:

Ten Thousand Demand Justice for Russia, *bulletin of the People's Council of America.*

25. THE MARCH OF SOVIET GOVERNMENT

Following the end of World War I, Soviets were set up in Berlin, Hamburg and throughout Bavaria. Workers demonstrated in Paris, London and Rome. In March 1919, a Soviet Republic was formed in Hungary, followed in April by the proclamation of a Soviet Republic in Bavaria. "The whole of Europe is filled with the spirit of revolution," declared David Lloyd George. The Negro Socialist monthly, The Messenger, *carried the following comment on these developments.*

Still it continues! The cosmic tread of Soviet government with ceaseless step claims another nation. Russia and Germany have yielded to its human touch and now Hungary joins the people's form of rule. Italy is standing upon a social volcano. France is seething with social unrest. The triple alliance of Great Britain—the railroad, transport and mine workers—threaten to overthrow the economic and political Bourbonism of "Merry Old England." The red tide of socialism sweeps on in America. South America is in the throes of revolution.

Soviet government proceeds apace. It bids fair to sweep over the whole world! The sooner the better. On with the dance!
——The Messenger, *May–June 1919.*

We Want More Bolshevik Patriotism

We want a patriotism represented by a flag so red that it symbolizes truly its oneness of blood running through each one's veins. We want more patriotism that surges with turbulent unrest while men—black or white—are lynched in this land. We want no black and white patriotism, which demands separate camps, separate ships, and separate oceans to travel in. What we really need is a patriotism of liberty, justice and joy. That is Bolshevik patriotism, and we want more of that brand in the United States.

——The Messenger, *May–June 1919.*

26. NO CHAOS OR ANARCHY UNDER SOVIET

The following report was an antidote to the typical accounts of the "Reign of Terror" existing in Russia at the time of the Bolshevik revolution.

During the Bolshevik uprising, when press reports were being sent out from Petrograd to the effect that Russia was in chaos, industry paralyzed and the gutters running with blood, the Soviet government was opening schools, reorganizing industry, quelling the counter-revolutionists who were working with German military officials to re-establish the monarchist regime, according to Wilfred Humphries, American YMCA and Red Cross worker, recently returned from Russia.

"I saw more opera in Petrograd during the months it was supposed to be running knee-deep in blood than I ever did in all the rest of my life," said Humphries. "Besides the opera, there were Ibsen, Shaw, Tolstoy's, Shakespeare's plays and vaudeville. In two months that Maeterlinck's 'Bluebird' ran, I never succeeded in getting in line early enough to get a ticket. At this time schools were being organized all over Russia. I remember seeing a poster in Petrograd announcing the opening of a kindergarten that said the children would be served with a hot lunch. This was the chaos and anarchy you read about. . . ."

——*New York* Call, *June 2, 1919.*

27. RESOLUTIONS AT 1919 AF OF L CONVENTION

Several resolutions dealing with Russia were introduced at the 1919 American Federation of Labor convention. They called for withdrawal of American troops from Russia and those of the other Allied Powers, requested the lifting of the blockade of Russian ports so that food and clothing might reach the Russian people, and recommended the recognition of the workers' government in Russia. The resolutions were submitted to the Committee on Resolutions, dominated by the AF of L leadership, which recommended passage of a substitute resolution. It called upon the U.S. government to withdraw all troops from Russia "at the earliest possible moment," but refused to endorse the Soviet government and recommend its recognition. Although the substitute resolution was adopted by the Convention, the resolutions which follow did represent the thinking of a substantial section of the American labor movement.

Resolution No. 9 by Delegate Peter Bolenbacher of the Pennsylvania Federation of Labor:

Whereas, It is alleged that, due to a blockade of Russian ports, starvation is rampant in Russia, causing thousands of deaths and much suffering; and

Whereas, As laboring people, we believe that democracy calls for alleviation of suffering and that food should not be denied to any person or nation not at war with this country; and

Whereas, We hold further that, as a democracy, it is our duty to do nothing to interfere in the form of government desired by any people; *therefore, be it*

Resolved, By the Pennsylvania Federation of Labor that we recommend to the Annual Convention of the American Federation of Labor, that it take such steps as are necessary to lift the alleged blockade of Russian ports and to do all in their power to permit food, clothing, etc., to be forwarded to the Russian people.

Resolution No. 189 by Delegate James A. Duncan, by instructions of the Seattle Central Labor Council:

Whereas, The Workers of Russia are endeavoring to establish in their country a government of, by and for the workers, and

Whereas, We find the capitalists of the whole world seeking to annul their efforts by every conceivable, underhanded method known to them, such as starving the people of Russia by a blockade, intervention by Japanese, our allies and U.S. troops without the consent of Congress, and assisting financially the counter-revolutionists of the old tsarist regime; all of which methods are out of harmony with justice, progress, civilization and democracy; and

Whereas, We believe the workers of America have the power to prevent the capitalists of the United States from carrying out their part in the plans for the development of Russia; *now, therefore be it*

Resolved, That we, the Steam and Marine Fitters, Local Union No. 473, of Seattle, Wash., urge the Seattle Central Labor Council and the Washington State Federation of Labor to call upon Congress to immediately order the withdrawal of United States troops from Russia and give recognition to the Soviet government of Russia; *and, be it further*

Resolved, That the above-mentioned labor bodies be requested to join in calling upon the AF of L at its June 1919 convention to request all internationals affiliated to immediately prepare and send out ballots to all local unions to ascertain the sentiment of the membership upon the question of recognition by the United States Government of the Russian Soviet government, such ballot to contain nothing pertaining to the subject except the plain question—"Are you in favor of the United States Government giving recognition to the Russian Soviet government?"

With the usual provision for noting the expression, the result of such referendum to serve as a guide to the conduct of all labor officials and unionists generally regarding this question.

> STEAM & MARINE FITTERS LOCAL UNION NO. 473
> —Report of the Proceedings of the Thirty-Ninth Annual Convention of the American Federation of Labor, held at Atlantic City, New Jersey, June 9–23, 1919, *pp. 332–33.*

28. 4,000 IN GARDEN VOICE PROTEST

In April 1919, Ludwig C.A.K. Martens set up the Russian Soviet Government Information Bureau to counter anti-Soviet propaganda in the United States and tell the truth about Soviet Russia. Through its commercial department, headed by Abram A. Heller, a successful businessman and long-time Socialist, the Bureau sought to negotiate contracts with American business firms. On June 12, the Bureau was raided by the New York state police and private detectives led by Archibald E. Stevenson of the Union League Club, and leader of the anti-Soviet drive in the United States. The raids were initiated by the Lusk Committee, named for Senator Clayton R. Lusk of New York, which was a joint legislative committee to investigate seditious activities.

The attack on the Russian Soviet Government Information Bureau, the first in a whole series of harassments and indignities imposed on Martens and his staff, produced many protests.

4,000 men and women in Madison Square Garden last night adopted the following resolutions.

The resolution denouncing the raid on the Russian Soviet Bureau reads as follows:

"*Whereas,* The Russian Soviet Bureau established in New York

City to perfect friendly relations between the peoples of Russia and the United States of America, was raided Thursday, June 12, by members of the State Constabulary and private detectives headed by one Archibald E. Stevenson of the Union League Club; and

"*Whereas,* These persons without legal authority or right invaded the premises of the representative of the Russian Soviet government in this country, and have carried away papers and documents which are the property of the Russian Soviet government; and

"*Whereas,* Mr. L.C.A.K. Martens, the representative of the Russian Soviet government in this country and his associates, as well as his employes in his bureau, suffered indignities at the hands of the invaders who took possession of the office for 24 hours; *therefore be it*

"*Resolved,* That we, in mass meeting assembled at the Madison Square Garden on Tuesday, June 17, condemn this outrageous assault upon the Russian Soviet Bureau, and call upon the proper authorities immediately to take steps to return the papers and documents which have been removed from the offices of the bureau and to prosecute those who participated in this unwarranted and wanton attack upon the Russian Soviet Bureau; *and be it further*

"*Resolved,* That we extend our fraternal greetings to Mr. Martens and his associates and promise them our aid in their efforts to get the truth about Russia before the American people and to establish friendly relations between the two countries."

The resolution condemning Allied support of Kolchak follows:

"*Whereas,* It is reported that the Allied and associated governments at Paris have decided to extend financial, military and material aid to the Kolchak government in Siberia, and

"*Whereas,* Such aid means virtual recognition of the Kolchak clique as the government of Russia; and

"*Whereas,* Such recognition and aid has been extended for the purpose of helping the counter-revolutionary forces headed by Kolchak to continue their war upon Soviet Russia, in order to overthrow the Soviet government and to restore the monarchy; *therefore be it*

"*Resolved,* That we, in mass meeting assembled at the Madison Square Garden, Tuesday, June 17, 1919, brand this act of the Allied and assembled governments as an assault upon the working-class government of Russia, and call upon the workers of this country to rally to the support of the Russian workers who,

since the overthrow of the monarchy, have been struggling hard
to establish an industrial democracy."
                                    ——*New York* Call, *June 18, 1919.*

29. FRANKLIN AND MARTENS

by KENNETH DURANT

Hospitality to heralds is one of the most ancient and honorable
of international traditions. Under its sanction and encouragement, envoys of new governments seeking recognition always
have been freely admitted to the United States. Agents of innumerable Latin American revolutions have come to us in this
guise. Some we favored, and some we spurned; but to all, so long
as they did not abuse our hospitality, we accorded the courtesies
due their status. . . .

Americans have a special reason to be scrupulously observant
of these courtesies. Our oldest diplomatic tradition concerns the
envoy whom we sent to France seeking recognition of our independence, before we were sure of anything more than our determination to achieve it. To the traditional immunities which
guarded him in the pursuit of his mission we owe our very being
as a state. The success of our revolution depended no more upon
the military strategy of Washington than upon the foreign
propaganda of Benjamin Franklin.[15]

A few weeks after the Declaration of Independence, the Continental Congress sent Franklin to France with instructions to
"obtain as early as possible a public acknowledgement of the
independence of these states," and to conclude a commercial
treaty with France. Pending recognition, he was to arrange for
loans and for the immediate purchase and shipment of supplies.
Lord Stormont, the British Ambassador to Versailles. . . . raged
and demanded that Franklin be deported. Vergennes, the French
Foreign Minister, replied that "the government, notwithstanding
its desire to comply as far as possible with the views of the Court
of London, would not send him away, because of the scandalous
scene this would present to all France should we respect neither
the laws of nations nor of hospitality. . . ."

If Mr. Martens lacks something of the popular favor bestowed
upon Franklin in France, he may take comfort in the thought
that he shares similar tribulations. Franklin had to plea for a
revolutionary government of whose progress and success at arms

only scant news, and that generally bad news, ever reached him. It is to the credit of our censorships that they have reduced our communication with Europe to 18th century conditions. Like Franklin, Mr. Martens and the rest of us have to wait for slow ships and secret couriers for news of what passes beyond the ocean. Franklin had to meet all the fears of the absolutists of Europe, employing every means of slander and falsehood to obstruct his mission. Most of Europe doubted the success of the Revolution, and many Europeans desired its failure, seeing only anarchy and ruin in the revolutionary establishment of democratic forms. And when, with the news of Saratoga, Franklin won recognition for his government, there were gloomy forebodings among the privileged. But Franklin, signing a treaty of alliance with Louis XVI, did not ask him to subscribe to the Declaration of Independence.[16] Nor has Mr. Martens, seeking recognition for the Soviets, asked the United States government to adhere to the Communist Manifesto.

——*New York* Call Magazine, *June 29, 1919.*

30. ADDRESS TO U.S. BUSINESSMEN

In 1919 Raymond Robins testified before the Senate's Overman Committee and described his mission to Russia in great detail. In a speech to a group of American businessmen in June, he pointed out that they could not rely upon stories about the Bolsheviks published in the majority of American newspapers, and urged them to realize that they were dealing with a well-organized, disciplined movement and not with a band of wild terrorists.

by RAYMOND ROBINS

You believe that private property has a great and useful mission in the world. So do I. You believe that free capital is absolutely necessary to the world's best progress. So do I. That is why I am talking to you today. There is a bomb under this room and under every other room in the world; and it can blow our system—your system and my system—into the eternal past with the Bourbons and the Pharaohs.

I saw this bomb make its first explosion—in Russia. I am not responsible for any more brains than God has been willing to put into my head, and I cannot tell you the whole Russian situ-

ation in every part and in every light, but I have been saying
one thing about this bomb now for 18 months, and every new
big development in Russia has proved that I am telling the truth.
This bomb is a real bomb. It is not simply a lot of riots and
robberies and mobs and massacres. If it were, it would be no
bomb at all. We are talking now of something that can destroy
the present social system. Riots and robberies and mobs and
massacres cannot destroy the present social system or any social
system. They can be stopped by force. They can be stopped by
the strong arm of government in command of the physical power
of government. The only thing that can destroy a social system
is a rival social system—a real rival system—a system thought
out and worked out and capable of making an organized orderly
social life of its own.

Gentlemen, this bomb is that kind of proposition. The danger
of the Soviet social system to the American system is that the
Soviet system is genuinely a system on its own account.

There was more law and order, gentlemen, in Petrograd and
Moscow under the Bolshevik Nikolai Lenin than under the anti-
Bolshevik Alexander Kerensky. I saw it with my own eyes.
The methods used by the Bolsheviks to get law and order were
drastic. They were ruthless. I am not speaking now of the terror.
I shall speak of the terror later. Here I speak of the enforcement
of all law against all lawless elements, whether rebels or sneak-
thieves or highway robbers or persons insisting on drinking
alcoholic liquors when the drinking of alcoholic liquors was,
and is, forbidden. All such persons were pursued with a great
pursuit—altogether remarkable in a time of so many other
demands and troubles—and, when caught, they were dealt with
mighty shortly and suddenly. Orderliness was produced. I saw
it with my own eyes, down to May of 1918.

A year later Mr. Frazier Hunt of the Chicago *Tribune* and
Mr. Isaac Don Levine of the Chicago *Daily News* go to Russia.
It is 1919. There has been a terror. There has been a war. There
has been a blockade. There has been starvation. There has been
daily hell, with men's hearts stirred to frenzy by the sufferings
of their wives and children, and with men's hands reaching out by
the instinct of such circumstances to any stores of food and fuel
anywhere in any government warehouse or in any private cellar.
But what do Mr. Hunt and Mr. Levine see? They see what I saw.
They see a population in which the instinct of personal self-
preservation in hunger and agony is held in steady and successful
check by the social control of the Soviet power. They see a popu-

lation as orderly, fully as orderly, as the population of New York or of San Francisco.[17]

Gentlemen, the people who tell you that the Soviet system is nothing but riots and robberies and mobs and massacres are leading you to your own destruction. They are giving you your enemy's wrong address and starting you off on an expedition which can never reach him and never hurt him. To hurt Bolshevism you need at least to get its number. Bolshevism is a system which in practice, on its record, can put human beings, in millions, into an ordered social group and can get loyalty from them and obedience and organized consent, sometimes by free will, sometimes by compulsion, but always in furtherance of an organized idea—an idea thought out and worked out and living in human thought and human purpose as the plan of a city not yet made with hands, but already blue-printed, street by street, to be the millennial city of assembled mankind.

Gentlemen, it is a real fight. We have to fight it with the weapons with which it can be fought. Against idea there must be idea. Against millennial plan there must be millennial plan. Against self-sacrifice to a dream there must be self-sacrifice to a higher and nobler dream. Do you say that Lenin is nothing but Red Guards? Gentlemen, let me tell you something. I have seen a little piece of paper with some words on it by Nikolai Lenin, read and reread and then instantly and scrupulously obeyed in Russian cities thousands of miles beyond the last Red Guard in Lenin's army.[18]

——*William Hard*, Raymond Robins' Own Story, *New York, 1920, pp. 187–91.*

31. SOCIALISTS TO PROTEST WAR ON SOVIETS

At a conference in Paris, at which delegates from England, France and Italy were present, a plan was adopted calling for an international strike in these three countries on July 21 to protest the intervention of the Allied powers against Soviet Russia. The Southport Conference of the British Labour party, meeting on June 25, 1919, took a stand for solidarity with "the Workers' Socialist Republics of Russia and Hungary," and voted "that direct industrial action shall be used to stop capitalist attacks upon the Socialist Republics of Russia and Hungary." The Joint Executive of the Labour party then agreed with the French and

*Italian labor delegates to arrange anti-intervention demonstra-
tions for July 20 and 21 in France, Italy and Britain, the demonstrations to be "in the form best adapted to the circumstances
and to the methods of operation in each country."*

*In the United States the National Executive Committee of the
Socialist party endorsed the anti-intervention strike in Europe,
and called for demonstrations of sympathy with the movement.
The* Industrial Worker, *organ of the IWW, regretted the fact
that American workers were not joining the European strike,
but nevertheless called for a boycott of ships loading munitions
and supplies for Kolchak's army.*

Chicago, July 18.—Socialist locals all over the country are
ready to hold impressive demonstrations Sunday as a protest
against intervention of the Allied forces in Soviet Russia.

These demonstrations will be held in sympathy with the general strike of workers scheduled for Monday by the workers of
England, France, Italy and Scandinavia.

Each American local is asked by the National Executive Com-
mittee to adopt resolutions demanding of the President and
Congress the immediate withdrawal of United States troops from
Russia.

"Demand the immediate cessation of meddling in Russian
affairs," the committee's call read. "Demand immediate and
drastic action against the food gamblers who are constantly sending the cost of living skyward. Demand the immediate and unconditional release of all class war prisoners. These are the
demands of our European comrades.

"Join forces for international working-class solidarity!

"This great international protest demonstration by the proletariat of the Allied countries, under the banner of the Socialist
parties and the trade union federations of Great Britain, France
and Italy, in behalf of the Russian Socialist Soviet republic and
against the powers of reaction and counter-revolution, means the
beginning of the real practical work of the third international.

"It means the laying of the foundation for future joint action
by the European proletariat, irrespective of temporary differences of opinions and quarrels resulting from the world war. It
means the class struggle along international lines—the class
struggle in behalf of the eastern advance guard of the social
revolution, in behalf of Soviet Russia and Soviet Hungary.

"On June 27 the British Labour Congress met at Southport
and it was announced that the Socialists and trade unionists of

Britain, France and Italy had agreed to a general demonstration
July 20 or 21 to protest against Allied intervention in Russia.

"By vote of 1,893,000 to 935,000, the congress passed a resolution demanding industrial action to compel the British government to withdraw troops from Russia.

"The congress also adopted a resolution demanding industrial
action to compel abolition of conscription.

"The executive committee of the General Union of Operative
Carpenters and Joiners of England passed a resolution recom-
mending to their members, 'not to work on ships being fitted for
conveying troops and munitions to Russia and to seek the co-
operation of other unions connected with shipbuilding with the
view to direct industrial action.'

"The Italian Federation of Labor, together with representatives of the Italian Socialist party, met in Rome, July 5, and
made the final arrangement for the proposed 24-hour general
strike. The general strike order will be read at public meetings,
Sunday, July 20. The strike will be in protest against Allied
intervention in Russia; also against the high cost of living, the
censorship and the imprisonment of soldiers and labor leaders.

"The executive committee of the Confederation Generale du
Travail met on July 4 at Paris and made the official announce-
ment that after conferring with the comrades of Italy and Britain,
plans are being laid for an international labor manifestation on
July 21, when there will be a complete stoppage of all work in
France.

"The objects of the demonstration are the cessation of armed
intervention in Russia, the rapid demobilization of the armies,
full and absolute amnesty to all political prisoners."

——*New York* Call, *July 19, 1919.*

32. RESIGN FROM KOLCHAK'S ARMY!

The Workers of Italy, France and England are going on a
strike July 21, as a protest against intervention in Russia.

The Workers in America ought to be in on that strike, but
unfortunately they will not be.

However there are to be future strikes called by the Workers
OVER THERE and we can agitate and organize for participation when they occur.

The place to organize and agitate in this country is the Marine Transportation Industry.

The Seattle Longshoremen recently went on record favoring a strike or boycott against shipments of munitions destined to be used against the Workers of Russia. There is a strong sentiment everywhere similar to that of the Seattle Longshoremen.

Let us build up a sentiment against the shipment of munitions and supplies from the ports of America to be used to murder the Workers of Russia, who are struggling to lay the foundation for a WORKERS REPUBLIC.

Kolchak and the rest of the Capitalist tools who are leading armies against the Bolsheviks would collapse if shipments were cut off.

THE WORKERS IN THE PORTS OF AMERICA WHO ARE LOADING SHIPS WITH AMMUNITION AND SUPPLIES FOR KOLCHAK ARE AS MUCH A PART OF HIS ARMY AS THE SOLDIERS UNDER HIS PERSONAL COMMAND.

The time has come when the workers must resign from this army and refuse to work on supply ships that are for Kolchak, and the rest of the brigands who are attempting to strangle the workers of Russia.

BOYCOTT THE SHIPS LOADING FOR RUSSIA.

REFUSE TO BE A TOOL OR PART OF THE INDUSTRIAL ARMY THAT IS (BY SENDING MUNITIONS AND SUPPLIES TO KOLCHAK) A COMPONENT PART OF THE ARMY OF OPPRESSION, SEEKING TO STIFLE THE WORKERS REPUBLIC OF RUSSIA.

Don't work on a ship loading for Russia; if you do you are soiling your hands with the blood of workers who want to be free.

SHOW WHERE YOU STAND, WORKERS OF AMERICA!

Rather starve than receive wages for loading ships on a mission of murder.

THE WORKERS OF RUSSIA ARE FIGHTING FOR INDUSTRIAL DEMOCRACY. ARE FIGHTING YOUR FIGHT. DO NOT STAB THEM IN THE BACK.

———Industrial Worker, *Seattle, July 16, 1919.*

33. BLOODSHED IN SIBERIA—WHY?

The recent news from Siberia demonstrates dramatically what everyone with even a little knowledge of the situation has known for a long time. Our troops are in Siberia without any excuse or extenuation whatever, in obedience to no mandate from the American people, and are forced to co-operate with the reactionaries who are trying to impose something like tsarism on the Russians. The Americans are probably the best behaved troops in the world, but they could not possibly keep the friendship of peoples whose country they invaded and who felt that they were intruders. The best of Russians and the best of Americans must necessarily quarrel under such circumstances.

No more fertile ground could be found for the subtle propaganda and secret organization of the Bolsheviki. The fact that bitter struggles have taken place within fifty miles of Vladivostok, that forces of Bolsheviki, or of other Russians who resent the presence of foreign troops, are operating freely along the Trans-Siberian railroad in this region, shows that neither the Americans nor the Japanese nor Kolchak's band of émigrés are regarded with favor by the common people in Siberia. The evidence is that the Russians don't want to be "liberated" by outsiders. They want to be let alone.

No one in this country can feel anything but sympathy for the American soldiers who are engaged in this unequal and unexplainable struggle. They are shedding their blood and giving up their lives in response to a ukase from Washington—or Paris. For what? They don't know. The American public doesn't know.

———*San Francisco* Call, *July 20, 1919.*

34. SHOE WORKERS PROTEST ATTACK ON SOVIET

The United Shoe Workers' Convention, comprising 158 delegates, representing over 27,000 shoe workers throughout the country, adopted the following resolution yesterday at the Broadway Central Hotel in New York City:

"*Whereas,* American troops are now in Russia, and our government is conducting an economic blockade against the Russian Soviet government; and,

Whereas, no declaration of war has been made against that country; and

Whereas, there is evidence that gives rise to the fear that the object of the troops is to crush the aspirations of the working class in that country; *therefore be it*

"*Resolved,* That we protest against any interference by our government in Russia's internal affairs."

—*New York* Call, *August 30, 1919.*

35. SOVIET RUSSIA AND ITS CRITICS

by NORMAN THOMAS

The Bolsheviks are making an honest attempt to free men from the manifold slaveries of our profit system by organizing society for the benefit of producers rather than of investors. In this gigantic experiment they have made mistakes which the rest of the world ought to avoid. Nevertheless they are grappling fearlessly with an economic change essential to the further progress of mankind. It is for this reason that many Americans who keep their faith in Liberty and dedicate themselves to her service are nevertheless constrained, not only to denounce intervention and the distortion and the suppression of the facts about Soviet Russia and Hungary, but also to hail their positive achievements as steps along the road to the ultimate emancipation of the human race.

—The World Tomorrow, *August 1919.*

36. BOLSHEVISM, NOT LAWLESSNESS

The Challenge, a Negro monthly published in New York and edited by William Bridgetts, defended Bolshevism and urged anti-Bolshevik crusaders to stop worrying about Soviet Russia and "make America safe for Negroes."

America and, in fact, all modern states that are susceptible to the fertile possibilities of gluttonous exploitation existent in others, charged with being less modern, have apparently gone stark mad over the stern grip that new political doctrines, not lawless ones, have thrust aspiringly around the throat of "weeping" Russia. In all of this rankest of propaganda we might be able to discern a crumb of logic if we did not understand the methods and motives of Bolshevism. There is only one real obstacle in the way of a general understanding of them by everybody—not that after understanding them they will be under any obligation or compulsion to acquiesce in them, everybody still remaining free to reject or accept them as they now are, to accept or reject any political theory of which they do not altogether approve—which is that the millionaire press (everywhere that Imperialism survives the levelling of progress) prefers a dirty game of villainous distortion to that of telling the candid truth. Bolshevism is not bad. It is not nearly as prohibitory in dealing with the constitutional activities of society as are some putative Democracies. It is neither, as claimed by those who have and hold, take and steal, the negation of democratic ideas and ideals, nor subversive of the principles of "humanity." It is, to the contrary, a sort of positivistic confirmation of those very substances in the broadest manner.

Lenin and Trotsky, despite their personal ambitions, are not arch-fiends, else they would be slavishly driving the millions under them to death with the whip of political corruption and industrial degeneracy. Bolshevism is not an institution of lynching, segregation, and disfranchisement. It is an institution of security, equality, giving the ballot to every male and female 18 years old. Sovietry, its instrument of administration, is denounced. Is this, nevertheless, honest? Is it healthful criticism aimed solely at dissecting from the Russian body politic those elements that are dangerous to LIFE, LIBERTY AND PROPERTY; or at the re-enslavement of toiling masses to the same abominations inherent in the rotten corpse of the crushed Romanov dynasty? The fact that so many Negro men, women and children are killed lawlessly in the United States, while so many millions of other people are dominated by England shows clearly that all is not purely altruistic in the shaky camps of the accusers. Sovietry takes away nobody's freedom. It gives a larger freedom. Lenin and Trotsky, judging them fairly as all men should be judged, are not tyrannizing; they are democratizing, eliminating all waste and unproductive matter entirely, or compressing it within spheres of community usefulness. This incessant barrage of indignation directed at them and their system is piffle and punk, headlines, brainless, and bodyless; grist fallen from the PITYING mill of capitalism, a nasty mill always from which to expect propaganda dedicated to the uplift of the groundhog.

If America's Congressmen and notoriety seekers are truly desirous of accomplishing something reflective of credit to themselves, their Motherland and the world, let them focus their anti-Bolshevist grenades on the South, not on Russia; on Vardaman, Cole Blease, Hoke Smith and Bilbo,[19] not on Lenin and Trotsky.

Make America safe for Negroes. Never mind bettering Russian rule over Russians. It is not our business whether they adopt ballots or bullets. Let us better the rule of America over Americans.

——The Challenge, *August 1919.*

37. BORAH DEMANDS WITHDRAWAL OF TROOPS

On September 5, 1919, William E. Borah, Senator from Idaho, delivered a powerful speech on the floor of the Senate assailing the blockade of Soviet Russia and the Administration's policy of keeping troops in that country. Borah fought United States entrance into the League of Nations which was established at the Paris Peace Conference, and he stressed the connection between the League and the intervention in Russia. He was interrupted at one point in his speech by Senator McCormick who read from letters of American soldiers in Siberia.

by SENATOR WILLLIAM BORAH

It has been said, Mr. President, that the difficulty with reference to the Russian situation is that we have had no policy with reference to Russia, and therefore we have been moving without any concerted purpose or without any ultimate aim. I wholly disagree with that proposition. There has been for many months a policy with reference to Russia. The criticism to be lodged against those who are responsible for it is that it has not been made known to the American people. I venture to say that at no distant day there will appear to the American people the fact that for the last six months there has been with reference to Russia a settled, determined, and well-understood policy. It is a policy which, in my judgment, originated with Japan and Great Britain, and the United States as a co-ally or associated power has been willing to help effectuate. We have been dragged in as we have in other miserable affairs, and as we are going to be dragged in other affairs if the present program goes through.

The whole thing, Mr. President, is under British command. We are there under British command. We are there under the authority of Great Britain and Japan. We would not have a single soldier in Russia upon the volition of the United States itself.

I say, Mr. President, that we are engaged—those powers that are soon to be members of the League—in building up by far the largest military force, the greatest armament, that the world has ever known. We have before us a bill providing for a regular army of 500,000 men . . . and an establishment which will provide for reserves to the number of 600,000. We are also providing for the largest navy in the world, with the possible exception of Great Britain. Japan and Great Britain are carrying forward the same program with reference to military preparedness.

This cannot be for the purpose of taking care of Germany. This cannot be for the purpose of taking care of Austria-Hungary, or of Turkey. It is for the purpose of carrying out this other program of reducing to serfdom and holding there nearly 900,-000,000 people who will be subject people when this League of Nations is adopted. It is for the purpose of taking care of the 13,000,000 in Egypt now in open rebellion, for the purpose of taking care of the Balkans, for the purpose of taking care of Ireland, for the purpose of taking care of Korea; for when this League of Nations is organized the five principal powers will represent in population about 300,000,000 people, while the subject peoples over whom this League will have control will represent about 900,000,000 people.

What right have we to send soldiers into Russia, whether they are volunteers, or conscripted or of the regular army? The question is, what are we doing in Russia? What authority have we for being there? There is no condition in Russia except an internal one. There is no external attack upon Russia, even if we would presuppose the League of Nations in advance of its ratification. It is purely an internal affair, and yet Mr. Churchill says that though it is an internal affair it is one of the things, the first thing, which the League of Nations will be called upon to adjust.

Tell me how under the League of Nations you can go into Russia at all, except under Article 11? The contention which we have been making here, and which Mr. Churchill by his program substantiates, is that any war or threat of war, whether internal or external, is within the jurisdiction of the League under Article 11.

Mr. Churchill stated the other day in his speech in England the policy just as the Senator from Colorado states it, and that is that we are going into Russia to intervene with military power to adjust the internal affairs of Russia in accordance with what we think to be right.[20]

For what possible reason can we be recruiting soldiers to send into Russia to take the place of the volunteers except upon the theory that we have some policy of interfering in Russian affairs? This theory put forth that 100,000 Japanese, 10,000 Americans, and thousands of British troops are there to guard a railroad is not satisfactory. Besides the battles going on are not about or over railroads. Churchill stated the object of our being there and stated plainly that it is in accord with a policy agreed upon between the United States, Great Britain, and Japan.

I think it a most extraordinary situation, one that could hardly be conceived would ever happen in this country, that we have troops in Russia, a country with which we are at peace, and that conflict and battle are actually being waged, in which American troops are being shot down and in which American soldiers are shooting Russians. That is the situation which exists at this time, and it is against that, Mr. President, that I desire to protest.

The reports that come into this country, except under the control of the censored press, very clearly show who it is that is suffering by reason of our action in Russia. For instance, a few days ago a shipload of medical supplies which were bought some time ago in Scandinavia by the Russian Government was seized by the British naval forces while on its way to Petrograd for the relief of the suffering masses. The women and children and common people of Russia are being starved by reason of the blockade which is being maintained by the allied Governments. There is not anything which has happened in this war more cruel and pitiless than the suffering which has taken place among the Russian people as a mass by reason of the unjust and cruel blockade which has been maintained by the allied Governments since the war was over. We are starving helpless babes because there are Bolshevists in Russia. We are starving worn out and broken-down mothers because there are Bolshevists in Russia. We are as cruel as the Bolshevists and call it civilization. We are as brutal as the Bolshevists and call it Christianity.

What I want to know is why we are maintaining a blockade against the Russian people and causing suffering among the masses of the Russian people who have never been responsible for any of the hardships which have taken place in Russia, and a people who have always been friendly toward the United States? Why should we be so cruel and inhuman toward any people anywhere under any form of government? Have we lost faith in the healing, conjuring power of humanity and justice? Must we resort to force and inhumanity in all affairs of life? I reject the hideous and hellish creed.

What I said was that Mr. Churchill and those who were in favor of military intervention were in favor of it for the reason that some form of government had been set up there with which they were out of harmony, and, therefore, they desired to uproot and destroy it. So far as I am concerned, I am not in favor of fighting any form of government which the Russian people see fit to set up. I am in favor of them settling their own difficulties and setting up any kind of government which they want.

It is a peculiar thing to me, Mr. President, if Lenin and Trotsky do not represent the great mass of the Russian people, why it is that Admiral Kolchak and others claiming to represent the Russian people can get no support from the Russian people themselves, but depend entirely for their support upon people from abroad? There are 180,000,000 people in Russia, and if the Lenin and Trotsky government is not representative of the masses, and if they are not in sympathy with it and do not believe in it, they would overthrow it and submerge it within a fortnight.

Mr. McCormick. Mr. President, I interrupt to read from a letter from a soldier in the Siberian Army. It bears upon the discussion which has been going on before the Senate. He says, "It took us a very brief time to learn that the word 'Bolshevik' was merely the name of the economic faith and of the political party of the mass of the people."

Describing a battle, he says, "The American troops, at the command of an officer, fired at the horses, though many of the men had the sense to fire high. Luckily for our conscience and our repute, the old men, women, and children who remained had taken refuge in cellars.

"In all, there were 8 or 10 victims.

"In Katanka, Lieut. Vejar fired on a huddled mass of unarmed men and women, and town's population, who had been herded together. One bullet hit a woman who, falling to the ground bloody and dying, gave birth to a stillborn child."

That is the duty which has been imposed upon American troops in Siberia.

(Senator Borah continued:) Reflect for a moment, Mr. President. After the war is over, after all conflicts are ended, after fighting with the enemy has ceased, we are maintaining a block-

ade against these people which is more cruel and more remorseless than many of the activities which we took up arms against Germany to end. There is no possible justification for a Christian people not permitting the Russian people to be fed, the same as other human beings. I wish to say that if it were not for Japan and Great Britain, in my judgment the President of the United States would never have sent a single soldier to Russia; in my opinion, he would have withdrawn them long ago; and, in my opinion, he would have long ago raised the blockade. If the President had not been caught in this scheme of trade and barter for a League, our soldiers would not be in Russia at this time, and the Russian people would be permitted to enjoy whatever assistance would come to them by reason of opening up channels of trade and business.

Mr. President, if there is anything that is settled beyond peradventure in the American mind it is that every people have a right to set up their own form of government and to establish their own system and method of living. If they see fit to have a soviet government, it is their business. They must settle it for themselves. While I would prefer to see a different kind of government from that which apparently prevails in Russia, nevertheless it is for the Russian people to settle it.

I say, then, in conclusion, let us raise the blockade against the Russian people. Let us show the Christian spirit of the American people toward those struggling, suffering, starving masses, and let us bring every soldier not only out of Russia but out of Europe.

———Congressional Record, *Vol. 58, Part 5, pp. 4896–4900.*

38. THE BULLITT REPORT

William C. Bullitt, an attaché of the American delegation at the Peace Conference, was sent by the State Department to Russia in February 1919 on a private mission, to acquaint the Peace Commissioners with "conditions, political and economic, therein." He was accompanied by Lincoln Steffens who had first suggested the mission and by Captain Walter W. Pettit, an army intelligence officer. The result of this inquiry was submitted to the Peace Commissioners about April 1, 1919, but was not approved. President Wilson, pleading a headache, refused to see

Bullitt and then prohibited publication of his report. On Sep-
tember 12, 1919, Bullitt's testimony before the Senate Foreign
Relations Committee created a sensation, and his report was
made public. Included in the report was the Soviet government's
proposal, made by Lenin, for peaceful relations with the Allies,
among other things, calling for gradual evacuation of all anti-
Soviet forces from Russia, raising of the Allied blockade, the end
of Allied military support for any Russian groups, and a general
amnesty by the Soviet government for those who had supported
the Allies. These proposals were contained in a document in the
form of an Allied proposal to the Soviet government, and Bullitt
was assured that if this proposal was made by the Allied govern-
ments not later than April 10, it would be accepted by the
Russians.

When the Soviet's proposals were rejected by the Peace Com-
missioners, Bullitt resigned his post in the State Department in
protest. He predicted that the actions of the Peace Conference
would "deliver the suffering peoples of the world to new oppres-
sions, subjections, and dismemberments—a new century of war."

The following are some excerpts from Bullitt's report.

Social Conditions. The destructive phase of the revolution is
over and all energy of the Government is turned to constructive
work. The terror has ceased. All power of judgment has been
taken away from the extraordinary commission for suppression
of the counter-revolution, which now merely accuses the suspected counter-revolutionaries, who are tried by the regular, established, legal tribunals. Executions are extremely rare. Good
order has been established. The streets are safe. Shooting has
ceased. There are few robberies. Prostitution has disappeared
from sight. Family life has been unchanged by the revolution,
the canard in regard to "nationalization of women" notwithstanding.

The theaters, opera, and ballet are performing in peace. Thousands of new schools have been opened in all parts of Russia and
the Soviet Government seems to have done more for the education of the Russian people in a year and a half than tsardom did
in 50 years.

Political Situation. The Soviet form of government is firmly
established. Perhaps the most striking fact in Russia today is the
general support which is given the government by the people in
spite of their starvation. Indeed, the people lay the blame for

their distress wholly on the blockade and on the governments which maintain it. The Soviet form of government seems to have become to the Russian people the symbol of their revolution. Unquestionably it is a form of government which lends itself to gross abuse and tyranny but it meets the demand of the moment in Russia and it has acquired so great a hold on the imagination of the common people that the women are ready to starve and the young men to die for it. . . .

The following conclusions are respectfully submitted:

1. No government save a socialist government can be set up in Russia today except by foreign bayonets, and any government so set up will fall the moment such support is withdrawn. The Lenin wing of the Communist party is today as moderate as any socialist government which can control Russia.

2. No real peace can be established in Europe or the world until peace is made with the revolution. The proposal of the Soviet Government presents an opportunity to make peace with the revolution on a just and reasonable basis—perhaps a unique opportunity.

3. If the blockade is lifted and supplies begin to be delivered regularly to Soviet Russia, a more powerful hold over the Russian people will be established than that given by the blockade itself—the hold given by fear that this delivery of supplies may be stopped. Furthermore, the parties which oppose the Communists in principle but are supporting them at present will be able to begin to fight against them.

4. It is, therefore, respectfully recommended that a proposal following the general lines of the suggestion of the Soviet Government should be made at the earliest possible moment, such changes being made, particularly in Article 4 and Article 5, as will make the proposal acceptable to conservative opinion in the allied and associated countries.

(From the Appendix)

Terror. The Red Terror is over. During the period of its power, the Extraordinary Commission for Suppression of the counter-revolution, which was the instrument of the terror, executed about 1,500 persons in Petrograd, 500 in Moscow and 3,000 in the remainder of the country—5,000 in all Russia. These figures agree with those which were brought back from Russia by Major Wardwell, and inasmuch as I have checked them from Soviet, anti-Soviet and neutral sources, I believe them to be approximately correct. It is worthy of note in this connection that in the White Terror in Southern Finland alone, according to official figures, General Mannerheim executed without trial 12,000 workingmen and women.

Order. One feels as safe in the streets of Petrograd and Moscow as in the streets of Paris or New York. On the other hand, the streets of these cities are dismal, because of the closing of retail shops whose functions are now concentrated in a few large nationalized "department stores." Petrograd, furthermore, has been deserted by half its population; but Moscow teems with twice the number of inhabitants it contained before the war. The only noticeable difference in the theaters, opera and ballet is that they are now run under the direction of the Department of Education, which prefers classics and sees to it that workingmen and women and children are given an opportunity to attend the performance, and that they are instructed beforehand in the significance and beauties of the production.

Morals. Prostitutes have disappeared from sight, the economic reason for their career having ceased to exist. Family life has been absolutely unchanged by the revolution. I have never heard more genuinely mirthful laughter than when I told Lenin, Chicherin and Litvinov that much of the world believed that women had been "nationalized." This lie is so wildly fantastic that they will not even take the trouble to deny it. Respect for womanhood was never greater than in Russia today. Indeed, the day I reached Petrograd was a holiday in honor of wives and mothers.

Education. The achievements of the Department of Education under Lunacharsky have been very great. Not only have all the Russian classics been reprinted in editions of three and five million copies and sold at a low price to the people, but thousands of new schools for men, women and children have been opened in all parts of Russia. Furthermore, workingmen's and soldiers' clubs have been organized in many of the palaces of yesteryear, where the people are instructed by means of moving pictures and lectures. In the art galleries one meets classes of workingmen and women being instructed in the beauties of the pictures. The children's schools have been entirely reorganized and an attempt is being made to give every child a good dinner at school every day. Furthermore, very remarkable schools have been opened for defective and over-nervous children. On the theory that genius and insanity are closely allied, these children

are taught from the first to compose music, paint pictures, sculp
and write poetry, and it is asserted that some very valuable results have been achieved, not only in the way of productions but
also in the way of restoring the nervous system of the children.

Morale. The belief of the convinced Communists in their cause
is almost religious. Never in any religious services have I seen
higher emotional unity than prevailed at the meeting of the
Petrograd Soviet in celebration of the foundation of the Third
Socialist International.[21] The remark of one young man to me
when I questioned him is characteristic. He replied very simply:
"I am ready to give another year of starvation to our revolution."

The hold which Lenin has gained on the imagination of the
Russian people makes his position almost that of a dictator.
There is already a Lenin legend. He is regarded as almost a
prophet. His picture, usually accompanied by that of Karl Marx,
hangs everywhere. In Russia one never hears Lenin and Trotsky
spoken of in the same breath as is usual in the Western world.
Lenin is regarded as in a class by himself. Trotsky is but one of
the lower order of mortals.

When I called on Lenin at the Kremlin, I had to wait a few
minutes until a delegation of peasants left his room. They had
heard in their village that Comrade Lenin was hungry. And they
had come hundreds of miles carrying 800 puds of bread as the
gift of the village to Lenin. Just before them was another delegation of peasants to whom the report had come that Comrade
Lenin was working in an unheated room. They came bearing a
stove and enough firewood to heat it for three months. Lenin is
the only leader who receives such gifts. And he turns them into
the common fund.

Face to face, Lenin is a very striking man—straightforward and
direct, but also genial and with a large humor and serenity. . . .

——The Bullitt Mission to Russia: Testimony before
the Committee on Foreign Relations, United States Senate, of William C. Bullitt, *New York, 1919, pp. 49–65.*

39. LABOR BUCKS ARMS SHIPMENTS

Pacific Coast longshoremen will tie up the coast from Seattle to
San Diego before they will load rifles or munitions for Siberia or
any part of Russia, declared delegates from the Riggers' and

Stevedores' Local No. 38-12 at the Wednesday (September 17, 1919) meeting of the Central Labor Council.

Stating that efforts are being made to load vessels with munitions in cratings innocently marked "sewing machines" or otherwise, the delegates lent their arguments to the support of a communication to the council from the longshoremen's local, asking its financial and moral support to keep the rifles out of Russia. Amid a wild burst of cheering, a motion that full support be given carried.

One delegate said it was well known that 17 carloads of munitions were in Seattle ready for shipment.

Cases believed to contain ammunition, rifles and machine-guns consigned to Russia are sitting unmoved on Pier 5, the Frank Waterhouse & Co. dock, Thursday, as the result of a car gang of 12 men walking off the job following their demands to know what the cases contained.

This action follows the passage of a resolution by the Central Labor Council indorsing the action of waterfront workers in their planned refusal to ship munitions to kill Russian workers.

According to the men, they reported to work Thursday morning as usual and began loading the cases when the question was asked as to their contents. After some further questioning a customs officer was called and opened some of the cases, one of the workers declared, displaying their war-like contents. The men immediately got together and refused to continue the loading.

Longshoremen on the waterfront have been warned to keep a careful watch for rifles concealed in innocent appearing packages.

———*Seattle* Union Record, *September 20, 1919.*

40. WILSON ON RUSSIA

In his speeches at Des Moines, Iowa, and Billings and Helena, Montana, and other places throughout the West, President Wilson took occasion to attack the Soviet government. He painted Lenin as an autocrat and the Soviet government as a tyranny equal to, and, indeed, worse than that of the Tsar. The New Republic *took Wilson to task for this comparison.*

Woodrow Wilson was once an historian.[22] He was not, perhaps, distinguished for assiduous devotion to his muse, but he acknowledged obeisance to the rules she had laid down since old times. If it was ever necessary for him to employ a fact, instead of rhetoric, he was at some pains to assure his place that the fact existed. If it was necessary for him to institute a comparison between two historical phenomena, he acknowledged the obligation of illuminating his criticism with the light of attendant circumstance. He recognized himself as an imposing figure in the assemblies of his craft, but he knew that this fact did not make it safe for him to occupy positions out of which the veriest tyro could rout him, to the laughter of the whole confraternity of scholars. But all that has changed. Woodrow Wilson is no longer the servant of history, but has become her master.

And so he stands up bravely before her and asserts that the Soviet regime in Russia is more cruel than was that of the Tsar. Does anyone imagine that Woodrow Wilson ever made the least effort to ascertain the facts of either term of his comparison? Does he know how general was the use of "Stolypin's neckties"[23] in the suppression of the liberal revolution of 1906? Has he any acquaintance with the statistics of Siberian exile, or any knowledge of the conditions under which transportation to Siberia was carried on? Has he examined the relation between tsaristic officialdom and such affairs as the massacre of Kishinev?[24] No, of course not; he has been too busy. But of course he knows all about the spirit and the practice of the Soviet regime? No; he has been too busy to listen to Raymond Robins, Colonel Thompson, Mr. Thacher. He has been too busy to listen to anything but carefully selected and prepared reports justifying the policy he had already adopted under British and French pressure. . . . We envy him the sense of power he must enjoy as he yanks his former mistress around by the hair. But it occurs to us that he is overlooking one rather important consideration. She will have the last word.

———The New Republic, *September 20, 1919.*

41. SOVIET ABOLISHES RACIAL OPPRESSION

The September and October 1919 issues of The Messenger, *Negro Socialist monthly, carried the following articles dealing with Bolshevism and the new Soviet government. W. A. Domingo, author of the first article, was editor of the* Emancipator, *a Negro magazine published in New York City whose motto was "to preach deliverance to the slaves." The second piece, written in answer to an attack by James F. Byrnes, the racist Congressman from South Carolina, appeared as an unsigned editorial.*

by W. A. DOMINGO

Racial oppression in its various forms of disfranchisement, lynching, and mob murder prevails in non-Bolshevist Russia, but has been abolished in the territory dominated by Lenin and his followers. The Allies who are today fighting Soviet Russia in the name of freedom have colonies which they exploit, and sections of their own countries in which they at times permit the unrestrained passions of white majorities to run riot upon Negro minorities. In contrast to this racial failure on the part of self-righteous Allies and non-Bolshevik governments to protect small racial groups it is noticeable that all minorities are successfully protected in Soviet Russia.

The question naturally arises: Will Bolshevism accomplish the full freedom of Africa, colonies in which Negroes are the majority, and promote human tolerance and happiness in the United States by the eradication of the causes of such disgraceful occurrences as the Washington and Chicago race riots?[25] The answer is deducible from the analogy of Soviet Russia, a country in which dozens of racial and lingual types have settled their many differences and found a common meeting ground, a country which no longer oppresses colonies, a country from which the lynch rope is banished and in which racial tolerance and peace now exist.

———The Messenger, *September 1919.*

42. A REPLY TO CONGRESSMAN BYRNES

You take to task the editors of *The Messenger*, A. Philip Randolph and Chandler Owen, for being Bolshevists. While you are generally adept at distortion of facts and misrepresentation of circumstances, you have not very greatly misrepresented us. We would be glad to see a Bolshevist Government substituted in the South in place of your Bourbon, reactionary, vote-stolen, misrepresentative Democratic regime. In Russia the franchise, the right to vote, is based upon work, upon the performance of useful service. Negroes perform most of the service in the South. According to Professor Albert Bushnell Hart, of Harvard, three-fifths of the wealth of the South is produced by Negroes. Practically all Negroes in the South work. Under the Soviet system their right to vote would be based upon their service, and not upon race or color. Again, they would be rewarded according to what they produced, and not be robbed in peonage—a system with which you are well acquainted. So here goes: If approval of the right to vote, based upon service instead of race or color, is Bolshevism, count us as Bolshevists. If our approval of the abolition of pogroms by the Bolsheviki is Bolshevism, stamp us again with that epithet. If the demand for political and social equality is Bolshevism, label us once more with that little barrack behind which your mental impotency hides when it can not answer argument.

——The Messenger, *October 1919.*

43. UNIONISTS CHEER PLEA TO AID RUSSIA

Much applause greeted Albert Rhys Williams when he denounced the Allied governments for their attempts to starve and oppress the Russian people and destroy the Soviet government, at the meeting Friday night of the Central Federated Union of New York at the Labor Temple, 247 East 84th Street.

Williams told how members of the Central Federated Union of Vladivostok had been beaten and shot under the Kolchak regime.

After relating the conditions under which the people of Russia had been kept in servitude for centuries under the tsars, Williams declared England, France and Wall Street interests were now doing everything in their power to overcome the Soviet government, because, though ready to purchase more than a billion dollars' worth of machinery, it insisted that every piece of this machinery should bear a union trademark.

He appealed to members of the unions to join with the workmen in Seattle and refuse to make munitions of war to be shipped to Russia's enemies, just as Seattle longshoremen had refused to load supplies upon ships to Russia's enemies.

"The Russian revolution," he explained, "was one of the working people. It was that class that overthrew the tsarist despotism and set up Kerensky, who later proved too weak to satisfy their needs.

"It is the working men and the peasants who, through their unions or councils, called soviets, are ruling Russia today, and who are now being attacked on 25 fronts by their enemies.

"The soviet idea of government is dominant in Russia. Three days after the revolution soviet governments sprang up throughout the country as far as Vladivostok. It took on a national form, representing in democratic fashion every workingman and peasant and every political party.

"Only those who work with their hands and their brains can participate in the government."

Williams denied nationalization of women had been ordered and branded such stories as lies.

"Instead of this condition being true," he emphatically declared, "I found and others who have been in Bolshevik Russia have found that women have been raised to a higher plane. Instead of nationalization, prostitution has disappeared from all Russian cities. Russia under the new regime has become clarified, with model cities for decency.

"The rumored chaos that has been spread falsely throughout this country, is untrue. Streets in Moscow and Petrograd are today far safer than streets here in New York or Chicago."

Williams explained the Soviet government had not only brought order within its dominions, but had also gone ahead to educate the masses of ignorant people. Schools and universities have been established everywhere. Where despotic Russia had six universities, Soviet Russia has now 16 universities. Where under the tsars, Moscow contained only 23 libraries, today it has 49. Not only is the Soviet government educating the children, but posters containing general knowledge useful to all are put up in public places, he said.

"Cruelty is being practiced throughout Siberia by the invading armies of Japan and France and England," Williams declared. "Thousands have been massacred for no other cause than that they were in sympathy with the Soviet government. Trade unions in Siberia have been stamped out. Everything is being done to break up the Soviet government and restore the old tsarist regime under Kolchak and Denikin.

"Everything is being done to sabotage the workers' government. French agents with special passes and safe conduct have gone through Russia putting emery into machinery, and British spies have been blowing up bridges throughout the country.

"The only solution of the problem," he concluded, "can be effected by the co-operation of America. It is only from the workers throughout the United States taking the stand of the Seattle longshoremen that hope of relief may come. The United States must not only be forced to withdraw her troops, but she must also stop sending munitions of war to Russia's enemies."

——*New York* Call, *October 5, 1919.*

44. POLICE BRUTALLY ATTACK PROCESSION

The following account of a police attack on a peaceful demonstration in New York against the blockade of Soviet Russia illustrates both the obstacles placed in the way of those seeking "fair play" for Russia, and the scope of the anti-Red hysteria sweeping the nation.

by LOUISE BRYANT

I witnessed the most disgraceful scene of my life yesterday afternoon, and I have seen men die on two fronts—I have been on the barricades—I lived through the darkest days of the Russian revolution. Nothing in any country could compare with the brutality with which the mounted police broke up the Protest-Against-the-Blockade-in-Russia procession on Fifth Avenue.

As I stood there and watched that hideous spectacle of brutality it seemed to me that I would burst with shame. One thought kept running through my brain: So it has come to this in America; so it has come to this!

I did not know beforehand about the procession. It was only by chance that I found myself a witness and a participant in this terrible affair. I was on an 8th Street crosstown car. At Fifth Avenue the car stopped and we could see the banners.

One caught my eye: SAVE THE STARVING CHILDREN OF RUSSIA! I jumped off the car. A crowd was already on the sidewalk. In the middle of the street a band of working people was passing. They were poorly dressed. That was the first thing that impressed me —and they were foreign born.

Every age was represented. I saw men and women, old men, old women, very young boys and even small children. The banners were mild enough. I remember I thought of that. I wondered at their mildness. Here is an example: THE BLOCKADE IS UNAMERICAN —IT IS AGAINST ALL THE PRINCIPLES OF THE CONSTITUTION!

We read the banners and looked at the solemn faces of the marchers. . . . Then I heard the clatter of horses' hoofs, I heard screams and blows, the crowd surged round me, hemmed me in, took me along. I caught at the handle of a taxicab and hung there.

After that there was the wildest confusion. The mounted police galloped along the sidewalks. There was nowhere for that big crowd to hide. . . .

From everywhere policemen on foot came running, striking out with their heavy clubs right and left, and plainclothes men appeared. The latter armed themselves quickly with stout poles from the fallen banners. And they also began beating the people.

Their method was this! They would pull a man from behind the iron fence or from the edge of the sidewalk and begin to club him. He would try to protect himself, but would soon find it no use. A whole mob of plainclothes men and police would attack him; then he would run, and as he ran he would receive blow after blow.

One poor fellow was running with his wife. He was so bruised that he fell to the ground, and his wife, quite a young girl, unable to bear the sight any longer, fell face down in the middle of the street and began sobbing hysterically. . . .

"Get him on the head! Knock out his brains! Kill him!" And the sickening noise of heavy clubs coming into contact with soft flesh, screams, sobs. . . . This is what it was over and over again. Will they ever forget it, those simple folk from over the sea who came to America to find peace and freedom?

———*New York* Call, *October 9, 1919.*

45. BREAK THE BLOCKADE OF RUSSIA!

In late August and early September 1919, two Communist parties were organized by left-wing Socialists who had been expelled by the right-wing from the Socialist party. The first, formed on August 31 in Chicago, was the Communist Labor party, and the second, the Communist Party of America, was organized on Sep-

tember 1 in the same city. Both parties supported Soviet Russia and opposed the intervention.

It is nearly one year since the armistice was signed. Peace! It was what an agonizing world had yearned for. Peace! It sent a thrill through the world, a thrill of joy and promise. . . . No more dead. No more maimed. The mother could again clasp her son and the sweetheart her lover.

In all this joy at the coming of peace there was promise of finer things, of a new world, of international fraternity and a more human civilization.

Peace was granted Germany and Austria, Turkey and Bulgaria; but peace was not granted to Soviet Russia, where the workers were in control.

Why this war against the Russian people? They starved during the war; their dead and injured are more than of all the Allies put together. If the dead are the price of peace, then Russia paid the price in full.

But the "why" of war against Soviet Russia immediately was apparent. The diplomats of the Allies in the Peace Conference repudiated the ideals used during the war to make the people fight. The Peace Conference was not concerned with making the world safe for peace and democracy; it concerned itself with dividing the world economically, financially and territorially among the Great Powers—France, England, Italy, Japan and the United States. The Peace Conference divided the spoils; it was a peace of plunder, an imperialistic adjustment of power, a dagger thrust at the heart of the peace and liberty of the world.

Soviet Russia was a menace to this peace of plunder and oppression. Soviet Russia has repudiated Imperialism; it has repudiated annexations and wars of plunder; it believes in liberty of the peoples. Soviet Russia, in crushing its own Capitalism, is an inspiration to the workers of the world to crush all Capitalism.

So the Peace Conference declared war against Soviet Russia.

When the workers and peasants of Hungary organized their own Communist Government, the Peace Conference declared war against Soviet Hungary; and today the workers and peasants of Hungary are being starved and butchered by the Rumanian army, acting under the orders of the Peace Conference.

The military war against Soviet Russia proved a miserable failure. The Red Army, inspired by the ideal of Communist liberty for Russia and the world, has beaten back the counter-revolutionary forces.

But this war that Soviet Russia is compelled to wage in self-defense is a terrible agony. Instead of the factories producing shoes and clothes and agricultural machinery, they are forced to produce munitions. Instead of the men working in factory and mine, they are compelled to fight. Instead of the people's energy being used to build their new and finer civilization, they must use this energy for war against counter-revolution and aggression of the Allies.

But the worst feature of all is the blockade of Soviet Russia maintained by the Allies.

The Allies and the Peace Conference are deliberately starving the men, women and children of Russia—starving them in a brutal purpose to restore tsarism and maintain the workers of the world in slavery.

Food intended for Russia is rotting in the ports of Europe, but the Allies refuse to allow this food to enter Russia, while women and children die the terrible death of starvation.

Why?

Soviet Russia is a Communist Republic. A Communist Republic is a republic in which the power of the capitalists to sweat the workers is broken, where the workers control industry; a republic in which life is supreme and not profits. The Communist Republic of Russia is the promise of a new world and a finer culture of life, liberty, and peace to all the peoples.

Capitalism maintains that the Communist Republic of Russia is a failure. On the contrary, Capitalism knows that the Communist Republic of Russia is a success; that is why international Capitalism wages war against the Communist Republic of Russia, starves it and tries to crush it. For if the Russian Republic lives and flourishes, the workers of the world will say: "why can't we have a Communist Republic of our own?"

The war against Russia, the blockade of Russia, is an expression of the international class struggle between the workers and the capitalists. Force is used against the Russian workers, but force is also used by these governments—British, French, Italian, Japanese, American—against their own workers. The war against Soviet Russia is a war against the workers of the world.

Let the workers determine: We must break the blockade of Soviet Russia!

In Italy, the workers have compelled the government to withdraw all troops from Russia, while the Italian sailors refuse to allow ships to sail that bring munitions to Kolchak & Co.

In Sweden the workers are organizing a blockade of the Allies as a means to break the blockade of Soviet Russia.

In Seattle American longshoremen refuse to transport munitions bound for Russia to slaughter their fellow workers.

The blockade of Soviet Russia must be broken! The workers alone can break it. Agitate against the blockade. Organize mass demonstrations against the blockade. Organize strikes against the blockade.

Workers, men and women! The struggle of the Russian workers is your struggle. If they are crushed, you will be crushed.

On November 7 it will be two years since the Russian workers conquered power. During two years, in spite of starvation, in spite of war and blockade—in blood and tears and agony—the Russian workers have held firm to their Communist ideals. They have shown the workers of the world the means to power. They are constructing a new civilization—the new civilization that you also will soon begin to construct. They call to the workers of the world for aid.

Workers, men and women! Come to the aid of your fellow-workers! Break the blockade of Soviet Russia!

> ——*Declaration issued by the Executive Committee of the Communist party,* The Communist, *Chicago, October 18, 1919.*

46. INTERNATIONAL WOMEN'S CONGRESS
PROTESTS BLOCKADE

Washington, Nov. 6—The first International Congress of Working Women concluded its deliberations here today after an eight-day session. . . .

A resolution protesting against the Russian blockade was introduced by Margaret Bondfield and unanimously adopted. The resolution follows:

"*Whereas,* neither the United States nor any of the Allied and Associated Powers is officially at war with Russia, and

"*Whereas* the blockade of the greater part of Russia in Europe

is in effect directed against millions of women and children, and
has brought death to countless victims; *therefore*

"We protest against this blockade and we demand removal of
all restrictions upon the shipment of food and necessities to
Russia."

——*New York* Call, *November 7, 1919.*

47. LONG LIVE THE SOVIET REPUBLIC!

*The second anniversary of the Bolshevik revolution was greeted
by numerous editorials, resolutions and declarations. The following four documents reflect the views of Socialists, Communists,
and militant labor groups.*

On the second anniversary of the establishment of the Socialist
Soviet Republic of Russia, the Socialist party of the United States
sends its hearty greetings and reaffirms its solidarity with the
workers and peasants of Russia. In all the annals of history there
never has been a more heroic struggle of the masses against such
tremendous odds as that waged by the revolutionary republic of
workers and peasants.

From the hour of the proclamation of the Soviet republic it has
met the hostility of the world imperialists—German, Allied and
neutral alike. Our Russian comrades have decreed the abolition
of the rule of capital, finance and landed Junkers in the life of
Russia. They have repudiated the crimes of the imperialist
statesmen and renounced the proposed annexations of the former
criminal regime.

Against the counter-revolution they have stood in arms, defending the Socialist fatherland, the only fatherland the workers
can ever have to defend. The Soviet republic's repudiation of
the intrigues and crimes of the imperialist diplomats has provoked the hatred of the ruling classes of the world.

Menaced by German bayonets at first, they now face the armed
mercenaries financed and supported by the Allied governments.
The vassal border states sustained by the Allied diplomats are
used as so many mercenary tools to serve the finance oligarchy
which seeks to destroy the Soviet republic.

Surrounded by a ring of bayonets, blockaded and denied the

foodstuffs and raw materials essential for its economic and social life, interned from the world by the lying bourgeois press of the capitalist nations, forced to divert its energies to military defense, menaced within by the intrigues of the counter-revolutionists, maligned and slandered by the infuriated international thieves, the Socialist Soviet Republic of Russia bears aloft the banner of internationalism and serves as an inspiration to the workers of all countries.

The imperialist diplomats, with an assumption of holy indignation, charge the Soviet power with confiscating bourgeois property, while at the same time they have looted China, Egypt, India and the former German colonies in the interest of Allied exploiters. They charge the Soviet power with suppressing the rights of the citizen, while in their own countries thousands of citizens are imprisoned for their opinions.

They charge the Soviet power with internal repression of counter-revolution, while in Ireland, Egypt and India they hold down whole populations with the mailed fist.

They charge the Soviet power with being a bloody regime, while they make the Finnish assassins their accomplices and supply arms to bandit armies in the Baltic and Siberia. They charge the Soviet power with ambitions for world dominion, while they have organized a world union of imperialists which they parade as a League of Nations.[26]

For two years the masses of Russia have held back the international looters and have appealed to the workers of all countries to renounce the aims of the imperialist governments. The Socialist party is proud of its record of service in behalf of the beleaguered Socialist Republic of Russia. To the extent of its power it has demanded withdrawal of troops from Russia, the lifting of the blockade, resumption of trade, and the settlement of all internal questions by the Russian masses themselves.

On this second anniversary of the birth of the Socialist republic we reiterate these demands and call on the masses to protest against the attacks upon Russia and demand the lifting of the cowardly blockade which condemns thousands to a miserable death this winter. It calls upon them to remember our own revolutionary traditions and the 15 years required to stabilize the new republic.

Greetings of solidarity and internationalism to the tried and suffering workers and peasants of the first Socialist republic in history! Long live the Russian Socialist Soviet republic! Long

live the international brotherhood of the workers of the world!
——*National Executive Committee, Socialist party, New York* Call, *November 7, 1919.*

48. SOCIALIST RUSSIA VS CAPITALIST WORLD

by Morris Hillquit

Seven hundred and thirty days the first proletarian republic of the world has lived, and each day has been a day of titanic struggle.

When the Socialist workers and peasants of Russia assumed control of the government of the vast domain of the former tsars, the hapless people of the country were miserably succumbing to the cumulative weight of age-long oppression and rapacity, a monstrously voracious war and a treacherous and incompetent bourgois regime. The class-conscious workers of Russia determined to take the government of their country into their own hands, and to make a clean sweep of all exploitation and all exploiters of human toil. The class-conscious capitalists of Europe and America were fully alive to the challenge of their rule.

Thereafter it was war between Socialist Russia and the capitalist world, a war of aggression on the part of the foreign capitalist governments, a war of defense on the part of the Russian people. The world has never seen a war so desperate and persistent, so ruthless and brutal as the unconfessed, unsanctioned and uncivilized war which the capitalist powers have been waging against Soviet Russia in the two years of its existence. From open warfare without declaration of war to secret plotting with counter-revolutionary adventurers; from armed support of tsarist reactionaries to coercion of neighboring countries into active hostilities; from a shameless press campaign of calumnies and lies to an indiscriminate savage food blockade; no weapon has been too base or dastardly in the desperate effort of the predatory powers to throttle the first effective revolt against their tottering rule.

And the Socialist Republic of Russia lives. The second anniversary of its birth finds it strong and stable, confident and invincible, dreaded and cursed by the oppressors of all lands, acclaimed and cherished by the forward-looking workers of all nations and races.

Hail, Soviet Russia! The bright proletarian hope, the symbol of the new world spirit and new world order.

——*New York* Call, *November 7, 1919.*

49. NOVEMBER 7, 1919

On November 7, 1919, the Workers Republic of Russia will be two years old. The combined forces of world capital, by using the military butchers of their governments, have for two years attempted to crush the Russian workers and have failed. The revolution is still victorious. The capitalist class and their bloody governments are trembling. November 7, the Second Anniversary of the Soviet Government of Russia, will be the occasion for workers the world over to demonstrate their class solidarity and loyalty to their Russian brothers. The workers will on that day proclaim to the terror of the capitalist class their determination to end the greedy rule of world capitalism. The Russian Revolution was born out of the bloody carnage of the world war. When capitalism was using workers as cannon fodder, when the products of labor were consumed in ruthless slaughter of human lives, when homes were shattered by shell and destroyed, when women and children were starved and every vestige of civilized conduct was abandoned, there came the Russian Revolution with its defiant challenge to the capitalist world order.

——The Voice of Labor, *official organ of the Communist Labor party, November 7, 1919.*

50. "FIGHT ON!" SAYS SEATTLE LABOR

Seattle, Wash., Nov. 6—James A. Duncan, secretary of the Central Labor Union of Seattle, in anticipation of the second anniversary of the birth of the Soviet government of Russia tomorrow, issued the following statement today:

"No single event throughout the whole world today can, from the standpoint of the workers everywhere, compare in importance with the successful piloting of the Russian Soviet Republic past the treacherous rocks of international capitalist greed and the determination of these plunderers to ruin when they cannot rule.

"Labor the world over will some day realize the service rendered it by the heroic stand of their Russian brothers against untold odds in their tremendous struggle against the earth's most powerful highwaymen.

"In shame and humiliation over our weakness and inability to render the assistance our conscience dictates, we should—at the risk of appearing cowards—urge them to continue to bear a burden, part of which we ourselves should bear.

"We say to our Russian fellow-workers: 'Fight on, fight on!' accepting Woodrow Wilson's word and your own experience to back it, that right is might, and your cause will conquer."

——*New York* Call, *November 7, 1919.*

51. THANKS TO U.S. LABOR

In spite of the fact that the Allied and counter-revolutionary White troops were still conducting major offensives against Russia, Ludwig C. A. K. Martens assured the friends of Soviet Russia that they need have no doubt about the continued existence of the Soviet Union. He expressed the thanks of his government for the support of American workers.

by LUDWIG C. A. K. MARTENS

The second anniversary of the proletarian revolution in Russia finds the Russian Socialist Federal Soviet Republic stronger than ever before and victorious on all fronts.

The historian of the future will marvel at the superhuman achievements of the workers of Russia during these two years of a life-and-death struggle against the combined forces of world imperialism.

The workers of Russia have given an effective answer to all those faint-hearted souls who have doubted the ability of the Russian working class at this stage of capitalistic evolution to establish a communistic regime.

But the work in Russia is by no means ended. Still greater tasks confront the comrades of Russia—long years of incessant working out of details. But the main work—the fundamental work—is done. The foundation has been laid—a foundation which cannot be destroyed.

While the two years of a life and death struggle against external attacks and internal plots have brought Soviet Russia and the Russian workers much suffering, on the other hand, and in spite of the capitalists, these years of trial have been of great value to the Russian revolution.

The grave necessities of the situation have built up such discipline, and a determination to overcome all obstacles, that under more peaceful conditions it would have taken more time to develop. In this, as in everything else which the capitalist class undertakes against the workers' revolution in Russia, we find that every policy adopted by that class itself contains the germ of its destruction.

The days of anxiety about the very existence of the Russian Soviet Republic have passed. Soviet Russia stands firm, ready to enter the third year of its existence—a year which we hope will afford greater opportunities than heretofore for the most important work of social reconstruction.

Again, on this occasion I want to thank the American workingmen and women in behalf of Soviet Russia for the sympathy and helpfulness which they have shown during the past year in their protests against the attacks on Soviet Russia. I feel confident that the more the American workers learn the truth about the republic of the Russian workers, the stronger will be our bonds of sympathy and solidarity.

——*New York* Call, *November 7, 1919.*

52. LABOR ENDORSES PROTEST OF BLOCKADE

A mass meeting of 15,000 people called by the People's Freedom Union to protest the blockade against Soviet Russia was held in New York's Madison Square Garden on November 9, 1919. It was supported by the Central Federated Union and other labor organizations. Two of the invited speakers, who were unable to attend, sent messages to the meeting. One was Congressman William E. Mason of Illinois. The other was Helen Keller, the deaf, blind and mute woman, whose triumph over her disabilities had made her an inspiration to the entire world and who, as a militant Socialist and foe of imperialism, supported the Bolshevik revolution from the beginning. Helen Keller's letter, sent from Alabama where she was lecturing, was read to the meeting, as was Congressman Mason's message.

Ernest Bohn, secretary of the Central Federated Union, in speaking of the Madison Square Garden meeting tonight to protest the Soviet blockade, said:

"The Central Federated Union has adopted a resolution urging the United States government to raise the blockade and to withdraw our troops from Russia on the ground that this country is not at war with Russia and that, according to President Wilson's declaration, the people of a country have the right of self-determination.

"The meeting tonight has been indorsed by the Central Federated Union, which represents 350,000 working people, and will, in my opinion, go a great way in inducing our government to raise the blockade."

The Joint Board of Furriers has also indorsed the meeting. Many other labor groups, including the Women's Trade Union League, the Amalgamated Clothing Workers of America and the International Ladies' Garment Workers' Union have taken boxes and blocks of seats.

——*New York* Call, *November 9, 1919.*

53. CONGRESSMAN MASON DENOUNCES BLOCKADE

Congressman William E. Mason of Illinois was to have spoken last night at the Madison Square Garden meeting protesting against the blockade of Soviet Russia, but was unable to be present. The following telegram, read at the meeting, was received from him:

"Nothing but a last minute engagement of imperative importance keeps me from being with you tonight in Madison Square Garden. Please accept my keen regrets to those assembled. The blockade which will starve women and children of Russia this winter is a crime against humanity. The American troops in Siberia without a declaration of war by Congress is a violation of the Constitution of the United States. Let us, as loyal American citizens, do all we can within the law to correct these great mistakes. I intend to keep up my fight in Congress along these lines."

——*New York* Call, *November 10, 1919.*

54. "END THE BLOCKADE OF SOVIET RUSSIA!"

by HELEN KELLER

I am glad to join the People's Freedom Union and other friends of liberty in condemnation of the blockade of Russia by Japan, Great Britain, France and the United States of America. This outrage upon a people who are trying to work out their form of government, their ideas of life, upon their own territory, is one of the blackest crimes in history. The Allied and associated governments which are guilty of this infamy violate every principle of civilization, every rule of common honesty.

For our governments are not honest. They do not openly declare war against Russia and proclaim the reasons. They are fighting the Russian people half-secretly and in the dark with the lie of democracy on their lips and the indirect weapon of the blockade in their hands.

We cannot remain silent while the government for which we are partly responsible assists in starving women, children and old people, because forsooth, our political rulers and perhaps a majority of the American public do not approve the ideas which underlie Russia's experiment in a new type of society. No thinking American can be silent, can fail to be on one side or the other. There can be no middle ground. Those who are not for fair play to Russia, for the removal of all alien soldiers from Russian soil, for the lifting of the blockade, are Russia's enemies. And Russia's enemies are the friends and upholders of Tsarism, of oppression, of exploitation, of the plunder of one people by another. Silence in this case is not neutrality in a mere problem of politics and trade. Every word of sympathy for the men, women and children of Russia, whom the Allied governments are trying to starve into submission to the interests behind those governments, is a word on the side of humanity and progress.

What quarrel have our people with the Russian people? We may disagree with their ideals and we have a right to disagree. If their ideals are not ours, we need have no fear of them, for they cannot supplant our own ideals, whatever our own may be.

Has the truth been told about Russia? The whole truth cannot be known because it is too vast and complicated and involves rapidly developing events. But have not our people been deliberately supplied with falsifications appealing to their fears and their prejudices to make them hostile to Russia and its present government?

Hold any opinion you may happen to hold about Russia and its government. It is wrong to attack Russia without an open declaration of war and an avowal of the true causes. That is simply honest politics in accordance with the Constitution of the United States.

Above the Constitution and the laws of politicians are the laws of humanity, justice and right, embodied in the Declaration of Independence and so often eloquently invoked by President Wilson when he was urging us into a war against Germany, with Russia as one of our Allies. And now Germany is being urged to join our Allies and associates in a war against Russia. Can all this shifting of alliances, this change of partners in a few months, any longer deceive us? We fought and helped win a war to make the world safe for democracy, for ideals. That war is finished and our ideals are, of course, established. What ideal is served by this war, this actual war against Russia, denied by the State Department and carried on by the War Department? And of the generous vocabulary of liberty and justice and humanity, which has been strained and worn during the past few years, what is left to apply to this war to make it seem right to the heart and conscience of Americans?

It is not enough to express our feelings about the treatment which our government is according Russia. It is not enough to defend one part of democracy. All democracy must stand together. All humanity must be humanitarian or all will perish. We cannot divorce an unrighteous intervention in Russia, nor the attack of France and Rumania on Hungary, from the theft of Shantung. For they are only specific evils in a world-wide evil, and we must cure them to maintain ourselves and all mankind in health and happiness. We must oppose hypocrisy, greed, murder, wherever we find them in order to save ourselves and the rest of humanity. If the President and his administration will not apply to Russia and to every other country, including the United States of America, the principles which he has expressed over and over again, we must bring pressure to bear upon our government. We must appeal to the citizens of America to regard with suspicion the news from and about Russia which is printed for them every day, and to demand the enforcement of the President's own proposition, that every nation has a right to govern itself, to self-determination.

——*New York* Call, *November 10, 1919.*

55. HANDS OFF SOVIET RUSSIA!

The imperialists of the world are continuing their infamous armed intervention in Soviet Russia. The counter-revolutionary Tsarist generals, backed by allied troops, allied ammunition and allied money continue shedding the blood of the Russian workers and devastating the territory of the proletarian Republic. Moreover, the Allies are tightening the iron ring of the blockade around Soviet Russia, thus dooming millions of women and children to unheard-of misery, starvation and disease.

All this is being done because the workers and peasants of Russia have cast off the yoke of exploitation and oppression and have devoted themselves to the task of reconstructing their life on such foundations as will eliminate all oppression of the poor by the rich, all exploitation of the toilers by the capitalists. This is why the capitalist countries where all the power is concentrated in the hands of the big commercial and financial interests, are waging this predatory war against Soviet Russia. Defending their class in Russia they are thereby protecting their own interests, for they know that the example set by the Russian workers will inevitably be followed by the workers of their own countries.

Hence, America's participation in this war against Russia!

American troops still on Russian territory and American ammunition and money are still being used for the purpose of strangling the only proletarian Republic in the world.

America's intervention in Russia is frequently referred to as President Wilson's private war. This is correct only insofar as the formalities required for the waging of the war have not been complied with; it is being carried on without the consent of Congress. Yet, as a matter of fact, it is not altogether President Wilson's private war. It is rather the class war of the American plutocracy, the class war of the international money bags. American capital is vitally interested in crushing Soviet Russia and it does not stop at mere technicalities, even if it means the violation of laws of its own creation. In waging this war, President Wilson plays the part of the faithful servant of the American plutocracy.

American workers, you must realize this and bear it firmly in mind. You must know that every American soldier sailing for Russia, goes there to shed the blood of the Russian workers and peasants who are now engaged in a desperate struggle against the capitalists of the world—those brigands of the international highways. You must bear in mind that every rifle, every cannon, every machine gun which is being sent from the United States to Russia means death for the many Russian workers and peasants who are sacrificing themselves in order that the workers the world over may be liberated from the yoke of international capital.

Workers of America! It is not sufficient to know and to bear all this in mind—*you must act accordingly. Hands off Russia!*

This slogan has already been adopted by the British, French and Italian workers. In Great Britain, in France and in Italy the workers are refusing to load ships with ammunition and provisions destined for the foes of Soviet Russia.

American workers, you must follow their example! To every invitation to play the part of Cain toward your Russian brothers, to every request of the American government to enlist for active service in Russia, or to load ships for the bloodstained Russian White Army, there must be one answer: "HANDS OFF SOVIET RUSSIA!"

——*The Communist Labor Party of America,* in The Ohio Socialist, *November 19, 1919.*

56. FRIENDS OF SOVIET RUSSIA LEAGUE

In the fall of 1919, the Friends of Soviet Russia League was organized in New York City with Edas Flower as President, Charles Kruse as Vice-President, and Henry C. Petit as Treasurer. The League concentrated on work among the trade unions, pointing out that "if the workers' government of Russia, that is the Soviet government, falls, what a misfortune that would be for organized labor in America and all over the world." A three-page leaflet issued by the League is reprinted below.

The League of the Friends of Soviet Russia is a voluntary organization of liberty-loving Americans whose main purpose is not so much helping Soviet Russia but saving from utter destruction the last vestige of American tolerance and international fair play. Its purpose is not to spread the doctrines of Bolshevism but to secure fair play for the Russian people by obtaining in a legal way, and more especially through a direct appeal to the American people, the withdrawal of all American troops, both drafted and volunteer, from any and all parts of the territory of the former Russian Empire that have not been assigned to the newly created nationalities by the Paris Peace Treaty and the League of Nations.

The League of the Friends of Soviet Russia also asks that recognition of any of the contending factions now struggling for supremacy in Russia proper, be withheld by the American Government, until such time as the free conscience of the peoples of the world has unmistakably determined where and in whose hands the legitimate government of that country lies. The League must avow, however, as a token of its good faith, that while it refrains from agitating in favor of the recognition of the Soviet Government it firmly and honestly believes that that government is now and has been for nearly two years the only legitimate expression of the popular will of the Russian people.

Why we demand the withdrawal of our troops:

1. Because it is not the business of the American Republic to interfere in the private affairs of any nation whose people are trying to remodel its government and institutions in such a way as they believe best suits their new needs and aspirations. This President Wilson has repeatedly stated.

2. Because the right of revolution is sacred and intangible, and it is so declared in the Declaration of Independence of the United States, where it is even held up as a duty. Mr. Wilson has stated this, unasked, in his St. Louis speech on September 5, 1919.[27]

3. Because the United States of America is not at war with the Soviet Government, the joint houses of Congress and the Senate, the sole constituted bodies in which the right of declaring war is vested, never having taken such action.

4. Because America has received no mandate over Russia by any competent international body, neither the Peace Conference, nor the League of Nations, allowing that the latter is in operation.

5. And now finally, because if there are any disputes or controversies between the United States and the Soviet Government, such disputes or controversies can be adjusted at any time peaceably and amicably and without any further shedding of blood, the Soviet Government having declared on many occasions that it is ready to make peace with the whole world even to the extent of making all kinds of concessions, several unwarranted.

These arguments seem to us unanswerable. Unless it can be proved that the President of the United States is the sole arbiter of the foreign policy of the Government and has the absolute power to wage war without even consulting the duly elected representatives of the American people, it is quite clear that the soldiers of the United States have no legal business in Russia. The other alternative would be for Congress to declare war openly and honorably.

However, it may be argued that the withdrawal of our troops would prove detrimental to the cause of the majority of the Russian people, as represented by the so-called government of Kolchak, and that they are there not to fight a bona fide government of the Russian people, but rather to protect it. This bona fide government is represented as being that headed by Admiral Kolchak. Setting aside the fact that even if this were the case, Congress and not the President is the sole arbiter of the question involved, such a position is absolutely untenable. If there is any government in Russia that truly represents the will of the large majority of the Russian people, such government is that of the Soviet Republic.

Why we believe that the Soviet Government is the legitimate expression of the will of the Russian people:

1. Because it has been established and remained in power over nine-tenths of the territory of European Russia for about two years.

2. Because it is founded on a charter or constitution adopted by the majority of the duly elected representatives of the Russian people and it is now functioning in strict accordance with said constitution.

3. Because it is upheld by the free suffrages of *all* the Russian people now within its jurisdiction, that is by the votes of all men and women, unrestricted by any qualifications of race, color, religion or previous social position, provided every elector is above 18 years old and is engaged in *useful social labor*. The only requisite for voting in Russia is that the elector *works with-*

out exploiting other human beings, nor is in open armed rebellion against the State.

4. Because no other so-called government in Russia comes up to these requirements. Neither the Omsk Government,[28] nor that of Denikin have ever held a general election throughout the territory they occupy. Kolchak, whose recognition is now being urged, is generally suspected of actually attempting to restore dead Tsarism on the throne.

5. Because the Soviet Government is now fighting for its life on nine fronts against reactionary and absolutist forces, and is the sole power in Russia today which has an army of two million disciplined soldiers, all of whom are volunteers. All the other elements opposing the Soviet have no more than 200,000 Russian soldiers, their mainstay being mostly made up of foreign bayonets.

6. Because, in fine, if the Soviet Government did not express the will of the Russian people, the one hundred odd millions that are living under it would be quite sufficient to sweep it off the earth, without outside assistance, as they did with the Tsar.

For these reasons, which we believe to be good and sufficient, the Friends of Soviet Russia League call upon all liberty-loving Americans to join them in their earnest and respectful petition to the Congress and the Senate of the United States, that American troops be withdrawn from Russia without any further delay, that the blockade that is starving to death millions of Russian women, children and old men, be lifted, and that the Russian people be left entirely alone to work out their own salvation and achieve their destinies without any interference, save that of friendly advice and benevolent help.

> ——*November 1919; copy of four-page leaflet in possession of author.*

THE THIRD YEAR

November 1919–November 1920
(and Developments to January 1921)

1. MANUFACTURERS SEEK TRADE WITH RUSSIA

Ludwig C. A. K. Martens reported that from April to December 1919, 941 American firms in 32 states "expressed a readiness to enter into trade relations with Soviet Russia." The State Department, however, opposed all plans to promote Soviet-American trade and establish diplomatic relations with the Soviet Union. The following document reflects the protest movement among American business groups against the State Department's policy.

Denouncing the organized attacks on the Soviet government and the Allied blockade of Russia as "fanatical," E. P. Jennings, president of the Lehigh Machine Company of Lehighton, Pa., one of the largest machine shops in the United States, has openly declared himself in favor of non-interference with the Socialist republic and the opening of commercial intercourse with it. . . .

That thousands of manufacturers in the United States are anxious to take advantage of the unlimited commercial opportunities that Russia offers through the Soviet Bureau here can be reasonably assumed, although few have openly declared their attitude. . . .

Jennings' letter sent to *The New York Times,* but which has not appeared to date, is perhaps the first public expression of a manufacturer. The New York office of the Lehigh Machine Company is in the Singer Building.

The letter follows in part:

"I think it is pretty nearly time that the fanatical attacks upon Russians in this country ceased. I am in thorough harmony with the attitude toward Russia as expressed by the President of the United States in a statement which I understand was issued in Paris about January 22, 1919, in which he outlined our attitude toward Russia, and in which he said that we recognized the absolute right of Russia to direct her own affairs, and also said that it was our sole and sincere purpose to do what we could to bring Russia peace and an opportunity to find her way out of her present troubles.[1]

"It is evident that Great Britain does not sympathize with the President's statement of our attitude toward Russia, as it has been expending millions of money and hundreds of the lives of its citizens to try and compel the Russian people to adopt a form of government satisfactory to the reactionaries of Great Britain.

"Russia cannot dictate the kind of government that America will have in the future. This can safely be left to the intelligence of the 100,000,000 people of the United States, and the campaign of misrepresentation inaugurated by powerful financial interests of this country, which largely control the press, can only have a detrimental effect when the truth is known by the American manufacturers, the American businessmen and the American public.

"I have been interested in Russia from a business standpoint, because I have looked upon that country, with its vast resources in natural wealth and tremendous population, as one of the most likely markets for the products we manufacture. I have taken occasion to investigate and get the truth in regard to the Russian situation, and have not been satisfied to base my judgment of the situation upon the many contradictory reports that have been published in your paper.

"If governmental agencies would spend some time investigating how much of the tax-payers' money had been turned over to the representatives of the former Kerensky regime which now represents no government at all (so far as Russia is concerned), and what has become of this money, and how it has been used for arms, ammunition and other materials to support troops in Russia, that have not been fighting Germany, but who have been making war upon a part of their own people, it would undoubtedly bring out facts that would be very interesting to the great mass of American people and a great many of the American manufacturers.

"There is no consistency between the President's statement of our attitude and the present attitude of the State Department in its refusal to grant export licenses to manufacturers, and in the refusal of other governmental agencies to permit the transfer of monies from Russia to the United States for the purchase of food, machinery and other materials.

"We are not officially at war with Russia. War has not been declared on Russia by Congress. We have no reason to go to war with Russia. We have every reason in the world for trying to prove to the Russian people that the people of America are their friends.

"And I wish to make my position emphatically clear as an American manufacturer that I, for one, wish to go on record as being disposed to co-operate with the people of Russia in the re-establishment of their war-torn country and in the furnishing of machinery and such other valuable aid as I can render to them as an American manufacturer, without any inclination on my part to dictate to the people of Russia the kind of government they must adopt in order to secure my co-operation.

"It is evident that this is not the attitude of *The New York Times* toward Russia, nor is it the attitude of the Associated Press—which has been carrying on propaganda of falsehood and misrepresentations for many months past in regard to the situation in Russia. For many months I have read in *The New York Times* every morning of Kolchak victories, only to learn at the end of months of 'victories' that the Kolchak army was driven back about 800 miles.

"From my investigation of the facts, I am convinced:

"First, that the Soviet government of Russia is firmly established and has the support of the majority of the people of that part of the country which it controls;

"Second, that it will ultimately be victorious over all of its enemies, notwithstanding all the Associated Press 'victories' to the contrary;

"Third, that it will need millions of dollars worth of machinery and supplies from sources outside of its own borders;

"Fourth, I am convinced that the majority of American businessmen and American manufacturers have not taken the trouble to investigate for themselves and learn the truth regarding the Russian situation, and if they will do so their attitude will be very greatly changed.

"Fifth, German and English manufacturers are both anxious to get a very substantial amount of this Russian business, and the diplomacy of our State Department in connection with Russia for the last six to nine months, in my opinion, is not such as would be for the best interest either of the American manufacturers, the American people or the American financial interests.

"From what I know of the facts, it seems to me that our diplomacy is about on a level with the Kaiser's of 'force to the utmost' which got Germany into war with us. I do not believe that the American people, as a whole, want war with Russia or the Russian Soviet government. We have had enough wars in this world, and it is pretty nearly time, not only for the United States but for European countries as well, to settle down to producing the necessities and luxuries of life, and to cease destruction and murder.

"Sixth, as an American citizen whose ancestors fought in Washington's army to free our country from the domination of British rule, I am not at all pleased with the apparent tendency of our State Department to tie us on as a tail to Great Britain's kite a century and a half after the signing of the Declaration of Independence.

"Seventh, as an American citizen, I am convinced that the great strides in the last century, in the means of production and distribution and in the means of transportation and communication, have brought the world so closely together that some form of international government is desirable, but that form of international government should take in all the people of the world, and should not be of a character that will be destined to divide the world into two great armed camps, with a possibility of Russia, Germany, Austria and the Balkans and Eastern nations on the one side, and England, France, Italy and the United States with various smaller nations on the other side.

"If there are going to be two camps of fighting forces in the world, I, as one of the 100,000,000 population of this country, feel that we would be better entirely out of any alliance, with an established friendly attitude toward all the people of all the world.

"Eighth, as an American citizen, I can see no consistency in the appeal for funds to relieve the starvation and terrible suffering in the war-torn sections of Europe and Russia, which has been

"Checkmate, Gentlemen!"

The Liberator, February 1920

—BOARDMAN ROBINSON

put out by the Jewish Relief Association and others, and the support of our State Department of the starvation embargo which is being enforced against Russia by the British and French governments at the present time.

"In closing I wish to say that I have not sought publicity in this matter, but that, since you have taken the liberty of quoting from my letter to President Wilson and of publishing the name of the Lehigh Machine Company as connected with this Russian situation, I trust you will be kind enough to print this letter, presenting my personal views as president of this company, to your readers.

"Very truly yours, E. P. Jennings, President, Lehigh Machine Company."

——*New York* Call, *November 23, 1919.*

2. UNDIVIDED SUPPORT TO SOVIETS PLEDGED

In December 1919, a successful Red Army counter-offensive against Generals Denikin and Wrangel was reported. Denikin's troops fled in panic and disorder, and soon ceased to exist as a fighting force. Even before this, Admiral Kolchak's army had been routed by the attacks of the Red Army. In November, Kolchak evacuated his capital at Omsk, and took flight. He was captured at Irkutsk, and was executed on February 7, 1920, on the charge of treason. The national executive committee of the Socialist party hailed these reports from Russia.

The National Executive Committee of the Socialist party adopted the following proclamation on Russia before it concluded its sessions:

"The proletarian revolution in Russia, now in its third year, has demonstrated to the entire world that it rests upon the revolutionary consciousness of the great mass of the Russian people. Begun in November 1917, it has during the past two years taken deep root among the workers and peasants of Russia who, through their Soviets, have been forging a state based upon industrial democracy.

"All plots to undermine the trust of the Russian workers and peasants in their chosen leaders and attempts to overthrow the Soviet government by means of a counter-revolution have hopelessly failed, because the system of government which the revolutionary workers and peasants have established is of their own creation and is controlled by them.

"Besides the attempts of the internal enemies of the proletarian revolution to overthrow the workers' government, all the reactionary powers of the world have banded themselves together to destroy the Soviet republic.

"Armed intervention, starvation, blockades, financing of counter-revolutionary elements and other heinous methods are used to frustrate the accomplishments of the political and economic conquests of the Russian workers and peasants.

"The revolutionary Russian democracy has withstood all these nefarious attempts. The Soviet government is now stronger than ever. The Soviet army has defeated the armies of the counter-revolutionary bourgeoisie, and Kolchak, Yudenitch, Deniken and the other tsarist leaders of hired military bands have been almost completely annihilated.

"The Allied powers, which sent invading armies into Russia and raised the hopes of the counter-revolutionists for a return of tsarist rule, are now announcing the withdrawal of their troops and the support of the reactionary groups in Russia.[2] This was made possible because the Russian workers and peasants were united in their determination to defend their Socialist fatherland from foreign invasion and counter-revolution, and also because the organized Socialist and labor movements of the world have come to the aid of the Russian workers' republic, and have served notice upon their governments that they will not permit the sacrifice of the Soviet republic on the altar of world imperialism.

"A special representative of the United States government in Russia, who recently made public his report before the Senate Committee on Foreign Relations, has informed the government[3] that: '(1) No government save a Socialist government can be set up in Russia today, except by foreign bayonets, and any government so set up will fall the moment such support is withdrawn; (2) No real peace can be established in Russia or the world until peace is made with the revolution.'

"And now the workers of the world, inspired by the accomplishments of their Russian fellow workers, are celebrating the second anniversary of the proletarian revolution, and are renewing their pledge of co-operation and solidarity.

"The Socialist party of America, which has, from the very

beginning of the Russian revolution, supported the Russian
workers in their attempts to establish a Socialist commonwealth,
again sends its greetings to the valiant champions of political
industrial liberty, and wishes them success.

"In common with the Socialists of other countries, it pledges its
undivided support to them. It promises that it will continue to
carry the message of the Soviet Republic to the workers of this
country, and so enlist their aid in the demand that the American
government shall immediately withdraw its armed forces from
Russian territory, that it shall not give any material or moral aid
to the reactionary Russian elements, and that it shall forthwith
lift the blockade against the Soviet republic.

"LONG LIVE THE RUSSIAN FEDERATED SOCIALIST SOVIET REPUBLIC,
THE HOPE AND INSPIRATION OF THE WORKERS OF THE WORLD."

——*New York* Call, *December 12, 1919.*

3. WOMEN STIR FINANCIAL DISTRICT

*In October 1919, the American Women's Emergency Com-
mittee was organized for the purpose of sending a relief ship of
milk, medicine, shoes and food to starving women and children
in Soviet Russia. When this was denied by the government, the
committee turned its attention to a campaign to lift the embargo
against Russia, staging demonstrations such as the one described
below.*

Many American women took part in the protest demonstration
against the blockade of Soviet Russia, staged in the financial district by the American Women's Emergency Committee during
the noon hour yesterday. . . . Leading the parade, or picket line,
Miss Lucy Branham carried a large silken American flag. Behind her, for four city blocks, the protesting women followed,
each wearing a sash which read "Lift the Blockade." Some of the
marchers carried signs. Inscriptions on these read: "Milk for
Moscow." "Why Starve Russian Babies?" "Blockade Unconstitutional." "Millions Starve. Why?"

Slowly wending their way through the large crowds, and before
a battery of cameras, the women marched east on Wall Street to
William Street, passing the House of Morgan, where an army of

clerks, attracted by the procession, gathered before the door and gazed in open-mouthed amazement. . . .

Delegations from Washington, Philadelphia, Baltimore, Detroit and Hartford, Conn., took part in yesterday's protest.

"We will keep up our demonstrations until food and medicine and clothing are permitted to enter Russia," declared Mrs. Harriet Stanton Blatch of the Women's Emergency Committee. "The starving women and children are innocent of implication in this hideous crime. In my opinion, the economic blockade is a substitute for war. We women intend to wage a fight against this purely masculine brutality, and our fight will disclose the same unremitting persistence which marked our century-old battle for suffrage.

"It is our intention to arouse public indignation against the Russian blockade to a pitch which will cause no little perturbation among those whose criminal minds are responsible for it. We think it criminal to remain silent in the face of this monstrous inhumanity."

———*New York* Call, *December 13, 1919.*

4. THE CRIME OF THE BLOCKADE

by NORMAN THOMAS

Surely if Christmas brings any message of good will to the hearts of Americans, they will make it a solemn duty both to protest to the President and to Congress on their own account, and to organize mighty mass protests against the continuance of the crime of the blockade and against the whole policy of interference in Russian affairs. If compassion for the starving will not avail, enlightened self-interest ought to end the tragic folly of our Russian policy.

———The World Tomorrow, *December 1919.*

5. RUSSIA AND THE ALLIES

The headlines in The New York Times *of January 17, 1920, read: "No War With Russia, Allies to Trade With Her, Blockade Suddenly Lifted by Paris Council." The blockade had been lifted*

by the Supreme Allied Council meeting in Paris. Two weeks
before, on January 4, the New York World *had predicted the*
action, noting in an editorial entitled "What Next in Russia?":
"There can be no stronger evidence of the failure of the blockade
than the fact that the Soviet Government flourishes in spite of it."

Nevertheless, the U.S. State Department did not announce the
lifting of the blockade against Russia until July 7, 1920, and even
then it was only a nominal lifting since no commercial trans-
actions between the United States and Russia were permitted.

Justice, official organ of the International Ladies' Garment
Workers' Union, carried an editorial on the lifting of the block-
ade as did The New Solidarity, *eastern organ of the IWW.*

There are three perfectly good reasons which impelled the
Allies in their decision to lift the blockade against Russia: first,
the utter collapse of all the campaigns to crush the Soviets;
second, the growing discontent among the peoples; third, the
alluring economic prospects in Russia.

These reasons have during the last several months become
so compelling as to make this decision inevitable. Soviet Russia
has been asking for peace since it came into power. Since August
5, 1918, the Soviet Government has approached the Allies 21
times on the subject of peace; that is, the Allies were reminded
of the Soviet readiness for peace every three weeks. The terms
were moderate. Russia wanted to be left in peace and return to
peaceful production, trade and commerce with the outside
world. The Soviet leaders were ready to compromise; they were
even prepared to pay the debts contracted by the Tsar. In reply
to these offers, the Allies have suppressed, distorted, lied about
them; forged documents to "prove" their mud-flinging, slanderous accusations; indulged in indecent, perverted tales of "nationalization of women"; organized "loyal" governments in Siberia,
in Archangel, in south Russia; incited, threatened, coddled border countries to attack the Soviets; surrounded Soviet Russia with
a barbed wire fence, thereby starving defenseless men, women
and children.

These "measures" had their effect. The Allied Powers were
constantly being undermined. The Soviet power became stronger.
They could only go on with the war in Russia at great risk of
revolutions in their own countries. The Italian Government has
been forced to abandon the capitalist crusade against the Soviets.
The British Government has been growing more and more

uncertain of its very existence. The defeat to Clemenceau shows a weakening of the blood and thunder policy. The flimsiest pretense for further military campaigns against Russia has vanished. On the other hand terrible fears arose in the heart of the British imperialists with the approach of the Red Army to the Near East. Bolshevik activities around Turkey, Afghanistan, Turkestan, Persia, India are menacing to the British Empire.

Another reason which made the Allies uneasy about their undertaking is the suspicion, distrust and rivalry smoldering beneath the polished surface of the alleged love and harmony. America distrusts Japan. England distrusts America. They all distrust one another. . . . But in the face of the Soviet idea these nations would gladly join hands and conduct a new war in Russia to a finish—if they could only be sure of their peoples. But the rulers were pretty certain that they would soon need armies for suppressing the revolutions in their own countries. . . .

The statement issued by the Supreme Council is not, of course, a frank offer of resuming relations with Russia. It has many loopholes and evasions. It is attended by other acts which makes the situation extremely uncertain. They conclude their statement by saying that the new stand implies "no change in the policies of the allied governments toward the Soviet Government." They are merely trying to remedy "the unhappy situation of the population in the interior of Russia, which is now deprived of all manufacturing products from outside of Russia." The Supreme Council has discovered that the Russian people are "in sore need" of clothing, medicine, agricultural machinery, etc. It has also discovered that Russia has some things like grain, flax, lumber in which the Allies are "in sore need." The Allies can do profitable trade with Russia. But they cannot deal with the "autocratic" Soviets so they will deal with the "people." They will only trade with the co-operative societies. It is surprising why the Allies did not think of the co-operatives before.

But our press caught on to the trick that this was intended merely to save the face of the governments. It is admitted that the Russian people, the co-operative societies, cannot be dealt with outside of the Soviets. But there was no way out of this situation. Consolation is found by many in the fact that this is merely a new strategy to defeat the Soviets.

This, no doubt, is the underlying idea of the Allied decision. It was merely a change in tactics, but the end remained the same.

In raising the blockade they hope to accomplish what they had hitherto failed to do—to crush the Soviets.

——Justice, *January 23, 1920.*

6. ALL HAIL TO THE BOLSHEVIKS!

The lifting of the blockade against Soviet Russia by the Allied supreme council is a confession of ignoble defeat. The disgusting hyprocrisy of the pretense that concern for the sufferings of the Russian population influenced the council's decision will deceive no one. The Soviet armies had, to a very great extent, relieved those sufferings by annihilating the counter-revolutionary mercenaries of the Entente and opening up the food, fuel and other material sources of nearly the whole territory of the old Russian empire, before the supreme council capitulated. The latter need not hope at this late day to escape the undying infamy which is theirs for their attempt to destroy the first free government in history by systematic slow starvation.

What men and what women these Russian Communists are! Anti-militarists, they have put to rout a world in arms against them. Beset by invasion from without and treason from within, and stalked by the ever present spectres of hunger and cold, they have conquered. The proletarians of other countries will in their turn achieve emancipation; but the glory of the Russian workers they can never share. Thanks to these same Russian pioneers the others may be spared much of the agony that Free Russia has undergone. To the Russians, from the leaders to the humblest unlettered Red Guard or factory worker, is due an homage that is scarce short of hero worship. But he is a blind fanatic indeed who would wish to duplicate in any other land every phase of their revolution—the disasters, the false steps and the desperate expedients made inevitable by their terrible unpreparedness. It is one of the strangest paradoxes of history that the Communist revolution came first in the country which seemed least ready for it. That the revolution finally surmounted what appeared to be unsurmountably adverse conditions is the next thing to a miracle—and a testimony not alone to the glowing faith and heroism of the Red Russians, but to the invincibility of the Communist system.

With all military resistance practically ended and the blockade raised, Soviet Russia now enters the second period of the revolution—the period of construction. And the working plan of the new social order which she shall build will be—the industrial unionism of the IWW. It was necessary that Russia should pass through a frightful cataclysm before this work of building could begin. If the Industrial Workers of the World have their way in America and elsewhere, the building will be done first; and there need be no cataclysm.

——The New Solidarity, *Chicago, January 24, 1920.*

7. BUSINESS WITH RUSSIA

On January 24, 1920, 45 American business firms met in Washington and organized the American Commercial Association to Promote Russian Trade. The conference, presided over by E. P. Jennings, sent a committee to interview Secretary of State Lansing, but the businessmen were told that Lansing was ill and could not see them. The New York Times, a leading opponent of resumption of trade relations with Russia, reported that the "Washington Conference was largely composed of Soviet sympathizers" (Jan. 27, 1920). The following documents deal with the newly-founded Association.

A new organization urging the resumption of relations with Russia was formed last Saturday in Washington. This organization does not consist of aliens and Bolsheviks but of hard-headed American businessmen. The first conference was attended by a group of 45 representatives of American business firms in various parts of the country, for the purpose of devising ways and means for bringing pressure to bear upon the Administration to the end that present restrictions may be lifted against trade between Soviet Russia and America.

The name of the new organization is the American Commercial Association to Promote Russian Trade. The statement issued by this organization is in part as follows:

"This is a movement of manufacturers, importers and exporters representing the first organized attempt of American business interests to make a demand on the officials of this country to permit the shipment of American goods into Russian ports or to ascertain why such trade relations are not permitted.

"England, France, Italy and even Germany are making strenuous efforts to corral Russian trade. We know that England is on the job, that British representatives have been closing contracts with the Russian Soviet Government for trade and that German agents have been after Russian contracts. American firms have placed orders, but are unable to trade with Russia in the present illogical attitude of the State Department."

Accordingly a committee was appointed to "ask Secretary Lansing for a definite and positive statement of attitude. . . . It is a question of taking steps to hold our own interests in Russian trade against foreign competition." This is no sentimental issue. It is a proposition of dollars and cents. It is business.

But the committee appointed to meet Secretary Lansing failed in its mission. They could not see Secretary Lansing? Why? Because he would be asked to do something which he cannot do, that is, to speak plainly. So the august Secretary of State resorted to the banal excuse—sickness, indisposition.

It is significant that in the published statement of the Supreme Council to the Russian co-operatives there is not a word mentioned about American business. The entire plan is made out as if the United States had not existed. It is no wonder that American business is "taking steps to hold our own interests in Russian trade against foreign competition."

——Justice, *January 30, 1920.*

8. FIRMS DEMAND TRADE WITH RUSSIA

American business threw down the gauntlet to the State Department yesterday on the subject of trade with the Soviet republic. At a meeting at the Hotel Knickerbocker [in New York City], where more than 250 firms were represented, it was demanded in unequivocal terms that trade relations with Russia be re-established at once. If that necessitates recognition of the Soviet government, then the United States should recognize the Soviet government at once, those present declared.

A committee of six was appointed to call on Secretary Lansing and inform him that if clearance papers for ships to Russia are not granted at once, the American Commercial Association will go to the Federal courts and obtain an order of mandamus, compelling the Department of State to grant permission for trade with the Soviet republic.

A permanent organization to be known as the American Commercial Association to Promote Trade With Russia was established. E. P. Jennings of the Lehigh Machine Company of Lehighton, Pa., was elected president. . . .

The meeting expressed the sense of the members in the following resolutions:

"The American Commercial Association to Promote Trade With Russia has been organized by American businessmen for the purpose of re-establishing friendly relations with Russia, a country with which we are not and have never been at war, and against which we have not participated in any blockade.

"It has always been a recognized policy of the United States government that its citizens have the right to travel in and trade with all countries with which we are not at war and that the government facilitate this right.

"It has always been a well-known American principle that we do not interfere in the internal affairs of other peoples.

"In accord with these traditional American doctrines, the members of this association insist that American businessmen who desire to trade with Russia be given every opportunity and facility for opening and pursuing trade with Russia. All the other great nations of Europe are already completing these commercial relations, and it is ridiculous that American businessmen be forced to stand aside impotently while their European rivals skim the cream of this tremendous market."

While the vast majority of American businessmen are keenly anxious to resume trade with Russia on any terms, it was said that powerful interests are for various private reasons attempting to block re-establishment of such relations and the accompanying recognition of the Soviet government.

Among these, it was stated, are the American Manufacturers' Export Association, the National Foreign Trade Council, the National Association of Manufacturers and the Russian and American Chambers of Commerce.

In answering attacks made by spokesmen for such organizations, J. B. Fox, an exporter and importer of San Francisco, declared that American business must have the best markets for its surplus capital and emphasized the fact that Russia offers the most advantageous commercial field today. "The country which is greatest in natural resources, man-power and gold, has been

permitted to fall into the hands of America's commercial rivals,"
he protested.

——New York Call, *February 3, 1920.*

9. A PLEA FOR RECOGNITION

When the Senate Committee on Foreign Relations finally held hearings on Senator France's resolution (see p. 46), Lucy Branham and Mrs. Harriet Stanton Blatch came to Washington for the American Women's Emergency Committee. They brought with them the following statement by Helen Keller.

by HELEN KELLER

I am amazed that any thinking, liberty-loving man or woman should remain silent in the face of such an inhuman policy toward a starving and bleeding people. I hope, I trust, I pray that my country will not remain silent.

America was the friend of Russia during the long years in which the Russian people were denied opportunity for political expression. I do not believe that impulse of sympathy has died in American hearts. We still wish to be friends and brethren to the people of Russia. If we had a more enlightened press in this country—a press breathing the spirit of the founders of this nation, the spirit of 1776, there would be no blockade of Russia. There would be no doubt of America's purpose to help the forces of progress to prevail there. Our attitude would be one of encouragement and not of hostility to the daring experiment which is being tried out in Russia. American history and traditions would tend to deepen our interest in an experiment to abolish autocrats and privilege, to prove whether the workers can rule themselves, and maintain their position against internal dissensions and external aggressions.

The principle of the right of every nation to choose its own form of government is the very breath of democracy. In obedience to this principle America severed its relations with England and declared its political independence. Every American should feel a partnership in the struggle for human freedom that Russia is going through with such fortitude and sacrifice. If we could see the facts without the misrepresentation with which the newspapers obstruct them, we should be the champions of Russia, her steadfast friends in her hour of need.

But championship and co-operation have been checked and made difficult by sinister and corrupt intrigue and falsehood. These are the true facts: Russia had no quarrel with any one outside her own borders. She sought no nation's territory. She coveted no neighbor's goods. And yet all the strong nations have struck out at her with hatred in their hearts. Her stern, noble resolve to build a real democracy upon the ruins of the old autocracy of Russia was her only crime, and for that she has been maligned as if her people were the vilest on earth. Her territory has been invaded by marauders. Her women and children have been starved and murdered. She has been harassed and persecuted. She has been denied medicine and industrial machinery. And America has stood by silently while these atrocities were being perpetrated. But the most insidious propaganda cannot blind the conscience of humanity forever. I have a confident hope that our policy of hostile obstruction will not long continue. Surely this country will not much longer stand silent and see crimes committed in its name that should never have been tolerated by any nation which claimed to be civilized.

Let us, individually and collectively, express our condemnation of the cumulative wrongs done to the Russian people. What we have to do is not merely to protest against the starvation blockade, but also to assert a right—the right which is ours by the sacrifices this nation made upon the battlefields of Europe—the right of peoples to peace and security. We gave our treasures and the lives of our young men in vain if we fail now in this supreme moment, if we tolerate the further hindrance and betrayal of Russia. We unseated the Kaiser, but the imperialistic spirit of conquest and greed is still in the saddle everywhere in Europe. We have a right to demand the Entente guarantee Russia's freedom to develop and govern itself in the manner that shall seem good to the Russian people, without interference from any foreign power. We owe it to our children, to our country, to the generations which will come after us, that we shall not silently countenance open, flagrant, contemptuous violation of the rights for which we entered the world war. The Russian question is the acid test of our national integrity. It is also an opportunity for us to promote world peace and unity. Here is a fair cause, a just cause, a cause of reconstruction. Statesmen and premiers never labored for higher ends.

It should be remembered also that the recognition of Russia is perhaps of greater importance to America than to Russia itself. To be on the side of friendly relations with Russia is to march with the events and laws of world development. Co-operation with Russia will be the triumph of brains and spirit over stupidity and passion, and in this triumph all reasonable beings have a vital interest.

The thought that we, the members of the American Women's Emergency Committee, who will appear before the Foreign Relations Committee of the United States Senate, are a part of the great, justice-loving American people, should give us courage and steadfastness. When we protest with the power of 100 million Americans, who shall resist the push and sweep and might of that flood of public opinion? Together, we can speak so clear and so high and so insistent that the world must hear us. And hearing us, all right-minded, compassionate men and women will join us, and once more, with God's help, America will take up the championship of the disinherited and oppressed. We have had dreams of a world better, freer, happier, nobler because America was a democracy. Let us go to work in earnest with our hands, our voices, our lives to make that better world a reality.

——*New York* Call, *February 27, 1920.*

10. U.S. WORKERS TO HELP REBUILD RUSSIA

The first of a long series of movements by American workers to aid with their special skills in building socialism in Russia is described below.

Recently there was formed in New York City a Society for Technical Aid for Soviet Russia, composed of workers exclusively. It has already enlisted 1,200 members, who are ready and willing at a moment's notice to leave for Russia and lend their brains and brawn to the construction of the new society. Three-fourths of these people are technical experts in various trades and professions, such as civil, mechanical and electrical engineering, chemistry, dentistry, agriculture, motion picture photography and tailoring. They could be of very great service to Russia immediately; it is only the blockade and the lack of transport facilities which is preventing their exodus.

It is true that the great majority of those who have enrolled with the Society for Technical Aid, and who wish to go and be of service to Russia, are Russians by birth. Very many of them, however, are either American citizens or long residents of this country. There is even a good-sized number of native-born Americans in this organization who are as anxious as the rest to go and put their superior technical skill at the service of the Soviet Government....

According to Julian Leavitt, the active and enthusiastic secretary of the Society for Technical Aid, there are many members in the society who have made successful careers for themselves in this country as scientific experts, but who prefer to put their training at the disposal of the Soviet Government. There are, for instance, no less than 90 practicing civil engineers in the organization, about 50 mechanical engineers, an instructor in plant designing and operation, and an instructor in electrical engineering. As a matter of fact, college graduates in the Society for Technical Aid comprise the vast majority of its members....

——*New York* Call, *April 25, 1920.*

11. ILGWU CALLS FOR TRADE RELATIONS

At its 1920 convention, the International Ladies' Garment Workers' Union unanimously adopted the following resolution condemning the blockade and calling for trade relations with Soviet Russia.

Whereas, The people of Soviet Russia are suffering very much through the international blockade against that country; and

Whereas, Through the lack of medicine and lack of daily necessities of life, thousands of innocent victims are dying in that unfortunate country through that blockade, and

Whereas, The workers the world over are unanimously for the raising of the blockade and are for the immediate establishment of commercial relations with Soviet Russia in order to relieve the sufferings of the people of Russia, *be it therefore,*

Resolved, That the Fifteenth Convention of the International Ladies' Garment Workers' Union, assembled in Carmen's Hall, Chicago, Ill., requests the government of the United States to immediately enter into trade relations with Soviet Russia, *and be it further*

Resolved, That copies of this resolution be sent to the next convention of the American Federation of Labor.

————Report and Proceedings of the Fifteenth Convention of the International Ladies' Garment Workers' Union, *May 3, 1920, p. 106.*

12. RESOLUTIONS AT 1920 AF OF L CONVENTION

As at the 1919 Convention, several resolutions were introduced at the 1920 AF of L Convention dealing with Russia. Once again they called for lifting of the blockade, the resumption of trade relations, and recognition. They were again referred to the Committee on Resolutions which reported out a substitute resolution. This time the Committee did not even call for withdrawal of American troops from Russia, but devoted its entire resolution to a condemnation of the Soviet government. The resolutions which had been rejected by the AF of L leadership expressed the opinion of many members of the Federation.

Resolution No. 14, by Delegate Luigi Antonini of the International Ladies' Garment Workers' Union:

Whereas, The people of Russia, having arisen from their millennial oppression, have overthrown the old tsarist government as well as the oligarchy of the capitalist class, and have established a free and equitable government based on the universal duty to work, and the right of all toilers to have and enjoy the full product of their labor, thereby doing away with industrial slavery and economic injustice, the elimination of which we hold to be the ultimate aim and finality of the organized labor movement; and

Whereas, The imperialistic nations of the world, terrorized at the thought of this most glorious example spreading through the earth, have encircled the Russian nation with an iron ring of bayonets and are attempting to starve our Russian brothers into failure, submission and humiliation, through a most inhuman, brazen and cowardly economic blockade; and

Whereas, The Government of the United States has openly been, and now still covertly is an accomplice and an abettor in this most heinous crime against a free sovereign people with whom the American people have always been at peace and for whom they never felt but the warmest feelings of sympathy and friendship; and

Whereas, The downfall of the Russian Socialist Federated Soviet Republic would mean the defeat of the age-long aspirations of the workers throughout the world and would inevitably redound to the everlasting shame of organized labor, whose indifference and apathy alone would be held responsible for such a monstrous offense against humanity; *therefore be it*

Resolved, That the American Federation of Labor in Convention assembled in Montreal, Canada, goes hereby on record as favoring and urging most earnestly and emphatically the complete, final and thorough lifting of all blockades, obstacles and barriers of any character whatever that in any way encroach upon the natural rights of the Russian people to travel and take their goods through all the land and sea routes of the earth; while, at the same time it calls upon the Government of the United States to take at once the necessary steps to reopen commercial and diplomatic relations with Russia and officially recognize the Soviet government as the only true expression of the will of the Russian people, chosen by their free suffrages, defended and hallowed by their blood.

Resolution No. 28, by the Delegation of the International Ladies' Garment Workers' Union:

Resolved, By the American Federation of Labor, in Convention assembled, that we urge upon Congress and upon our government, in conformity with the principle of national self-determination and the spirit of fair play, the lifting of the blockade against the much-suffering people of Russia, and the renewal of commercial relations with that country.

Resolution No. 105, by Delegate James A. Duncan of the Seattle Central Labor Council:

Whereas, The noble defensive fight waged against tremendous odds by the workers of Russia for the right to work out their own salvation without outside interference, commands the admiration of all lovers of liberty throughout the world, so much so that it now appears impossible to induce soldiers of what we are accustomed to term enlightened nations to take the field against them; and

Whereas, The continued attacks of Japanese and other armies is compelling the use of transportation facilities to move soldiers, which are greatly needed to move food, thus causing endless suffering to be endured by the starving millions of people, largely women and children; and

Whereas, Truthful reports, furnished the United States Government by such reliable personages as William C. Bullitt, Capt. W. W. Pettit, Lincoln Steffens and Raymond Robins, and accepted as authentic by our peace delegates, including President Wilson, show that the workers of Russia are the most slandered of any in the world and, contrary to the stories circulated, are among the most considerate of their womenfolk and children, giving them every preference in order to minimize the evil effects of under-nourishment; and

Whereas, It is conceded upon all sides that the Russian Soviet Government cannot be crushed by force; and the world cannot have the peace that humanity demands as long as war continues in Russia; *now therefore be it*

Resolved, That the Fortieth Annual Convention of the American Federation of Labor respectfully urges the Government of the United States to exert its best influence to the end that Japanese and all other foreign troops be immediately withdrawn from the territory of the former Russian Empire and the blockade lifted: that peace be established with and between all the peoples of that great land and such steps taken as can be mutually agreed upon to furnish them with food and credits; *and further, be it*

Resolved, That the Executive Council select a suitable committee to present this matter to President Wilson and such other officials as they deem proper.

> ——Report of Proceedings of the Fortieth Annual Convention of the American Federation of Labor, Montreal, Canada, *June 7–19, 1920, pp. 265–66, 270, 294.*

13. METHODISTS OPPOSE BLOCKADE

The fact that the churches of the country are beginning to call upon our government to lift the blockade against Russia is a hopeful sign that America will cease fighting a nation upon which war has not been declared, a nation that is just as much one of our allies as is England or France.

Officials that high-handedly and without authority thus carry on hostilities against a friendly nation—whether these officials be Democrats or Republicans or Socialists—ought to be swept out of office with a bang that will be heard from Hell's Gate to the Golden Gate.

When is added the fact that this blockade is actually bringing starvation to tens of thousands as well as keeping up confusion and unrest among all nations, the continuation of the blockade and other hostilities is a crime that beggars description.

The Methodist Federation for Social Service urges people everywhere to pour their cries into the ears of our officials. If they will not listen to justice, perhaps because of the people's importunity, "the unjust judge will get up and open the door."

The Methodist committee states that "millions of people are suffering; the hate and bitterness of the world is daily growing; the wounds of Europe are being opened afresh; the United States is participating in the blockade, that just now is a chief cause of the evil situation."

The Methodist committee urges the president and congress to refuse to participate in the blockade, and urges the citizens by letters, etc., to besiege our government with petitions.

————*Seattle* Union Record, *July 3, 1920.*

14. FOR A U.S. LABOR MISSION TO RUSSIA

The article below was written before the National Executive Committee of the Socialist party named James Oneal, Alexander Trachtenberg, Joseph E. Cohen, Algernon Lee and Mrs. Victor Berger as members of a mission to study Russian conditions at first hand.

by ALEXANDER TRACHTENBERG

The Russian revolution is entering a new phase. The Soviet Republic has proved invincible against the counter-revolutionary plots of the domestic and foreign reactionary and imperialist interests. Kornilov, Deniken, Yudenich, Kolchak, Semenov and their bands of conspirators have been annihilated. The sulking middle classes, who aimed to undermine the proletarian rule through sabotage, have mended their ways and are now offering their services to the Soviets. The governments of Finland, Lithuania, Lettland [Latvia] and Estonia, who waged war on Soviet Russia to ingratiate themselves with the imperialist powers and to create a nationalist feeling among their peoples, had to give up their adventures and sue for peace.

And now Poland, the hired assassin, carrying out the bidding of its master, is crumbling before the mighty proletarian hosts of Soviet Russia.[4] The combined material, military and moral support of international black reaction could not help the Polish mercenaries in their counter-revolutionary task.

With the danger of military intervention removed, Socialist Russia will turn to the work of reconstruction and oragnization. Even during the darkest days of military aggressions and counter-revolutionary plots, the Soviets have been able to devote a good deal of attention to the social and industrial problems, attendant upon the great change.

A great many fundamental transformations in the social and economic life of the people have been made, and their results carefully surveyed and analyzed. The experimental stage has already been passed in many of the domains and constructive work is going on in different fields.

Born in the throes of the revolution, Socialism in Russia has become a living thing. The inspiration which has come to us from the heroic struggles of the Russian proletariat will be intensified when we learn of the great deeds of social reconstruction carried on in Russia since the establishment of the Soviet Government.

Conscious of the glorious achievements of the Soviets, as well as desirous of paying homage to the vanguard of the international proletariat, Socialist parties and labor bodies in various countries have sent official representatives to Russia. These missions have brought the Russian workers greetings from their brothers in other lands, have obtained first-hand knowledge of affairs and returned full of inspiration and praise of the indomitable spirit and unswerving idealism of the Russian proletariat. . . .

The Socialist movement of this country evinced from the very beginning of the Revolution an enthusiastic interest in Russian affairs. The American Socialists watched with suspense the tribulations of their Russian comrades and rejoiced in the success over their adversaries. The official declarations of the

Socialist party are full of praise of their accomplishments and sympathy for their sufferings. . . . The progressive labor organizations, following the lead of the Socialists, hailed the Russian Revolution with joy and also gave moral support to the Russian Soviet Bureau in the United States. The Federations of Labor in Illinois, Pennsylvania, Wisconsin and other states, and the city central bodies of New York, Boston, Bridgeport, Milwaukee, Chicago, Butte, Seattle and many national labor organizations emphatically condemned the blockade against Russia and demanded recognition of the Soviet government. Only the American Federation of Labor remained mute and, when it spoke, as it did at the recent Montreal convention, it sneered at the idea of a workers' control of government or industry in Russia and praised the outlived reactionary bourgeois democracy.

The writer proposed that a Socialist and labor mission be organized to visit Russia. The Socialist party at its last national convention went on record instructing its national executive committee to dispatch three delegates to Russia. The labor organizations which have shown their sympathetic interest in the struggles of the Russian workers, could jointly choose a delegation which would be representative of the progressive labor movement in this country. The Pacific coast, where the workers struck to prevent the sending of munitions to Kolchak; Butte, Chicago, New York and other industrial centers, where the hearts of the workers throb for their Russian brothers; and several international unions could organize a conference and choose a delegation which will represent that portion of American labor which disagrees with the officials of the AF of L that the Russian Soviets are a replica of the Tsar's government. . . .

A Socialist and labor mission from America will, I am sure, be welcomed in Soviet Russia. It will also give concrete expression to all we feel and hope about the Soviet republic. As an expression of international solidarity it will be a source of inspiration and will fire the rank and file of the Socialist and labor movement in this country with greater faith in the future, and will redouble the activities in behalf of working-class emancipation.

American Socialism and labor should join hands and together see the rising of the sun, the birth of an age-long dream—a Workers' Republic.

——*New York* Call, *July 12, 1920.*

15. SEATTLE LABOR OPPOSES WAR ON RUSSIA

The following documents illustrate some of the activities in support of Soviet Russia taking place during the months of August, and September 1920. The stand of the Seattle Central Labor Council was endorsed by the Chicago Federation of Labor which also called for a general strike if Russia were invaded, a stand which infuriated Samuel Gompers.

The General Executive Board of the IWW expelled the Philadelphia Marine Transport Workers' Union after receiving reports that the branch had loaded munitions for the White Russian General Wrangel, who was receiving Allied help in the war against the Bolsheviks in the Ukraine. The branch protested that its members were innocent, and the report in the New York Call that the Philadelphia local, the majority of whose members were Negroes, had called for tying up all shipments of munitions to Wrangel, would seem to bear out its protest. However, the document issued by the IWW executive body, in support of its expulsion order, is an indication of the strong feeling among militant workers on this issue.

Seattle labor is against war with Russia. Unequivocally and by a unanimous vote, the Central Labor Council Wednesday night voted to oppose war by any military step to aid the tottering imperialists of Poland, and took its stand with British labor in threatening to take definite steps to block any move which might place American soldiers in Poland, fighting the wars of the European plunderbund.

The adoption of the resolution was moved and carried without opposition, and a committee of five appointed to draw up suitable plans for action in case military preparations continue for sending American boys to Poland. In the meantime the American Federation of Labor is asked to take immediate steps to declare the policy of the American labor movement on President Wilson's latest imperialistic enterprise to aid the freebooters of Central Europe. Samuel Gompers was requested by telegraph Thursday morning to call the executive council of the A.F. of L., which is in New York City, into special session to consider the position in which Wilson has placed America.

The action of Seattle labor is probably the first move made by any American labor body to send forth a call for opposition to the proposed war to aid the beaten, allied-supported government of Poland, whose troops are being forced back to the fortifications of Warsaw by victorious Soviet Russian forces. Delegates consider that the council's action will be a clarion call for other councils throughout the land to take similar action, to express absolute opposition to sending troops or supplies across the seas to aid in the preservation of the Polish government.

"All women are against war," declared Jean Stovel, women's organizer for the State Federation of Labor, in a ringing appeal which voiced the unalterable opposition of Seattle working women to another European war. "We are not only acting in defense of our own boys in refusing to have them sacrificed for a government with whose aims we cannot sympathize, but we are against any of our boys, no matter what nationality, being killed or wounded in more wars. None of our ammunition, none of our supplies, but most of all, none of our boys, must be sent to the defense of the crumbling Polish government."

"The hosts of labor throughout America feel as we do, and are awaiting definite action by Seattle workers on the Polish question," James A. Duncan, Secretary of the Central Labor Council asserted. "This war must never be allowed, and drastic action, if necessary, must be taken to avert it."

———*Seattle* Union Record, *August 14, 1920.*

16. IWW EXPELS BRANCH LOADING WRANGEL ARMS

On August 11, 1920, the General Executive Board of the Industrial Workers of the World learned, for the first time, of the treasonable action of the Philadelphia branch MTW No. 8. This situation is the result of circumstances over which the General Executive Board had no control.

This branch was immediately expelled from membership and their charter revoked.

We consider that these misguided longshoremen have been guilty of a crime against the working class. They have betrayed the international labor movement by loading shrapnel shells consigned to the infamous Allied catspaw, Wrangel, for the purpose of drowning the Russian revolution in a sea of blood.

Such action is diametrically opposed to every principle of working-class honor that the IWW has stood for, fought for and bled for from its inception.

Workers who load munitions of war at the behest of any capitalist government, to help defeat any working class revolution, are guilty of high treason to their class.

The IWW has stood for unqualified industrial solidarity to defeat such ignoble ends and it stands for it now. The organization would rather face death and dismemberment than stand the disgrace of having its members render any assistance in keeping its workers enslaved to the Moloch of capitalism.

The IWW has always expelled members who were not true to the basic principles of the world revolution. We would expel members for aiding in the overthrow of a working-class government in Poland as readily as for aiding in the overthrow of the working-class government of Russia. We look forward joyfully to the day when the proletariat of Poland will cast into oblivion the imperialistic fakirs who now dominate the nation.

The IWW has proved by deeds that it is willing and eager at all costs to fight and sacrifice for the cause of international solidarity. It still keeps the faith.

The organization was designed to make it impossible for one group of workers to be used against another group in the great struggle of the classes. We do not want and will not tolerate in our membership men who can stoop so low as to aid and abet any capitalist government or any other national or international section of the common enemy in keeping the working class in slavery.

We look with horror and disgust upon the action of the Philadelphia longshoremen in loading high explosives on ships for the purpose of butchering our brave fellow workers in Russia who have established the first working-class government in the world.

The IWW has stood the brunt of the fury of master class hatred in America. More of our members have been imprisoned, murdered and brutalized than all other revolutionary organizations combined. The reason is that we stand and have always stood for the use of militant direct action to overthrow the dictatorship of the capitalist class.

The IWW wishes to keep its fair name untarnished in the eyes of the world's proletariat.

We call upon the membership of our organization to use their utmost power to assist the Soviet government of Russia in fighting the world's battle against capitalism.

We pledge ourselves and our organization to help overthrow capitalism and everything that stands for capitalism.

We appeal to the working class in general and to the United Communist Party in particular to take a stand in industry and help build up a revolutionary organization that will make forever impossible repetition of the dastardly action of the Philadelphia longshoremen.

The IWW holds out the clean hand of brotherhood to the revolutionary workers of the world.

GENERAL EXECUTIVE BOARD OF THE IWW
——Industrial Solidarity, *Chicago, August 14, 1920.*

17. SAILORS ASK RECOGNITION

The New York branch of the Eastern and Gulf Sailors' Association last night instructed Louis Thomas, its delegate to the annual convention of the State Federation of Labor to introduce a resolution calling for the immediate recognition of the Soviet Government in Russia, and to vote for any similar measure which may be presented. The resolution which the sailors' delegate is to present to the Syracuse convention reads as follows:

"*Whereas,* The experiment in cooperation now being conducted in Soviet Russia will, if successful, be of inestimable benefit to its own and indeed to the working people of all the world; and

"*Whereas,* This experiment in cooperation and its conductors have been systematically vilified and misrepresented by practically the entire press of this country, which have in turn openly charged the agencies distributing from European sources concerning this experiment with unjustified censorship and deliberate falsification; and

"*Whereas,* We have every reason to believe from the length of time which the government of Soviet Russia has been in power, as well as from the accounts of returning travelers from that country, that the experiment is successful and will continue to be successful; *be it hereby*

"*Resolved,* That the New York State Federation of Labor, in convention assembled, demand that the United States Government immediately recognize the Government of Soviet Russia and extend to that government and people all the privileges due those of a great and friendly power."

——*New York* Call, *August 17, 1920.*

18. IWW TIES UP ARMS SHIP FOR WRANGEL

Philadelphia, Aug. 18.—To every branch of the Marine Transport Workers, Local No. 8, Industrial Workers of the World, today went out a brief and decisive order to cease handling material for any war at once.

This order affects 8,000, the majority of whom are Negroes, throughout the entire Delaware district, touching the three states of Pennsylvania, Delaware and New Jersey.

As a result of this action the steamship *Westmore,* loaded with a part cargo of rails and expecting to take on shells, ammunition and additional rails for the support of the anti-Soviet leader, General Baron Peter Wrangel, is tied up at Point House here today, having come from Wilmington with the rails.

Polly Banker, business agent of the IWW marine transport workers, carrying out the order of the local union, appeared at the Broad Street station early today and called a gang of 40 workers off the job of handling war material destined for a ship at Edditson, Pa. The men who had been awaiting definite instructions, obeyed the order.

These developments are the result of a resolution passed unanimously at the last regular meeting of Local No. 8 at the headquarters last night.

——*New York* Call, *August 19, 1920.*

19. HANDS OFF SOVIET RUSSIA!

(Many progressive labor bodies have adopted resolutions similar to the following. The American working class may have to decide very soon whether they will support the International Brigands in a war on the Workers' Republic of Russia. Put your union on record by making a copy of this resolution and presenting it for adoption. Inform *The Toiler* of the result.)

The workers and peasants of Russia, after long years of suffering under the autocratic rule of tsaristic government, which represented capitalists and land owners, overthrew that government and established the rule of the workers through the Soviets.

The Soviet Government has since November 1917 been striving to rebuild Russia to insure the happiness and well-being of the workers of that country. In spite of the blockade and the unceasing war against it, Soviet Russia has succeeded in improving the conditions under which the workers and peasants live. It has achieved wonders in raising Russia out of the disorganization and chaos into which it had been plunged by the world war and the government of the tsar.

Today in Russia the great masses of the workers control the government. The labor unions are represented in all phases of the work of production and have a part in determining wages, hours, and all matters which directly concern the workers in the factories. No longer do a few capitalists and land owners control the mines, mills and factories, the land and all other means of production and distribution for their profit. The workers and peasants are conducting the work of society for the service of society, not for the profit of the few.

Understanding that the success of the rule of the workers in Russia will inspire the working class of other capitalist countries to follow their example, the capitalist governments of the world have leagued themselves against Soviet Russia, and are seeking to destroy it. They blockade Soviet Russia and starve innocent women and children. The governments of France, England and the United States have financed one tsarist general after another and incited them to make war against the workers and peasants of Russia. When these generals and their armies were destroyed, England, France, and the United States turned to Poland and urged that country to war upon Soviet Russia. Now that Poland has been beaten they threaten Soviet Russia with direct use of their power.

Because the workers everywhere realize that Soviet Russia is fighting *their* battle as well as the battle of the workers and peasants of Russia, they are rallying to its support. English and French workers have threatened a general strike and revolution if their governments attack Soviet Russia. Workers of Germany and Czechoslovakia are refusing to permit munitions for Poland to pass through their countries. English soldiers at Danzig mutinied when ordered to take the place of dock workers who went on strike rather than help the enemies of Soviet Russia.

We, the members of............give our heartiest endorsement to this demonstration of international solidarity of the workers and call upon all members of our organization and all workingmen and women of this country, to refuse to do any work that will help the enemies of Soviet Russia, but to stand solidly by the workers and peasants of that country in their struggle for freedom.

> ——The Toiler, *official organ Communist Party of America, New York, August 27, 1920.*

20. IWW ENDORSES BRITISH LABOR STAND

A resolution adopted at a regular session of the General Executive Board of the Industrial Workers of the World, August 31, 1920:

Whereas, The IWW has for 15 years been unalterably opposed to all wars in the interests of the imperialistic capitalist class, who are seeking through the international bankers trusts and the allied industrial groups to exploit the world's workers under a system bordering on industrial peonage; and

Whereas, They are now trying to crush the only real workers' government in existence, the Russian Soviet Republic, *therefore be it*

Resolved, That we the General Executive Board of the Industrial Workers of the World in regular session urge all members to refuse to give aid to the piratical designs of international capital or their attacks against the Russian workers, and *be it further*

Resolved, That we endorse the action of the special Conference of the Trade Union Congress of Great Britain in creating a council of action which has forced a reversal of attitude by Premier Lloyd George, in his attempt to send the British workers to another wholesale slaughter by giving aid to the Polish Government which had violated the integrity of Russia by invasion.

> ——Solidarity, *September 25, 1920.*

21. THE AMERICAN LABOR ALLIANCE

In the fall of 1920, trade union support for recognition of and trade with Soviet Russia and opposition to the blockade and intervention mounted sharply. This was influenced to no small extent by the stand of the British Labour party in favor of a general strike if the intervention did not end. Many affiliates of the AF of L, international unions, state federations of labor and city central labor bodies joined in the movement. The unifying organization was the American Labor Alliance for Trade Relations with Russia, originally called the American Humanitarian Labor Alliance.

Immediate action with a view to prevent further intervention in Russian affairs by the United States was called for by a conference of New York labor representatives under the name of the American Humanitarian Labor Alliance. Instigation of war against Russia by the Allies and the United States has created a situation which menaces the peace of the world, the Alliance declared. The program of the Alliance demands: (1) that all war against Russia be stayed; (2) that the last vestige of blockade and intervention be removed; (3) that all barriers interfering with communication, postal, telegraph and wireless be immediately removed; (4) that free and unrestricted trade relations be immediately re-established with Soviet Russia so that all obstacles to peace shall be removed.

The program also declares the intention of the Alliance to join with the organized labor movement in the United States and in Europe and Asia in taking necessary action which will prevent continuation of "unjustifiable and continuous attacks against Russia, interfering with the peace of the world and threatening to draw us into a new bloody war."

The Alliance has indorsed the resolution recently adopted by British labor, declaring for a general strike unless hostilities against Russia were abandoned.

The program adopted by the Alliance follows similar steps by the Chicago Federation of Labor and by the Seattle Labor Council. These bodies passed resolutions indorsing the action taken by the workers of England, Italy and France to prevent mobilization of military and naval forces to be used against Soviet Russia, and called for a general conference of representatives of United States labor to encourage and indorse the same action.

Twelve central labor organizations in the country have adopted resolutions demanding unrestricted trade relations and communications between the United States and Russia.

The facts upon which the Alliance bases its program are the result of a competent investigation of Russian affairs by the British Trades Union Congress and the Labour Party.[5] This investigation showed that an illegal blockade of Russia is being maintained and is causing not only endless suffering to helpless women and children, but is working against the return of Europe and America to settled conditions.

The provisional executive committee of the Alliance represents, besides labor unions, the American Women's Emergency Committee, and the Farmer-Labor Party.[6]

The provisional executive committee is made up of Percy J. Pryor of the Eastern and Gulf Sailors' Association; John Riley of the International Longshoremen's Association; J. T. De Hunt of the Brotherhood of Railroad and Steamship Clerks, Freight Handlers, Express and Station Employees; Sidney Hillman of the Amalgamated Clothing Workers; Abraham Baroff of the International Ladies Garment Workers; Valentine Bausch of the International Association of Machinists; Capt. William A. Maher of the Masters, Mates and Pilots; and officers of the Cloth, Hat and Cap Makers, the Fur Workers and the Painters.

————*New York* Call, *October 20, 1920.*

22. THE NEW YEAR OF WORKERS' REPUBLIC

From his cell in Atlanta Penitentiary where he was serving a 10-year sentence for anti-war activities, Eugene V. Debs paid tribute to Soviet Russia on the occasion of the third anniversary of the Bolshevik revolution. The message was received by the National Executive Committee of the Socialist party and released by the party's press service.

by EUGENE DEBS

Greetings, Comrades, in our glorious celebration of the third anniversary of the Russian revolution. The proletarian world and lovers of liberty everywhere thrilled with joy at the news of the great victory of the Russian people.

The triumph of the workers' cause in Russia is an historic milestone in the progress of the world, and its influence for good has circled the earth and shall direct the course of the future.

The emancipation of Russia and the establishment of the workers' republic is an inspiration to the workers of the world, and this people's government is a bright star in the political heavens and shall light the way of the world. It is the great hope of the human race and its example will lead to the emancipation of the workers of the world; all hail to those noble Comrades who carved out a people's government on an impregnable foundation of granite that shall stand for all time.

Comrades, you have weathered the storm, the faithful co-operation of Comrades has been able to defeat the world-wide alliance
of capitalism. I am sure that the same spirit that conquered capitalism will develop the geniuses that will conquer the devastating
diseases you inherited from capitalism in Russia, and combat the
present mad methods of alien capitalistic governments who seek
to destroy the newly emancipated people of Soviet Russia.

Have faith, Comrades, your triumph is complete. Other nations
will become liberated and together shall form a brotherhood of
the world.

————New York Call, *November 7, 1920.*

23. HILLMAN URGES UNION PROTEST

Sidney Hillman, general president of the Amalgamated Clothing Workers of America, yesterday issued an appeal to locals of
the union to send delegates to the conference of labor organizations which will be held November 21 to protest against the
blockade maintained against Soviet Russia. The American Humanitarian Labor Alliance, under whose auspices the conference
will be held, made public Hillman's letter, in which he said:

"The blockade of Russia is of immediate concern to the workers of this country, not only because it is our duty not to permit
our government to re-establish autocracy in that country under
the banner of Wrangel or any other tsarist adventurer, but also
because we here are affected by breaking off of trade relations.
While this country finds itself today in a condition of general
unemployment because there is no outlet for goods produced, we
are prevented from dealing with these markets that are in need
of the commodities that we have. Because of that the industrial
depression may be expected to assume even greater proportions."

————New York Call, *November 12, 1920.*

24. GREETINGS TO RUSSIA

It is under most auspicious circumstances that the Russian
proletariat goes to celebrate the third anniversary of the Soviet
Republic. There is small doubt that they are still hungry and
cold; that they have a hard battle with disease and other diffi-

culties; that innumerable problems are still unsolved and that others are daily arising; but the one all-important fundamental problem may fairly be said to be solved—Socialist Russia has acquired a position among—or we should say in the vanguard of —the nations of the world which not even the rankest and blindest champions of Allied imperialism dare any longer to dispute or question.

At this writing the last armed foe, General Wrangel, the last catspaw of the Entente, recognized by France as de facto ruler of Russia, aided by the British General Townsend and the highly reputed military genius of the French General Weygand, this last foe is just being driven into the interior of Crimea.

With its last foe conquered, Soviet Russia can start its fourth year of life, giving its entire attention to internal problems.

The Socialist Labor Party extends greetings and entertains the fondest hopes of rapid progress.

——Weekly People, *November 13, 1920.*

25. ACCOMPLISHMENTS OF THE REVOLUTION

by ALBERT RHYS WILLIAMS

1. It has destroyed root and branch the state apparatus of tsarism.

2. It has transferred the great estates of the crown, the landlords and monastic orders into the hands of the people.

3. It has nationalized the basic industries and begun the electrification of Russia. It has fenced off Russia from the unlimited exploitation of free-booting capitalists.

4. It has brought into the Soviets 1,000,000 workers and peasants and given them direct experience in government. It taught 40,000,000 peasants to read and write. It has opened the doors of tens of thousands of new schools, libraries and theatres and roused the masses to the wonders of science and arts. . . .

5. It has assured self-determination to a score of subject races formerly held in vassalage to the Russian Empire. It has given them free hand to develop their own language, literature, and institutions. . . .

6. It has not paid lip-service to "open diplomacy," but has made it a reality.

7. It has pioneered the way to a new society and made invaluable laboratory experiments in Socialism on a colossal scale. It

has quickened the faith and increased the morale of the working-classes of the world in their battle for the new social order.

Through the Russian Revolution, *New York, 1921, pp. 285–86.*

26. RESOLUTION ON INTERVENTION

Adopted at the conference of the American Labor Alliance for Trade Relations with Russia, November 21, 1920.

Whereas, The people of Russia have for the past three years been subjected to untold misery and privation because of an economic blockade maintained by the allied powers with the aim of forcing the Russian people to abandon a system of government which they saw fit to establish and continue to support, and which the avowed principle of self-determination declared by our Government guarantees them; and

Whereas, This inhuman blockade to which the American Government has given its approval and support is hindering the Russian people from organizing their industrial life in order to relieve the critical conditions created by six years of continued war; and

Whereas, In common with the Allies the United States Government has been participating in open warfare, or the support of invasions and internal assaults upon the sovereignty of the Russian Republic, although no war has been constitutionally declared by this country against Russia; and

Whereas, These attacks upon the Russian people have even led to the prohibition of the various relief agencies from sending medical and other aid to the sick and needy, and food to the starving women and children, while full support and aid was extended to the various counter-revolutionary forces; and

Whereas, Public opinion in the United States has been aroused against the monstrous murder of an innocent people so that the State Department announced on July 7, 1920, the nominal lifting of the blockade without, however, permitting the execution of commercial transactions between this country and Russia; and

Whereas, Growing unemployment in this country could be materially relieved if Russia were permitted to make purchases of clothing, tools, machinery, and various other supplies which are needed by the Russian people in large quantities, and this country could secure raw materials which Russia can supply; *be it therefore*

Resolved, That this conference of authorized delegates of labor unions of Greater New York assembled on Sunday, November 21, in Headgear Workers Lyceum, representing 600,000 organized workers, protests against the further participation of the American Government in the various plots against Soviet Russia and demands that all military, financial, and moral support be withdrawn forthwith from all these elements engaged in direct or indirect war upon Russia; *and be it further*

Resolved, That we demand that the State Department take immediate steps to remove all obstacles to trade with Russia, to establish communication by post, cable, and wireless, to restore the right to travel between the United States and Soviet Russia, and to permit the transfer of funds from Russia to be used in the purchase of American goods, to allow authorized representatives of the Soviet Government to act in its behalf regarding all commercial transactions, and otherwise establish complete and unrestricted relations with Russia, *and be it further*

Resolved, That copies of these resolutions be forwarded to the State Department and be given wide publicity.

TIMOTHY HEALY, *Chairman;* ALEXANDER TRACHTENBERG, *Secretary.*

———Relations with Russia. Hearing before the Committee on Foreign Relations, United States Senate, Sixty-Sixth Congress, Third Session, on S.J.Res. 164, A Resolution Providing for the Establishment of Trade Relations with Russia, And So Forth, *Washington, 1921, pp. 55–56.*

27. PROTEST DEPORTATION OF RUSSIAN ENVOY

The American Labor Alliance for Trade Relations with Russia sponsored a mass meeting in Madison Square Garden to protest the action of Secretary of Labor William B. Wilson in ordering the deportation of Ludwig C. A. K. Martens. Wilson took this action even while admitting that there was no evidence that Martens had ever personally advocated the use of force or violence for the overthrow of the U.S. government, or that he had ordered the dissemination of any literature containing such propaganda.

Ten thousand men and women poured into Madison Square Garden yesterday afternoon to voice a mighty protest against the deportation of Ludwig C. A. K. Martens, representative of the Russian Soviet Government in the United States. Long before the doors of the amphitheater opened, long lines of workers and liberal-minded citizens, who were incensed at the policy of the United States Government in regard to the Soviet Republic, were waiting for the moment to voice their long pent-up protest.

The meeting, called by the American Labor Alliance for Trade Relations with Russia, with which are affiliated large international unions of machinists, clothing and other workers, was the climax of the many demands which sprang up spontaneously when the rank and file of the labor unions and the general public realized that the discrimination against the Soviet Republic and the order to deport its representative was a violation of the fundamental principles of American justice and American tradition.

It was to these men and women that the speakers—among whom were such men as Senator Joseph I. France, Frank P. Walsh and President Timothy Healy of the Brotherhood of Firemen—addressed themselves.

"You are here today to formulate a foreign policy," said Senator France, "and to stop an illegal, unconstitutional war against Soviet Russia. For Ludwig Martens is being deported in pursuance of a policy of war, an unjustifiable war which is staining the honor of the people.

"This meeting will send a mandate from the people to the Foreign Relations Committee. It will demand action from a body which has kept my resolutions for trade with Russia sleeping in its file waiting for the President to dispose of it."

"The American people," said Mr. Walsh, "will get behind your demand. The American people will force the recognition of the Russian Soviet Republic. It is with a feeling of shame that we say good-bye to this representative of that government. I might say that if he had come in another day he would not have been thus treated, or if he had waited only a little while before he came. Just now he is the victim of the same forces that crushed the steel workers."

Two resolutions were enthusiastically adopted, the first demanding that trade with Russia be resumed and the second protesting against the deportation of Martens. They will be sent to the State Department, the Senate Foreign Relations Committee and the Department of Labor.

The text of the deportation resolution follows:

"*Whereas,* The Department of Labor has ordered the deportation of Mr. L. C. A. K. Martens, the accredited representative to this country of the Soviet Russian Government, whose activities were directed solely toward the establishment of friendly relations between the peoples of the United States and Russia; and

"*Whereas,* The decision of the Secretary of Labor in the deportation proceedings found Mr. Martens guilty only of the crime of being the representative of the Russian Soviet Government, and exonerates him of all other charges originally made against him; and

"*Whereas,* Section 3 of the Immigration Act of October 16, 1918, under which the order of deportation is used, provides 'that this act shall not be construed to apply to accredited officials of foreign governments"; and

"*Whereas,* The deportation of Mr. Martens removes further the possibility of the establishment of free relations between the two countries; *be it*

"*Resolved,* That we, 10,000 American workers, assembled in Madison Square Garden, January 2, 1921, condemn the action of the Department of Labor in ordering the deportation of Mr. Martens; *and be it further*

"*Resolved,* That we request Mr. Martens to take to the Russian workers the greetings of their American brothers, and the assurance that we are utterly opposed to the treatment by the administration of the accredited representative to this country of the Russian Soviet Republic, as well as to the policies of the administration regarding relations between the United States and Russia; *and be it further*

"*Resolved,* That copies of this resolution be sent to the State Department, the Department of Labor and Mr. L. C. A. K. Martens."

The resolution denouncing the American blockade against Soviet Russia reads:

"*Whereas,* The people of Russia have for the past three years been subjected to untold misery and privation because of an economic blockade maintained by the Allied Powers with the aim of forcing the Russian people to abandon a system of government which they saw fit to establish and continue to support, and which the avowed principles of self-determination declared by our government guarantees them; and

"*Whereas,* This inhuman blockade—to which the American

Government has given its approval and support, is hindering the Russian people from organizing their industrial life in order to relieve the critical conditions created by six years of continued war; and

"*Whereas,* In common with the Allies the United States Government has been participating in open warfare or the support of invasions and internal assaults upon the sovereignty of the Russian Republic, although no war has been constitutionally declared by this country against Russia; and

"*Whereas,* Public opinion in the United States has been aroused against this monstrous murder of an innocent people so that the State Department announced on July 7, 1920, the nominal lifting of the blockade without, however, permitting the effective execution of commercial transactions between this country and Russia; and

"*Whereas,* Growing unemployment in this country could be materially relieved if Russia were permitted to make purchases of clothing, tools, machinery and various other supplies which are needed by the Russian people in large quantities while this country could secure raw materials which Russia can supply; *be it therefore*

"*Resolved,* That this mass meeting of American workers assembled in Madison Square Garden, January 2, 1921, protests against the further participation of the American Government in the various plots against Soviet Russia and demands that all military, material, financial and moral support be withdrawn forthwith from all those elements engaged in direct or indirect war upon Russia; *and be it further*

"*Resolved,* That we demand that the State Department take immediate steps to remove all obstacles to trade with Russia. . . . ; *and be it further*

"*Resolved,* That copies of these resolutions be forwarded to the State Department, the Senate Foreign Relations Committee, and be given wide publicity."

——*New York* Call, *January 3, 1921.*

28. CHICAGO LABOR SUPPORTS TRADE

New impetus has been added to the agitation of the American Labor Alliance for Trade Relations with Russia by the decision of the Chicago Federation of Labor, representing over 400,000 members, to appoint a committee to co-operate with the Alliance. This co-operation will take the form of a conference of all Chicago unions to crystallize the growing demand of organized labor there for the resumption of commercial relations with Soviet Russia.

The International Machinists' Association, Local 113, has undertaken to organize the conference, and the Chicago Federation has sent resolutions for indorsement to all the local unions of the city, it was declared by the Alliance. The resolution authorizing this conference was unanimously passed, and calls on the State Department immediately to remove all obstacles to trade with Russia; to establish all means of communication with that country; to permit the transfer of funds from Russia to be used in the purchase of American commodities; and to "allow authorized representatives of the Russian Government to act in its behalf regarding all commercial transactions and otherwise establish complete and unrestricted relations with Russia."

The sponsors of the resolution argued that mills and factories have been shut down throwing multitudes of workers out of employment in all industries and sections of the United States, while the Russian Government stands ready to pay in gold for hundreds of millions of dollars' worth of manufactured products, "which, if our government would permit such sales, would result in sending back to work millions of men and women now walking the streets in search of work."

———*The New York* Call, *January 8, 1921.*

29. PHILADELPHIA UNIONS BACK TRADE BILL

Philadelphia, Jan. 9.—Organized labor of this city, represented by the Central Labor Union, today joined in the nation-wide campaign for the resumption of trade relations with Soviet Russia, initiated recently by the American Labor Alliance for Trade Relations with Soviet Russia. Entry into the movement for the lifting of the blockade against the Russian workers' republic was expressed by the adoption of a resolution calling upon the United States Government to remove all diplomatic barriers to the resumption of trade relations with Russia, and by a decision to send a delegate to attend the hearings before the Senate Committee, on the resolution of Senator France, which are scheduled to begin within two weeks.

The adopted resolution, introduced by Lodge 159 of the International Association of Machinists, reads:

"*Whereas,* A group of labor organizations in New York City under the auspices of the Central Trades and Labor Council have formed an organization known as the American Alliance for Trade with Soviet Russia; and

"*Whereas,* The object of this body is to crystallize and make effective the sentiment of the organized workers and the public generally, in favor of the removal of all trade restrictions against Soviet Russia through the medium of publicity and public meetings; and

"*Whereas,* We are now in the midst of an industrial depression with the number of unemployed workers growing daily, and there seems to be no immediate relief in sight except such as would result from the execution of immense contracts, which we are advised the Russian Government desires to place in this country as soon as trade restrictions are removed;

"*Therefore be it resolved,* That the Central Labor Union of Philadelphia warmly endorses the work of the American Labor Alliance for Trade with Soviet Russia, and goes on record in favoring organization of a branch committee of the Trade Alliance in this city;

"*And be it further resolved,* That the secretary of the Central Labor Union be instructed to send out a call to all affiliated local unions requesting them to elect delegates for a conference, to be called as soon as possible, for the purpose of effecting a permanent organization locally of the American Alliance for Trade with Soviet Russia, and in order that the work of arranging public meetings and carrying on such other educational work as may be necessary locally."

————*New York* Call, *January 10, 1921.*

30. SOVIET TRADE DEMAND GROWS

American labor's growing demand for the resumption of trade with Soviet Russia was accentuated yesterday by the following developments:

(1) James H. Walker, president of the Illinois State Federation

of Labor, on behalf of the federation, informed the American Labor Alliance for Trade with Russia that he and his organization endorsed the aims of the Alliance.

(2) The national headquarters of the International Association of Machinists announced that it will work for the adoption of Senator France's resolution calling for trade with Russia.

(3) The League of Free Nations wrote Norman H. Davis, Acting Secretary of State, appealing for friendly relations between the Soviet Government and the United States.

(4) The Schenectady Trades Assembly, representing 20,000 workers, addressed a statement to Congressman Frank Crowther of New York, calling on him to initiate at once action that will lead to commercial intercourse with Russia.

(5) The Central Labor Union of Hartford, Connecticut, elected a standing committee of four to speak for the reopening of trade relations at the forthcoming hearing in the United States Senate.

In its communication to Congressman Crowther, the Schenectady Trades Assembly said:

"The number of unemployed has been considerably augmented with the layoff in the General Electric. Schenectady has everything to gain and nothing to lose by the restoration of Russian trade and diplomatic relations, as the carrying out of the great electrification project of the Soviet Government necessarily involves the purchase of a vast amount of apparatus."

———*New York* Call, *January 18, 1921.*

31. COMRADE MARTENS' DEPARTURE

On January 22, 1921, Martens left the United States with his family, as thousands at the pier waved farewell. The Toiler's editorial marking his departure is interesting because of its prediction that sooner or later recognition of Soviet Russia would have to come. Twelve years passed before this prediction was realized.

When the United States of America set up its government after throwing off the monarchical yoke of Great Britain, it sent an envoy to Russia for the purpose of gaining "recognition" and establishing trade relations. But the Tsar and his government did not like the form of this government, it was an oppositional form and contained the elements of political liberty—with which tsarism was always at war. It was only after the American ambassador had knocked at the door of Russia's government for two years that recognition was granted.[7]

Today the reverse of these conditions obtains, or rather did until this government outstripped the Tsar in maliciousness by deporting Ludwig C. A. K. Martens, envoy of Soviet Russia, a few days ago. Tsarism is gone forever in Russia. That black cloud that shut out the sunlight from the oppressed masses of Russia has been lifted—consumed by the holy flame of revolution. In its place stands a government of the workers and for the workers. When bloody tsarism existed it received every courtesy this government could extend, no matter what its crimes or in what seas of human blood it drowned the aspirations of its people. Every year the President of the United States cabled his congratulations to the Tsar upon his birthday and expressed the hope that he would continue many years to rule over the Russian people.

The envoy of New Russia has been knocking at the door of the State Department in Washington for two years. He has exerted every resource to establish relations of friendship and commerce between the peoples of Russia and this country. The only official reply he has received is—deportation. In such manner has this government shown its attitude toward the Soviet government and the Russian masses. So officially ends this chapter of world history, a chapter that will always be white in the book of Russia and black as night in the book of the United States.

But it is only the ending of a chapter of a story that will continue. Comrade Martens and his official family left these inhospitable shores amidst the cheers and well wishes of thousands assembled upon the docks and piers of New York's harbor. Enormous masses of red roses were strewn over them, songs were sung in their honor, shouts were raised for Soviet Russia. In this manner did the people part from the first representative of a people's government that has ever set foot in this country. Their greetings, smiles and cheers blotted out the government's curse. The masses repudiated the government's action with their presence, their songs and cheers. They blessed the departing comrades and the whole cause of the toiling masses everywhere by these simple and human expressions of sympathy and good will.

The demand for recognition of and trade with Russia has not been stifled by this act of deportation. A matter of this importance is not settled in that manner. The causes which create the demand for a favorable settlement of this question are growing larger and larger. A country of the size and economic quality of Russia cannot be left out of this country's trade calculations, and all be well. Conditions demand the opening of trade relations; this, aside from humanitarian reasons, will have the say-so and settle the question in favor of trade.

———The Toiler, *February 5, 1921.*

The Allies (to Russia): "If you weren't so bloody we might recognize you."

—Maurice Becker

The Liberator, April 1920

"You gotta nerve, asking for a raise—suppose you were in Russia!
"Suppose YOU were."
—BARNS

The Liberator, March 1921

REFERENCE NOTES

INTRODUCTION

1. The correspondence of Marx and Engels is replete with references to their belief that Russia might become the first country to achieve a truly thorough-going revolution. On September 1, 1870, Marx wrote to F. A. Sorge, an American Marxist, of the "inevitable social revolution in Russia," and again, on September 27, 1877, he wrote to him: "This time the revolution will begin in the East, hitherto the unbroken and reserve army of counterrevolution." Engels shared this confidence. On December 1, 1884, he wrote to August Bebel, the German Socialist: "As things are at present an impulse from outside can scarcely come from anywhere but Russia." On April 23, 1885, Engels wrote to Zasulich: "To me the most important thing is that the impulse should be given in Russia, that the revolution should break out." On September 22, 1892, Engels wrote to Danielson: "At all events, I am sure that the conservative people who have introduced capitalism into Russia will be one day terribly astonished at the consequences of their own doings." (*The Selected Correspondence of Karl Marx and Frederick Engels, 1846–1895*, New York, 1942, pp. 301, 349, 434, 438, 501.)

2. In his work, *Two Tactics of Social Democracy in the Democratic Revolution* (1905), Lenin developed his theory of the revolutionary struggle in Russia, stating clearly his belief that the democratic phase of the revolution would grow into the socialist phase. (*See* U.S. edition, New York, 1935.) In his economic work, *The Development of Capitalism in Russia* (1899), Lenin proved, from an exhaustive study of Russian sources, that the development of capitalism in Russia was preparing the way for revolution. Engels, in his letter to Danielson, cited above, made precisely the same point. *See also* Engels to Danielson, October 17, 1893, op. cit., pp. 513–15.

3. Christopher Lasch, *The American Liberal and the Russian Revolution*, New York, 1962, p. 19.

4. Cable to N. S. Chkheïdze of the Russian Duma, April 1917, *American Labor Year Book*, New York, 1917, vol. II, p. 379.

5. "The Dawn of Russian Freedom," *American Federationist*, April, 1917, p. 286; *Knights of Labor*, March, 1917, p. 2.

6. See, for example, *New York Times*, March 24, 1917.

7. Philip Taft, *The AF of L in the Time of Gompers*, New York, 1957, pp. 444–45.

8. Resolution adopted by meeting held at Ferrer Center, New York City, April 29, 1917, copy of leaflet in possession of author.

9. Charles Louis (Louis C. Fraina), "The Seizure of Power," *The New International*, May 5, 1917, p. 30.

10. New York *Call*, April 1, 1917.

11. In December 1917, one month after the October revolution, the editor of the Socialist New York *Call* wrote: "We in America know little of Lenin and that little is probably wrong." (Dec. 7, 1917.) Leon Trotsky and Nikolai Bukharin were better known since they were in the United States briefly early in 1917. *The Class Struggle*, a left-wing

Socialist journal, published Bukharin's article, "The Russian Revolution and Its Significance," in its May–June 1917 issue. In it Bukharin called the February revolution "the first step in the revolution. . . . The old, semi-feudal noble, landowning class is overthrown. In its place stand the new rulers, the modern, capitalist bourgeoisie." He predicted that "the second step will inevitably follow," and it would transform the fatherland of the capitalist bourgeoisie "into the fatherland of the proletariat." (pp. 20–21.)

12. Mooney was a union organizer and Billings a member of the Shoemakers' Union. The reactionary open shop employers in San Francisco had long hated Mooney and Billings, and they were quickly indicted for the bomb explosion. Evidence favoring the defendants (such as a photograph which showed Mooney a mile from the scene of the explosion at the time indicated) and evidence that witnesses had been tampered with by the prosecution were ignored. Billings, who was tried first, was found guilty and sentenced to life imprisonment. Mooney's trial began in January 1917. He was found guilty without a recommendation of clemency. Mooney was sentenced to be hanged, and his execution was set for May 17, 1917. Most scholars agree that the action of the Russian workers saved Mooney's life, leading to his being sentenced to life imprisonment.

13. Bernard Mandel in his biography of Gompers claims that Wilson asked the AF of L President to serve on the Root mission but that "Gompers did not want to leave the country at that critical period." (Bernard Mandel, *Samuel Gompers*, Yellow Springs, 1963, p. 402.) But Wilson's letter appears to indicate that the President was reluctant to have Gompers serve on the mission.

14. On April 7, 1917, the day after the United States entered the war, an emergency meeting of the Socialist party was held in St. Louis. The convention finally adopted a series of resolutions which reaffirmed the party's "allegiance to the principle of internationalism and working-class solidarity the world over and proclaims its unalterable opposition to the war just declared by the government of the United States. . . . The mad orgy of death and destruction which is now convulsing unfortunate Europe was caused by the conflict of capitalist interests in the European countries. . . . The American people did not and do not want this war. They have not been consulted about the war and have no part in declaring war. They have been plunged into this war by the trickery and treachery of the ruling class of the country through its representatives in the national administration and national congress, its demagogic agitators, its subsidized press, and other servile instruments of public expression." (*American Socialist*, April 21, 1917.) Charles Edward Russell, along with John Spargo, A. M. Simons and other Socialists, opposed the resolution and continued to support the war.

15. Lasch, *op. cit.*, p. 44.

16. New York *Call*, June 11, 1917.

17. Ronald Radosh, "American Labor and the Root Mission to Russia," *Studies on the Left*, vol. III, No. 1, 1962, pp. 42–43.

18. *American Federationist*, Sept. 1917, pp. 744–45.

19. George Kennan, *Russia and the West Under Lenin and Stalin*, Boston, 1961, pp. 25-26.

20. William Appleman Williams, *American-Russian Relations, 1781–1947*, New York, 1952, p. 86.

21. The Socialist-Revolutionaries were a left-wing party formed in the 1890's, with support among the peasants in the provinces. They turned to terrorism, and their agents killed many well-known figures in the Russian ruling circles. Kerensky joined the Socialist-Revolutionaries before the February revolution.

Kerensky's career confirmed Trotsky's view: "Kerensky was not a revolutionist; he merely hung around the revolution." Reviewing *The Russian Provisional Government, 1917; Documents,* selected and edited by Robert Paul Browder and Alexander F. Kerensky (Stanford, 1961), Rudolf Schlesinger writes: "If anything is clear from these volumes, it is his [Kerensky's] complete unwillingness to interpret his task otherwise than as an agency of the Allied war effort." (*Science & Society,* vol. XXVIII, Summer 1964, p. 306.)

22. In his recently published autobiography, *The Kerensky Memoirs,* Kerensky concedes that "the main reason for the failure of the offensive . . . was that the Russian army was opposed by first class German troops," and that two-thirds of the Russian infantry had been killed or wounded during the preceding years. Nevertheless, he revives the old anti-Bolshevik accusation that the German General Staff had financed Lenin and the Bolsheviks, citing recently published diplomatic archives. (These are published in Z. A. B. Zeman, editor, *Germany and the Revolution in Russia, 1915–1918,* London, 1958.) But the truth is that not a single piece of evidence has been found to show that Lenin and the Bolshevik party ever entered into any secret contact with the Kaiser's government or accepted money from it.

23. Adam B. Ulman, *The Bolsheviks,* New York and London, 1965, pp. 347–48.

24. D. F. Fleming, *The Cold War and Its Origins, 1917–1960,* New York, 1961, vol. I, p. 14.

25. V. I. Lenin, *Collected Works,* vol. XXVI, Moscow, 1964, p. 236.

26. Karl Kautsky, "The Russian Revolution," *The Class Struggle,* vol. I, Nov.–Dec. 1917, p. 38.

27. *See* Document 51, p. 126.

28. *Proceedings, National Convention of the Socialist Party, 1920.*

29. Joseph Rappaport, "Jewish Immigrants and World War I: A Study of American Yiddish Press Reactions," unpublished Ph.D. thesis, Columbia University, 1951, pp. 265–67, 353–54.

30. Samson Freeman, County Organizer, Essex County SP, in New York *Call,* March 16, 1918.

31. These Federations had constituted 35 per cent of the party membership in 1916, but by 1919 their ranks had increased to 53 per cent of the party total. The Russian Federation, which had not been organized until 1915, had grown most rapidly. (*American Labor Yearbook, 1917–1918,* p. 340; Theodore Draper, *The Roots of American Communism,* New York, 1957, pp. 137–38.)

32. F. L. Paxson, *Post-War Years: Normalcy, 1918–1923,* Berkeley and Los Angeles, 1948, pp. 27–29.

33. Robert W. Dunn, *The Palmer Raids,* New York, 1948; Robert K. Murray, *Red-Scare: A Study in National Hysteria, 1919–1920,* Minne-

apolis, 1955, pp. 35–36; H. C. Peterson and Gilbert C. Fite, *Opponents of War, 1917–1918*, Madison, Wis., 1957, Chapters V, XV, XVII.

One gets an idea of the terror and intimidation of this period from the case of A. L. Hitchcock, a Cleveland Socialist, who was arrested, convicted and sentenced to ten years in prison on the complaint of a person not present for a remark he was alleged to have made while visiting a sick friend in his home. (Hitchcock to Seymour Stedman, Cleveland, May 28, 1918, Socialist Party Collection, Duke University Library.)

34. *Weekly People*, Dec. 15, 22, 29, 1918.

35. *Industrial Worker*, Jan. 26, Feb. 2, 1918.

36. *Ibid.*, Dec. 15, 1917.

37. *Ibid.*, May 4, 1918.

38. *Solidarity*, Aug. 14, 21, 1920; William D. Haywood, *Bill Haywood's Book*, New York, 1929, p. 360.

39. Paul R. Brissenden, *The IWW: A Study of American Syndicalism*, New York, 1919, p. 373.

40. *The New International* of June 30, 1917, carried the text of a speech Lenin delivered before leaving Switzerland for Russia in which he stated emphatically: "The difference between us and the anarchists is that we admit that the State is a necessity in the development of our Revolution." (*See* also *The Class Struggle*, vol. I, July–Aug. 1917, p. 138.)

41. Emma Goldman, *Living My Life*, New York, 1934, pp. 644–45.

42. *Ibid.*, p. 644.

43. Lasch, *op. cit.*, pp. 98–99.

44. Murray, *op. cit.*, pp. 35–36.

45. *New York Times*, Oct. 31, Nov. 6, 8, 1918; New York *World*, Nov. 11, 1918.

46. *New York Times*, Oct. 26, 1918; Lasch, *op. cit.*, p. 122.

47. Christopher Lasch has written an interesting analysis of the response by American liberals to the Russian Revolution. He divides the liberal community into "war liberals" and "anti-imperialist liberals." Both welcomed the February revolution, but for different reasons: the war liberals because it would induce the Russians to fight against Germany; the anti-imperialists because it brought democracy to the Russian people. They split over the October revolution; the war liberals hated the Bolsheviks for exposing the imperialist purposes of the Allied powers and for Brest-Litovsk; the anti-imperialists were friendly and thought that the Bolsheviks were making an important contribution in the field of economic democracy and would inevitably return to political democracy as it was understood in the United States. (*The American Liberals and the Russian Revolution*, New York, 1962.) While it is possible to question Lasch's lumping the anti-war liberals into the anti-imperialist camp without much distinction among them, he has presented a useful study of American policy toward Russia.

48. Ray Stannard Baker and William E. Dodd, *Public Papers of Woodrow Wilson*, New York, 1927, vol. II, p. 206; New York *Call*, May 19, 1918.

49. *Advance*, March 29, 1918; New York *Call*, April 21, 1918.

50. Lasch, *op. cit.*, p. 98.

51. Williams, *op. cit.*, pp. 105–06.

52. *See* Document 44, p. 118*f*.

53. U.S. Department of State, *Papers Relating to Foreign Relations of the United States, 1918, Russia, II,* Washington, 1932, pp. 324–34; K. K. Kawakami, *Japan and World Peace,* New York, 1919, pp. 79–80; William S. Graves, *America's Siberian Adventure, 1918–1920,* New York, 1931.

54. E. H. Carr, *The Bolshevik Revolution, 1917–1923,* New York, 1953, vol. III, pp. 127–28; James Bunyan, *Intervention, Civil War and Communism in Russia, April–December, 1918,* Baltimore, 1936, p. 277; Ulam, *op. cit.,* pp. 433–34.

55. William Appleman Williams, "American Intervention in Russia, 1917–1920," *Studies on the Left,* vol. IV, no. 1, p. 56.

56. Frederick L. Schuman, *American Policy Towards Russia Since 1917. A Study of Diplomatic History, International Law and Public Opinion,* New York, 1928, p. 137; Louis Fischer, *Why Recognize Russia?* New York, 1931, p. 248.

57. *The Communist,* Chicago, Ill., Oct. 18, 1919.

58. *The Ohio Socialist,* Nov. 19, 1919.

59. Quoted in Williams, *American-Russian Relations,* p. 154.

60. New York *Call,* Jan. 8, 1919.

61. Samuel Gompers, *Seventy Years of Life and Labor,* New York, 1924, vol. II, pp. 398–99; Margaret Hardy, *The Influence of Organized Labor on the Foreign Policy of the United States,* Liege, Belgium, 1936, p. 75; Taft, *op. cit.,* p. 416.

62. *National Civic Federation Review,* April 25, 1919, pp. 4, 11.

63. *Proceedings,* AF of L Convention, 1919, pp. 332–24.

64. *Proceedings,* AF of L Convention, 1920, pp. 357–63, 368, 371, 372.

65. International Ladies' Garment Workers' Union, *Report and Proceedings of the 14th Convention,* 1918, pp. 42–43.

66. *Justice,* Jan. 23, 1920, p. 2; June 4, 1920, pp. 2, 4; June 25, 1920, pp. 2–3; July 18, 1920, pp. 6–7; Nov. 19, 1920, p. 5; *Advance,* Nov. 19, 1920.

67. New York *Evening Call,* June 6, 1918.

68. *Advance,* June 14, 1918, p. 1; March, 1922, p. 4; Dec. 1922, p. 4.

69. Sidney Hillman, *Reconstruction of Russia and the Task of Labor,* New York, 1922, pp. 21–22.

70. The speech was originally published by the Socialist Rand School in New York under the title *The Soviets at Work* in an edition edited by Alexander Trachtenberg. (The *Union Record*'s edition omitted Trachtenberg's notes; it was edited by Anna Louise Strong who also wrote an introduction.) On November 22, 1918, after tens of thousands of copies had been sold by the Rand School, the U.S. Post Office informed the School that the pamphlet, "*The Soviets at Work* by Nicholas Lenine, is unmailable under the Espionage Act." (New York *Call,* Nov. 26, 1918.) Reprinting the exact letter sent by T. G. Patten, Postmaster, the *Call* commented:

"*The Soviets at Work* is a masterly address on government from the standpoint of the 'greatest good for the geratest number,' which our 'liberals' are so fond of talking about. Not a word in it that is in contradiction to the right of the people to govern themselves in their own interests. Not a word in it that would bring condemnation from any one but a kaiser, a tsar or a sultan.

"And yet in America, where the Declaration of Independence was proclaimed, where a great war was fought, resulting in the abolition of chattel slavery, an officer of the present Democratic administration has been found who dares, in the face of every tradition of American freedom, to forbid the people of this country the privilege of reading such a pamphlet as 'The Soviets at Work.'

"This is the same sort of thought control which the procurator of the Holy Synod exercised to the disservice of his master, the late Tsar."

In Seattle the anti-labor press charged that the general strike which gripped the city for five days (February 7–11, 1919) was an attempt to put the principles outlined in the pamphlet the *Union Record* published into practice. The strike was caused by the refusal of employers to increase wages to meet the tremendous rise in the cost of living. (Harvey O'Connor, *Revolution in Seattle: A Memoir,* New York, 1962, p. 119.)

71. Seattle *Union Record,* Sept. 20, 1919; *Industrial Worker,* Sept. 27, 1919.

72. Lasch, *op. cit.,* p. 121.

73. The American Archangel expedition cost more than $3,000,000, 240 men killed, and 305 wounded (Schuman, *op. cit.,* p. 34). General Graves concluded his book, *American Siberian Adventure,* with the following observation: "I doubt if any unbiased person could ever hold that the United States did not interfere in the internal affairs of Russia. By this interference the United States helped to bolster up, by its military forces, a monarchistically inclined and unpopular government . . . and gained by this act the resentment of more than 90 per cent of the people of Siberia." (*op. cit.,* p. 283.)

74. *Justice,* June 25, 1920, pp. 2–3; New York *Call,* Nov. 7, 1919.

75. L. Gvishiani, "The Martens Mission," *International Affairs,* Moscow, Oct. 1964, pp. 62–63; "Refusal of the Government of the United States to Recognize the Mission of L. Martens, Russian Soviet Agent in the United States," *Foreign Relations of the United States, 1919, Russia,* Washington, 1919, pp. 133–49.

76. Gvishiani, *op. cit.,* p. 63.

77. *Bankers' Magazine,* vol. LCVIII, Jan. 1919, p. 73; *Nation's Business,* vol. VII, Feb. 1919, p. 20; July 1919, p. 36. *See also* Meno Lowenstein, *American Opinion of Soviet Russia,* Washington, D.C., 1941, pp. 14–15.

78. *New York Times,* Nov. 15–17, 1919; New York *Call,* Nov. 14, 1919.

79. Louis F. Post, *The Deportation Delirium of Nineteen Twenty,* Chicago, 1923, p. 291.

80. Gvishiani, *op. cit.,* p. 65.

81. Martens reported this development to his government, writing: "The victories of the Soviet Army and the opening of peace talks with the Baltic countries are noticeably influencing both official circles in Washington and American opinion at large. Spirits are low in government circles, they feel that intervention has failed. At the same time the public is markedly inclining towards non-interference in Russia." (*op. cit.,* p. 65.)

82. New York *Call,* Jan. 3, 1921.

83. *New York Times,* Jan. 26, 27, 1920; *Justice,* Jan. 30, 1920, p. 2.

84. *Advance,* Dec. 17, 1920.

85. *Relations with Russia. Hearings before the Committee on Foreign Relations United States Senate, Sixty-Sixth Congress, Third Session, on S.J. Res. 164, A Resolution Providing for the Establishment of Trade Relations with Russia, And So Forth,* Washington, D.C., 1921, pp. 29, 55–60.

The national and international unions endorsing the objectives of the Alliance were International Assocation of Machinists; Amalgamated Clothing Workers: International Ladies' Garment Workers; International Fur Workers; United Cloth, Hat and Cap Makers; International Brotherhood of Firemen and Oilers; International Jewelry Workers; International Woodcarvers Association; International Federation of Hotel Workers; Grand Division of Sleeping Car Conductors; Amalgamated Textile Workers; Eastern Federation of the Brotherhood of Railway and Steamship Clerks.

Among the central labor unions endorsing the Alliance were the central labor bodies of Barstow, San Diego, Taft, Calif.; Denver, Col.; Bridgeport, Hartford, Meriden, New Haven, Conn.; Wilmington, Del.; Washington, D.C.; Council Bluffs, Iowa; Chicago, Springfield, Ill.; Portland, Shelbyville, Terre Haute, Ind.; Frostburg, Baltimore, Md.; Boston, Salem, Mass.; Albert Lea, Minn.; Omaha, Neb.; Berlin, N.H.; Fort Edward, Schenectady, N.Y.; Cincinnati, Ironton, Ohio; Altoona, Harrisburg, Jeannette, Philadelphia, Pittsburgh, Reading, Warren, Wilkes-Barre, Pa.; Charleston, S.C.; Ogden, Utah; Newport News, Richmond, Va.; Seattle, Tacoma, Wash.; La Crosse, Milwaukee, Wis.; Cheyenne, Greybill, Wyo.; Central Trades and Labor Council of New York. United Hebrew Trades of New York, Women's Trades Union League of Philadelphia, Women's Trades Union League of New York, and Italian Chamber of Labor of New York were also among the supporters of the Alliance's program.

86. *Relations with Russia, op. cit.,* pp. 7–30, 37.

87. Samuel Gompers and William E. Walling, *Out of Their Own Mouths: A Revelation and an Indictment of Sovietism,* New York, 1921, pp. 8, 218–21; Samuel Gompers to the National and International Unions, State Federations, Central Bodies and Labor Press, April 21, 1921, AF of L Archives, Washington, D.C.; *American Federationist,* May, 1921, pp. 86–90. Gompers also contacted Secretary of Commerce Herbert Hoover requesting the same information and received the same answer that Russia, as long as it was under Soviet rule, was not worth trading with. (Gompers and Walling, *op. cit.,* pp. 218–21.)

88. Lenin's letter was dated August 20, 1918. It was brought to the United States, at Lenin's request, by Pyotr Travin who had just returned to Russia after 12 years of exile in the United States. Arriving in the United States, he took the letter to John Reed who arranged to have it translated, and edited the translation. (Pyotr Travin, "How Lenin's Letter to the American Workers Was Delivered," *Soviet Woman,* No. 4, 1964, pp. 10–11.)

On January 21, 1919, Lenin wrote "A New Letter to the Workers of Europe and America" in which he repeated his equation of Gompers with Scheidemann. The first accurate translation of Lenin's letter to American workers was published in 1934. In this edition Lenin denounced Gompers as a social traitor, a member of the labor aristocracy bribed and corrupted by imperialists. (V. I. Lenin, *A Letter to American Workers*, New York, 1934, p. 22.)

89. *Proceedings*, AF of L Convention, 1921, pp. 90–102.

90. Eugene V. Debs, *The Negro Workers: An Address Delivered October 30, 1923, at Commonwealth Casino, 135th Street and Madison Avenue, NYC*, New York, n/d., pp. 28–29.

91. The AF of L leadership, however, refused to follow the lead of the government and still adhered to its anti-Soviet position. This had been predicted by *Justice* in its issue of July 16, 1920, when it wrote: "If the AF of L will wait much longer the American Government may go as far as to recognize the Soviet Government while the Federation will still persist in its uncompromising hostility to Soviet Russia."

92. *New York Times*, Nov. 17, 1933.

93. Although many of the Socialists who were early supporters of the Soviet Union changed their attitude after 1921, a number still continued to advocate recognition of the Soviet government by the United States. B. Charney Vladeck, managing editor of the *Jewish Daily Forward*, wrote in 1927 that "while disagreeing with the Soviet Union in many of its policies," he had "always advocated publicly and privately the recognition of the Soviet government by the United States." (B. C. Vladeck to I. I. Kitlin, Oct. 27, 1927, B. Charney Vladeck Papers, Tamiment Institute Library of New York University.)

How far the leaders of the Socialist party had moved from their early attitude towards the Soviet Union is illustrated by the following items which appeared in *The New Leader*, weekly organ of the Socialist party, in 1930–31. The first is a letter to the weekly by McAlister Coleman, a member of the Party and the biographer of Eugene V. Debs. He wrote in part:

"I now read that in the proletarian atmosphere of the Pennsylvania Hotel an organization was formed consisting of 'Labor, Socialist and Progressive Organizations' to protest against the 'reign of terror which prevails in Soviet Russia.' So, it seems, whether we like it or not, we Socialists who have not ventured an opinion on an extremely controversial subject are officially drafted as partisans in a dispute from which up to now we had studiously abstained. For my part, I have no objection to a fight. But I do like to choose my side. And in my humble and undoubtedly expert opinion, in this instance, I am decidedly on the wrong side.

"For despite all the assurances to the contrary on the part of those who organized this pointing-with-horror conference, I now find myself cheek by jowl with Ham Fish, Matt Woll, Ralph Easley, Archie Stevenson and other persons highly obnoxious to me and with whom I have had as little to do as possible. I do not like my new bed-fellows. I resent being forced to occupy the same room with them and I have the sneaking suspicion that my resentment is shared by a large majority of the Socialist Party who like myself have preserved a decent silence up to now.

"Talk and talk about it, as the backers of the conference will, there can be no other effect upon the American public at this time, as the result of the unhappy publicity which the Pennsylvania conference gained, but that we as a Party are definitely lined up with the foes of

Soviet Russia. The sooner we dig out of this mess into which we have been led by a little group of disgruntled and discredited prophets, sore because things are not going exactly according to their calculations, who have imported their personal and political feuds to this country and who have a Moscow phobia which blinds them to the facts, the quicker we will recover our Socialist integrity." (*The New Leader*, Dec. 27, 1930.)

Hamilton Fish was the New York Republican Congressman who made a political career out of attacking the Soviet Union and radicals and liberals in the United States. Matthew Woll, AF of L vice-president, was, together with Samuel Gompers, leader of the anti-Soviet elements in the Federation, and after Gompers' death in 1924, assumed the top position among the AF of L anti-Soviet bloc. He was a close associate of Ralph M. Easley, secretary of the National Civil Federation and a leading red-baiter. Archibald E. Stevenson, a prominent New York lawyer, had been a leading force behind the infamous and sensational Lusk investigation of radicalism in New York in 1918.

The second item was Norman Thomas's criticism of Morris Hillquit because the Socialist lawyer had become the counsel for the Standard Oil Company in its suit seeking compensation for confiscation by the Soviet government of oil lands disposed of by the tsarist regime to private owners. Thomas voiced his objection to a leader of the Socialist party serving as a spokesman for capitalist interests who challenged the right of a Socialist government to confiscate property belonging to capitalists. His criticism forced Hillquit reluctantly to withdraw from the case, but the incident revealed how far Hillquit had strayed from the position he had taken in the years immediately following the Bolshevik revolution. (*See The New Leader*, Aug. 22, 1931.)

THE FIRST YEAR

1. Red Guard was a voluntary organization made up of factory workers in the cities who armed themselves, collected in bands and supported the Bolsheviks. They were first formed in 1905, but played a much greater part after 1917.

2. The Cadets were a political party formed in tsarist days, which got its name from the Russian initials of its longer title, Constitutional Democrats. Composed mainly of liberals from the propertied classes, it aimed at political reform of a moderate nature, but by April 1917, it was on the right wing of the parties making up the Provisional government.

3. General Alexei Kaledin had organized a White counter-revolutionary army among the Cossacks in Southern Russia, proclaimed "the independence of the Don," and was preparing to march on Moscow to overthrow the Soviet government.

4. On November 29, 1917, Lord Lansdowne published a letter in the London *Daily Telegraph* in which he argued that the war had already lasted too long, warned that its prolongation would "spell ruin for the civilized world" since it would bring more revolutionary upheavals, and pleaded for an early end of the war on the basis of

compromise with the Germans rather than unconditional surrender.

5. Shortly after they came into power, the Bolsheviks disclosed the fact that the governments of Great Britain, France, Italy, Rumania and Japan had made a series of secret treaties by which the Allies in advance had divided among themselves the prospective spoils of victory over Germany and Austria. The Bolsheviks found the secret treaties in the archives of the Russian foreign office.

6. As early as April 1917, the Bolsheviks had advanced the peace proposals: No annexations, no indemnities, and the self-determination of all peoples. These proposals were endorsed by American Socialists and pacifists at a convention in New York City's Madison Square Garden, May 30–31, 1917, called the First American Conference for Democracy and Terms of Peace. The People's Council of America was organized at this conference.

7. The Constituent Assembly was convoked by the Provisional government after the February revolution. It adjourned for the last time on January 18, 1918. The following day the Central Executive Committee of the All-Russian Soviets proclaimed the dissolution of the Constituent Assembly.

8. In a letter to *Pravda* from Geneva in April 1917, Lenin wrote of "the conspiracy of the Anglo-French imperialists who encouraged Milyukov, Guchkov and Co. to seize power *in order to prolong the imperialist war,* and to conduct the war even more ferociously and stubbornly, and *slaughter new millions* of Russian workers and peasants, and so that Guchkov may obtain Constantinople, and the French may obtain Syria, and the English capitalists may obtain Mesopotamia." Milyukov, a long-time leader of the Constitutional Democrats, was Minister of Foreign Affairs in the Provisional government. Guchkov, a prominent industrialist and former president of the Duma, was head of the Ministry of the Army and Navy.

9. The reference is to the declaration of war aims issued by the Provisional government on April 10, 1917, in response to pressure from the Petrograd Soviet. In the declaration, it renounced its own claim to "annexations and indemnities" at the expense of Germany and her allies. Earlier Russia had signed treaties with Britain, France and Italy, in which each had promised not to make peace until the others had gained certain objectives. Although Russia now renounced her claim to Constantinople, this did not mean that she was leaving the war.

10. *The Masses* was a Socialist literary monthly edited by Max Eastman. It was famous for its art, verse and fiction.

11. Lenin was sent to exile in Siberia after his imprisonment in January 1896, in connection with the case of "The League of Struggle for the Emancipation of Labor," the precursor of the Russian Social-Democratic Labor Party.

12. Lenin began work on *The Development of Capitalism in Russia* while in prison and finished it while in Siberian exile. It was first published in 1899. For the English edition *see,* V. I. Lenin, *The Development of Capitalism in Russia,* Moscow, 1956.

13. Lenin did not escape from Siberia; he received official authorization to return to European Russia, and an official passport to go abroad. He left for Germany in July 1900, beginning his first period

of emigration abroad, which lasted for five and one-half years. After living in Munich, he moved to London in the Spring of 1902, and in the Spring of the following year to Geneva. From there, after the outbreak of the Russian Revolution of 1905, he returned to Russia in November of that year. The second period of emigration abroad began at the end of 1907. After a brief stay in Finland, Lenin came to Geneva in January 1908. He then lived in Paris (1909–12), Cracow (1912–14), Berne (1914–15) and Zurich (1916–17). He returned to Petrograd in April, 1917, after the outbreak of the February revolution. For his life and work in emigration, *see* N. K. Krupskaya, *Reminiscences of Lenin.* New York, 1967. For Lenin's important writings during this period, *see Selected Works of V. I. Lenin* (3 vols.), vol. 1, New York, 1967.

14. *Iskra* was first issued in Leipzig in December 1900, and later in Munich and Stuttgart. In November 1903 (not 1912, as the article states), Lenin resigned from the Editorial Board. From then until its last number of October 1905 it became the organ of the Mensheviks.

15. While in exile in Siberia, Lenin translated Sidney and Beatrice Webb's *The History of Trade Unionism.*

16. The *New Yorker Volkszeitung* was a German-language Socialist daily published in New York City.

17. Philipp Scheidemann, a German Social-Democrat, was also known as a "Kaiser Socialist." Together with Friedrich Ebert, first president of the German Republic, he later put down the workers' insurrection in Germany with the help of the army.

18. In the summer and fall of 1917, Socialists in Philadelphia were arrested for distributing a pamphlet entitled *Long Live the Constitution of the United States.* The pamphlet quoted from the Declaration of Independence in calling for the repeal of the Selective Service Act.

19. In his message to Congress, December 4, 1917, Wilson wrote that if the aims of the Allies "had been made plain at the very outset the sympathy and enthusiasm of the Russian people might have been once for all enlisted on the side of the Allies, suspicion and distrust swept away, and a real and lasting union of purpose effected." Wilson thus implied that the Allies themselves were to blame for the collapse of Kerensky.

20. The paper published by Maxim Gorky was *Novaya Zhizn* (New Life).

21. In late 1917 and early 1918, IWW leaders and members were arrested throughout the country, ostensibly because of their opposition to the war, but more frequently because employers, threatened by organization of their workers by the IWW, saw an opportunity to use the war to destroy the militant labor body. The press regularly reported frequent beatings and jailings of IWW's in many parts of the country.

22. On December 29, 1917, a Soviet peace delegation met with the Germans at Brest-Litovsk, headquarters of the German Eastern Army, to discuss German peace terms. Lenin had urged this step, convinced that to save the revolution, it was necessary to sign an immediate peace on the Eastern Front.

23. The reference is to the "Fourteen Points," Woodrow Wilson's program for peace, put before Congress on January 8, 1918. It asked

for "open covenants," freedom of the seas, a league of nations, adjustment of all colonial claims, based on the interests of the populations concerned as well as those of governments, evacuation of Russian territory and cooperation of all nations with Russia "in obtaining for her an unhampered and unbuttressed opportunity for the independent determination of her own political development and national policy and assure her of a sincere welcome into the society of free nations under institutions of her own choosing. . . ."

24. The Rand School of Social Science in New York City was the leading Socialist party educational center in the country.

25. The Red Guard was being recruited for military service in Russia to help stem the German military drive. The name was taken from the Red Guard in Russia which formed the nucleus of the new Red Army.

26. The Ferrer Association was named in honor of the Spanish educational reformer and philosophical anarchist, Francisco Ferrer, who was executed by the Spanish government in 1909.

27. The People's Council of America was organized at a conference of Socialists and pacifists in May 1917, with the aim of protecting labor's interests at home and advancing the Bolshevik peace proposals.

28. *Mother Earth* was an anarchist monthly publication founded by Emma Goldman in 1906.

29. In a message to the Russian people and an appeal to the people of Germany and Austria, made public on January 15, 1918, the British Labour party announced that the British people accepted the Russian principle of self-determination of peoples, and no annexations or indemnities. "The British people must proclaim to Russia and the Central Powers that its aim is identical with Russia's; that we, too, see no solution for the evils of militarism except self-determination and no indemnities."

30. On July 12, 1917, 1,200 workmen in the Arizona copper mines, engaged in a strike led by the IWW, were rounded up by vigilantes belonging to the Citizens' Protective League and deported to New Mexico. They were unloaded at the little desert station of Hermanas, New Mexico, abandoned by their guards and left to shift for themselves.

31. The Keating-Owen Act of 1916 attempted to regulate child labor by forbidding its products in interstate commerce when made by children under fourteen years of age or other conditions. The Supreme Court declared the law unconstitutional in the case of Hammer v. Dagenhart (1918).

32. The "Zabern Affair" occurred in 1913–14. German Lieutenant Forstner, stationed in the town of Zabern in Alsace, made offensive remarks about France, and incidents followed in which several people were wounded by German officers led by Forstner. The officers were acquitted by a military court, but the incident was regarded as a glaring example of the arrogance of the German officers.

33. Instead of collapsing, the intervention had only just begun.

34. On September 27, 1918, Wilson delivered an address in New York City in which he outlined the "particulars" of a peace treaty with Germany. There was no reference to Russia in the speech.

35. The reference is to the Sission documents. *See* pages 132–8.

36. In the elections of November 1918, the Democrats lost control of Congress. The Republican party captured the Senate (and with it the Foreign Relations Committee) by 49 to 47, and the House of Representatives by 239 to 194. Warren G. Harding, the Republican candidate, was elected President in 1920.

37. The first thing the German workers did in their peace demonstrations was to set Karl Liebknecht free from prison. Upon his release, Liebknecht organized the Spartacans, who hoped to emulate the Bolsheviks and overthrow the provisional republican regime set up by Friedrich Ebert and other conservative Socialists. Liebknecht was arrested with Rosa Luxemburg and both were murdered by the police.

38. For evidence that Sisson himself discounted the documents as proof that the Bolsheviks were German agents, *see* William A. Williams, "American Intervention in Russia, 1917–1920," *Studies on the Left,* vol. IV, no. 1, p. 56. For an analysis of the documents, *see* George F. Kennan, "The Sisson Documents," *Journal of Modern History,* vol. XXVIII, June 1956, pp. 125–52.

39. For evidence that Harper and Jameson were pressured by the administration to sustain the Sisson documents, *see* Samuel H. Harper, *The Russia I Believe In,* Chicago, 1945, pp. 111–12. For the Harper-Jameson report, *see* New York *Evening Post,* Nov. 11, 1918.

40. The Sisson documents were first published by the *Petit Parisien* on February 8, 1918. The attack on the documents in *New Europe* was by S. Poliakov-Litovzev, the British correspondent of the *Russkoe Slovo,* an anti-Bolshevik paper. It was reprinted in the New York *Evening Post* of March 13, 1918.

THE SECOND YEAR

1. The St. Louis *Post-Dispatch* of November 29, 1918, carried a brief account of the meeting and reported over 2,500 present.

2. In an interview with Colonel Raymond Robins soon after the Soviet government was formed, Lenin offered a program for cooperation with the United States. In return for American technical aid, the Soviet government would agree to evacuate all war supplies from the eastern front, thus preventing them from falling into German hands.

3. The Democratic-Republicans, the political group led by Thomas Jefferson, expressed sympathy for the French Revolution, and bitterly opposed the Federalists who were antagonistic to the revolution.

4. Theodore Roosevelt knew Colonel Robins well. Robins had supported Roosevelt for President in the "Bull Moose" campaign of 1912.

On May 2, 1918, Ambassador David R. Francis telegraphed the State Department from Russia: "Robins and probably Lockhart also have favored recognition of Soviet government but you and all Allies have always opposed recognition and I have consistently refused to recommend it, nor do I feel that I have erred therein." When Robins, who was ordered home by Secretary of State Lansing, reached Washington, he submitted a report urging recognition of Soviet Russia and condemning Allied intervention.

5. This excerpt from Wilson's "Fourteen Points" message eliminated the last phrase of the sixth point which read: "and, more than a welcome, assistance also of every kind that she may need and may herself desire."

6. The Peace Conference met early in January 1919 at the Quai D'Orsay in Paris, attended by the Big Four—Woodrow Wilson, David Lloyd George, Georges Clemenceau, and Vittorio Orlando. Russia, however, was not represented. Although Wilson urged the Conference to invite Soviet delegates to attend and reach a peaceful understanding with the Allies, this advice was rejected.

7. Johnson was a Republican. Senators Henry Cabot Lodge and Philander Chase Knox were leaders of the Republican party in the Senate who bitterly opposed the Bolshevik revolution and favored the intervention.

8. Vitoriando de la Huerta overthrew the government of Francisco Madero in the Mexican revolution which began in 1910 against the government of Porfirio Diaz. Huerta murdered both President Madero and his vice-president. The United States refused to recognize Huerta, and soon he, too, was overthrown by a successful revolt led by the Constitutionalists, under the leadership of Venustriano Carranza. Huerta fled to the United States where he was held a prisoner by the government.

9. Thomas Jefferson, the Democratic-Republican candidate, was elected President in 1800 over the Federalist candidate, John Adams. The Federalists and the Jeffersonians differed sharply over the French revolution, the former opposing and the latter supporting it.

10. This was a reference to the Soviet government's repudiation of the foreign debts incurred by the tsarist regime. Among the reasons the Bolsheviks advanced to justify this action was that the monies had been loaned as a means of aiding tsarism to suppress popular uprisings.

11. The Oneida community, established in 1847 in western New York by John Humphrey Noyes, became notorious as a "free love" colony.

12. The Mormons moved to Utah after being persecuted in New York, Ohio and Illinois. In Utah they developed a social system which practiced polygamy until it was abolished in the Thirteenth Amendment to the U.S. Constitution adopted in 1865.

13. In ordering the advance of the German army into Russia, Prince Leopold declared: "We want no annexations or contributions, but restoration of order. Russia is the center of anarchy. The contagion is spreading into Europe. Civilized Europe understands the Germans are defending order in Europe."

14. F. C. W. L. Metternich-Winneberg was an Austrian diplomat who, as Austria's Foreign Minister and Chancellor, played a leading role in mobilizing European reaction, especially at the Congress of Vienna, against the influence of the French Revolution.

15. On September 26, 1776, the Continental Congress decided to send a commission of three—Benjamin Franklin, Silas Deane, and Arthur Lee—to negotiate a treaty with France. Franklin's tremendous popularity in France contributed immensely to the success of his mission.

16. After the victory of the Americans in the Battle of Saratoga, Louis XVI, King of France, authorized negotiations for an alliance with the United States. The final treaties—a treaty of commerce and a treaty of "defensive alliance . . . to maintain effectively the . . . independence absolute and unlimited of the United States"—were signed on February 6, 1778.

17. Frazier Hunt's and Isaac Don Levine's reports from Russia were published in the radical and Socialist press as well as in the Chicago *Tribune* and the Chicago *Daily News*.

18. Robins was referring to his experience on his journey out of Russia back to the United States. He left Moscow on May 14, 1918, carrying the following pass from Lenin: "To all councils of deputies and other Soviet organizations; I beg you to give every kind of assistance to Colonel Robins and other members of the American Red Cross Mission for an unhindered and speediest journey from Moscow to Vladivostok."

19. Governor James Vardaman of Mississippi, Governor Cole Blease of South Carolina, Hoke Smith of Georgia, and Theodore G. Bilbo of Mississippi were leaders of the most vicious anti-Negro forces in the South.

20. Borah was referring to Winston Churchill's remark that "the League of Nations is on its trial in regard to Russia." "That," Borah declared in another speech, "is precisely the principle and policy announced by Metternich in 1822 with reference to the Holy Alliance. When Metternich declared that it was necessary for the Holy Alliance to take part in internal affairs of South America, of Spain, and other countries, he based it upon the proposition that unless democracy was put down in those countries, democracy would inevitably destroy the governments which were the pillars of the Holy Alliance."

21. In January 1919, the Soviet government issued a manifesto inviting 39 left-wing parties, groups and tendencies, from all over the world to send delegates to a congress in Moscow to found a new International. Four of the 39 groups invited were American. The Third International came into existence on March 4, 1919.

22. At Johns Hopkins University, Wilson was a member of the History Department. In 1902 he published *A History of the American People*, in five volumes.

23. Peter Arkadyevich Stolypin, Minister of the Interior under the Tsar, vigorously enforced a reign of terror in 1906. Court martials in which trial was secret, formal defense barred and sentences not subject to appeal, resulted in death sentences for many Russians. Stolypin's terror was directed especially against members of organized revolutionary groups whose detection was facilitated by a network of political spies and *agents provocateurs*.

24. In the spring of 1903 the whole civilized world was shocked by the bloody pogrom against the Jews of Kishinev, in the province of Bessarabia. Forty-five Jews were killed by drunken mobs, assisted by the Russian authorities and police; over 600 were wounded, and 1,500 houses or shops were destroyed or looted.

25. The Washington, D.C., and Chicago race riots occurred in 1919. In Washington mobs roamed the city for three days looking for Negroes

to lynch. A number of Negroes and whites were killed and scores were injured. The Chicago riot grew out of Negro resentment of exclusion from a bathing beach dominated by whites. One Sunday, while Negroes and whites scuffled on the beach, a Negro teenager drowned after being attacked in the swimming area. That attack was the most recent of a long series of assaults upon Negroes. A white policeman not only refused to arrest a white man allegedly involved in the drowning, but actually attempted to arrest one of the complaining Negroes. The officer was mobbed and soon the rioting was underway. Before it was over, 15 whites and 23 Negroes were killed, almost 600 wounded, and 1,000 families burned out.

26. The League of Nations to enforce the rule of law in international affairs was proposed by Woodrow Wilson in his "Fourteen Point" message, and was established at the Peace Conference. Although the Soviet government, through Maxim Litvinov, informed a special American agent, W. H. Buckley, that insofar as the League could prevent war "without encouraging reaction," it could count on Russia's support, it was not allowed to become a member until 1934. United States membership in the League was rejected by the Senate along with the Versailles peace treaty.

27. In the hope of winning support for the Versailles Treaty, Wilson on September 3 set forth on a country-wide tour, in the course of which he made some 30 speeches. He spoke in St. Louis on September 5, and while denouncing the Bolsheviks, upheld the right of revolution. On September 25, at Pueblo, Colorado, he suffered a physical breakdown, and was hastily brought back to Washington.

28. The capital of Admiral Kolchak's counter-revolutionary government was at Omsk.

THE THIRD YEAR

1. At the Peace Conference Wilson did try to obtain agreement from the other Allied powers to invite Soviet delegates and try to reach a peaceful understanding with the Soviet government. He was supported by Britain's David Lloyd George, but the other Allied representatives rejected Wilson's approach and insisted on an anti-Bolshevik crusade.

2. This was an over-optimistic statement. In spite of the reverses the counter-revolution had suffered, the Anglo-French interventionists launched new offensives against Soviet Russia.

3. The reference is to William C. Bullitt's report. *See* pp. 200–204.

4. In April 1920, in a drive to seize all the territory of the Western Ukraine and the town of Smolensk, the Poles attacked Soviet Russia. Assisted by the French and British with materials and a huge loan ($50,000,000) from the United States, the Poles drove into the Ukraine and occupied Kiev. Here they were halted and driven back by the Red Army into Poland. Later, however, a Polish counter-offensive, aided by the Allied governments, drove the Red Army back. The Soviet government was forced by the Peace of Riga to turn over the western sections of Byelorussia and the Ukraine to the Poles.

5. On December 10, 1919, the Labour party and the Trades Union Congress sent a British Labour delegation to Soviet Russia to conduct

"an independent and impartial inquiry into the industrial, political and economic conditions in Russia." In its report, the delegation said: "We feel it necessary to begin by pointing out that most accounts of Soviet Russia which we had seen in the capitalist press of our own country proved to be perversions of the facts. The whole impression gained was of a different character from that presented by those accounts." The delegation was extremely impressed by the support for the Soviet government demonstrated everywhere it went, the enormous advances in care of children, and the tremendous developments in the field of education. The delegation bitterly denounced the blockade of Soviet Russia, and wrote in its report: "We recommend that the entire British Labour Movement should demand the removal of the last vestige of blockade and intervention, and the complete destruction of the barrier which imperialist statesmen have erected between our own people and our brothers and sisters in Russia." (*British Labour Delegation to Russia, Report,* London, 1920.)

6. After the war, local labor and farmer-labor parties began to spring up in the United States, most of them modeled after the British Labour party. The Farmer-Labor party of New York was a union of Socialists and trade union groups.

7. Francis Dana was sent by Congress as a regular accredited minister to Russia. He stayed in St. Petersburg from August 1781 to September 1783, but did not present his credentials to the Russian government until March 7, 1783. The tsarist government refused to recognize Dana or the United States.

BIOGRAPHICAL SKETCHES

In many cases, personalities appearing in the documents are identified in the introductions or in the text. The following sketches cover most of the others.

ADDAMS, JANE, an outstanding pacifist and social worker; founder of the Hull House, a pioneer settlement house in Chicago.

BALDWIN, ROGER NASH, social worker and member of the Bureau for Conscientious Objectors and the Civil Liberties Bureau. Baldwin was one of the key figures in the civil liberties movement, and active in the organization of the American Civil Liberties Union.

BERGER, VICTOR L., born in Austria-Hungary, he became an influential leader of the Socialist party of the United States, after taking over the leadership of the Socialist movement in Milwaukee and the state of Wisconsin. A right-wing Socialist, he was the first Socialist to be elected to Congress, winning his seat in 1911.

BLATCH, HELEN STANTON, daughter of Elizabeth Cady Stanton, the pioneer women's rights advocate; she herself was a woman suffrage leader and a prominent figure in the Socialist party.

BLOOR, ELLA REEVE, began her long political career in Philadelphia during Bryan's "free silver" campaign in 1896, quickly joined the Socialist Labor party, and then the Socialist party, and became one of its leading women organizers. Later she became one of the leading figures in the Communist party.

BRANHAM, LUCY, was a member of the faculty of Columbia University.

DU BOIS, W. E. B., the distinguished Negro leader, Harvard-educated with a Ph.D. from that university, leader of the "Niagara Movement" which demanded full equality for the Negro people, and one of the founders of the National Association for the Advancement of Colored People, whose journal, the *Crisis*, he edited. Du Bois was also active in advancing the struggle for the independence of Africa, and was a key figure in the Pan-African movement.

EASTMAN, CRYSTAL, sister of Max Eastman, a Socialist and pacifist who helped organize the American Union Against Militarism.

EASTMAN, MAX, Socialist editor of *The Masses* and the *Liberator*. At first a champion of Soviet Russia, as an admirer of Trotsky, he became increasingly hostile to it.

FRAINA, LOUIS C., born in Italy, he came to New York and joined the Socialist party as a youth and, in 1909, moved over to the Socialist Labor party. He left the SLP in 1914 and became a prominent figure in the left-wing of the Socialist party, expressing his views through the *New Review* of which he was a member of the board of editors. One of the founders of the Communist party of America, he left the movement in 1922 and, using the name Lewis Corey, wrote a number of books dealing with social and economic problems.

GIOVANNITTI, ARTURO, poet and labor organizer, came to the United States from Italy in 1900, and later joined the IWW. He was one of the leaders of the Lawrence, Massachusetts, textile strike in 1912, and with Joseph Ettor was arrested and charged with being an accessory to murder during the strike. Both were acquitted after a great defense campaign.

GITLOW, BENJAMIN, one of the ten New York Socialists elected to the State legislature in 1917, he allied himself in the spring of 1918 with the left-wing Socialists, and later helped found the Communist Labor party. In later years he became a professional anti-Communist.

HAYWOOD, WILLIAM D. ("Big Bill"), a founder of the Western Federation of Miners and leader of the IWW. He was acquitted of murder in one of the most famous labor cases in American history, the Moyer-Haywood-Pettibone case of 1906. During World War I, Haywood was indicted for sedition and sentenced to 20 years in prison. In 1921 he went to Russia, where he died.

HILLQUIT, MORRIS, leader of the Socialist party, long its representative to the International Socialist Bureau in Brussels, and Socialist candidate for Mayor of New York City in 1917 on an anti-war platform.

HOURWICH, ISAAC A., a distinguished figure in the American Socialist and trade-union movements. Born in Vilna, Russia, in 1860, he was forced to flee his native land because of his revolutionary activity. Emigrating to the United States, he received his Ph.D. degree from Columbia University, and became a member of the New York bar. From 1900 to 1913, he was employed by the U.S. Bureau of the Mint, the U.S. Census Bureau, and the New York Public Service Commission. He was the author of many works, the most important being *Immigration and Labor,* published in 1912. He also translated Karl Marx's *Das Kapital* into Yiddish.

HOURWICH, NICHOLAS I., son of Isaac A. Hourwich, a leader of the left-wing of the Socialist party.

HOWE, FREDERIC C., reformer, writer and student of municipal government, was Commissioner at the Port of New York.

KATAYAMA, SEN, following his return to his native land from the United States in 1896, became active in the Japanese labor and Socialist movements. In 1906, after serving nine months of hard labor in Japanese prisons for anti-war activity, he returned to the United States and became active in the Socialist movement, allying himself with the left-wing.

KELLER, HELEN, stricken as an infant by a disease that left her deaf, blind and mute, she learned how to read and speak. After graduation from Radcliffe College, she lectured in behalf of the blind. She became a member of the Socialist party and wrote and spoke actively in its behalf. She was friendly to the IWW, opposed America's entrance into World War I, and defended the Bolshevik revolution.

KELLOGG, PAUL U., editor of *Survey,* a magazine for social workers; active in liberal and anti-war movements.

LIEBKNECHT, KARL FRIEDRICH AUGUST, son of Wilhelm Liebknecht; leader of the German Social Democratic Party and, like his father, an opponent of militarism and war. As a member of the Reichstag, Liebknecht fought to prevent the granting of war credits to the Kaiser, and was sentenced to prison. (He was the only Reichstag deputy to vote against the war budget in 1914.) Liebknecht was liberated following the collapse of the German Empire in November 1918 and, with Rosa

Luxemburg, led the revolution in Germany. Both were assassinated in the counter-revolution.

LOCHNER, LOUIS P., formerly Secretary of the Chicago Peace Society, he became the Executive Secretary of the Peace Council of America.

LOCKHART, BRUCE, an agent of the British diplomatic service in Russia, he was chosen by Prime Minister Lloyd George to go to Russia to work out some sort of relations—not including recognition—with the Soviet government.

LODGE, HENRY CABOT, conservative Republican Senator from Massachusetts, leader of the Republicans in the Senate, and of the Senate fight for rejection of the League of Nations.

LONDON, MEYER, a founder of the Socialist party who became one of its leaders. A right-wing Socialist, he was elected to Congress in 1914, lost in 1916, but was re-elected in 1920.

LOVETT, ROBERT MORSS, University of Chicago professor who became a distinguished liberal.

ROSA LUXEMBURG, the radical Polish socialist who rose to leadership of the German Social-Democratic Party. She was a noted critic of Eduard Bernstein, the socialist revisionist of Marxism. She was imprisoned in Germany during World War I for her anti-war activities. When the war ended in defeat for Germany, she and Karl Liebknecht launched the Spartacus League, father of the German Communist party. Arrested by soldiers of the conservative Socialist government on January 15, 1919, she was carried to the Eden Hotel in Berlin, and after being beaten over the head with rifle butts, bleeding profusely, more dead than alive, she was thrown into Landwehr canal. The corpse remained there for four months.

MAGNES, RABBI JUDAH L., distinguished Jewish leader in New York and member of the People's Council of America and of the American Union Against Militarism. He was chairman of the Jewish Kehillah (Community).

MARTENS, LUDWIG C. A. K., a mechanical engineer by profession, he was born in Russia of German parents. He joined the Russian revolutionary movement as a student, and after arrest, jail and deportation, settled in Germany and then in London. He came to New York in 1916 as the representative of a large Russian steel firm. He was a member of the "New York Section of the Russian Bolsheviks," and in 1919 was designated the Soviet government's first diplomatic representative to the United States.

MAURER, JAMES P., Socialist, president of the Pennsylvania State Federation of Labor.

MURPHY, CHARLES, as boss of Tammany Hall, he dominated New York City politics from 1902 to 1924.

MUSSEY, HENRY RAYMOND, professor of economics, he resigned from Columbia University in December 1917 in protest over the dismissal of two anti-war professors, Henry W. L. Dana and James M. Cattell.

NEARING, SCOTT, a young Socialist economics teacher who was dismissed from the Wharton School of Economics of the University of Pennsylvania and from the University of Toledo. He became an important Socialist lecturer and writer.

NOCK, ALBERT J., a single tax advocate and opponent of American intervention in World War I. He was a frequent contributor to liberal magazines.

NUORTEVA, SANTERI, a Finnish émigré, he became editor of the *Rayvaaja,* the Finnish-language Socialist organ in the United States and member of the National Executive Committee of the Socialist party. He was appointed American representative of the short-lived "People's Republic" of Finland which had gained power early in 1918, but which was overthrown by the counter-revolution in the spring of that year.

PENROSE, BOIES, U.S. Senator from Pennsylvania and leader of the Republican organization in that state from 1904 to 1921.

PINCHOT, AMOS, leader of the Progressive party, he left the party because he believed it was coming under the control of big business, and continued to be active in anti-war and civil liberties movements.

REED, JOHN, the son of an Oregon progressive, after graduation from Harvard, he was introduced to journalism by Lincoln Steffens. He wrote for the *American, Metropolitan,* and *The Masses.* He helped the IWW in the Paterson strike of 1913, organizing the Madison Square Garden Pageant. He reported the Ludlow, Colorado, strike of 1914, the Mexican revolution, and the war in eastern Europe, where he was convinced that, "this is not our war." The Bolshevik revolution, at which he was present, inspired his greatest writings, especially his famous work, *Ten Days That Shook the World,* published in 1919. After popularizing the cause of the Bolshevik revolution in the United States and helping found the Communist Labor party, he revisited Russia where he died in 1920.

SANGER, MARGARET, Socialist, pioneer advocate of birth control; she was indicted in 1915 for sending birth control information through the mail, and arrested the following year for opening a birth-control clinic. In 1917 she founded the American Birth Control Clinic.

SHELLY, REBECCA, a leader of the pacifist forces in the United States. She had been instrumental in interesting Henry Ford in sponsoring the peace ship *Oscar II* which left in December 1915 on a fruitless mission to persuade the Scandinavian countries to mediate the war.

STEFFENS, LINCOLN, famous muckraking journalist and reformer. He made his first trip to Russia in 1917 before the outbreak of the Bolshevik revolution.

STOKES, ROSE PASTOR, an immigrant girl active in the Socialist party, she married James G. P. Stokes, a wealthy New Yorker who was also interested in socialism. She separated from her husband because she opposed America's entrance into World War I while he favored it. She was indicted under the Espionage Act of 1917. Later she became a Communist.

THOMAS, NORMAN, Socialist and pacifist clergyman who edited *The World Tomorrow,* a magazine of progressive, pacifist and Socialist opinion. He became the successor to Eugene V. Debs as the Socialist party standard-bearer.

TRACHTENBERG, ALEXANDER, a native of Russia who had taken part in the Revolution of 1905, he emigrated to the United States the following year, and played an important role in the Intercollegiate Socialist Society, first at Trinity College and then at Yale University. He came to New York in 1915 to head the Research Department of the Rand School of Social Science and to edit the *American Labor Year Book.* He later became a Communist and founded International Publishers.

WALSH, FRANK P., liberal and well-known labor lawyer who gained national fame as chairman of the U.S. Commission on Industrial Relations.

YOUNG, ART, the great social cartoonist who appeared regularly in *The Masses,* the New York *Call,* and other Socialist periodicals and papers.

INDEX